THE ESSENTIAL INDIVIDUAL PENSION PLAN HANDBOOK

Peter J. Merrick, B.A., FMA, CFP, FCSI

LexisNexis®

FOREWORD

During the past number of years, the image of an accounting profession has evolved from one of a traditional, conservative, green eyeshade clad individual to today's dynamic, tech-savvy business advisor. This evolution has not been without its struggles and some triumphs along the way. This publication by Peter Merrick stands out as a shining marker of how the world in which accountants operate has changed.

Some of the forces that have pulled the accounting profession (sometimes screaming and kicking) into a new world include: ever-escalating client needs and expectations; the ever-increasing complexity of the marketplace; and the survival need for accountants to embrace new areas of business as the traditional attest and tax compliance lines of business have become increasingly commodified.

The very structure of this publication, which includes material from several different experts, reflects the complexity of today's financial world. Accolades should come Peter's way in recognition of his sensitivity to the interconnections amongst the practitioners from several different areas of the marketplace. Not only has Peter seen this network of relationships but he has obviously devoted much energy to organizing and marshalling practitioners from several different markets.

This publication should serve as a primer for practising accountants who are interested in knowing what this "financial services" world is all about. Public accountants owe it to themselves and to their clients to become knowledgeable of the broad range of products and strategies available to their clients. The material in this publication explores many creative and beneficial strategies that are generally unknown to practising accountants at this deeper level.

It is quickly apparent to the reader that although they may be aware of these products and strategies, they must find some way to forge relationships with those who possess the necessary expertise to formulate customized strategies for individual clients.

In this publication we see a template for today's commercial marketplace in which strategic alliances, affiliations and networks are commonplace. To properly serve most clients' needs, one must bring together a host of disciplines: law; accounting; tax; insurance; pensions; banking; and so on.

I see it as inevitable that the public accountant, the trusted business advisor, is the logical central force in creating these collaborations.

Preparing this foreword has been a particularly meaningful effort for me. Many years ago, as an accounting student, I had the pleasure of working with Peter's father, Marvin S. Merrick, CA, before either of us was designated. I am sure that he would be proud of this publication and would recognize the value of this material for the practising public accountant.

Morden Shapiro, B.Com., FCA, CMC
President of Morden S. Shapiro & Associates Inc.

PREFACE

Stop!

Don't read any further if you are not prepared for change. The information contained within these pages has the power to change your career and your life!

You have happened upon this book for a reason. It could be that you want to change the way you practice in the realm of financial planning, or you have plateaued at a certain level in your career and you desire to achieve greater and more fulfilling success.

Carl Gustav Jung, the Swiss psychologist who is considered to be one of the 20th century's most influential thinkers, coined the term "synchronicity" in the early 1930s. Jung believed that synchronicity happened when a person experienced two or more events or coincidences at the same time and found them to be meaningfully connected. Jung believed that there was no such thing as an accident — everything had a purpose — and modern physics over the past century has validated his claim. This book has the power to be the catalyst for meaningful change in both your life and career if you are ready for that change.

An advisor who gains one Individual Pension Plan (IPP) client, aged 49, today will create over $300,000 of commissionable and fee income over the next 15 years. An IPP is a defined benefit pension plan for usually one person, a husband and wife, a small group of employees or a family. Research indicates that the IPP market will experience unparalleled growth, from 8,500 registered plans in 2006 to over 300,000 within 15 years for Canada's richest Canadian households. Three hundred billion dollars of new investable assets are now up for grabs.

The only thing holding financial professionals back from capitalizing on this new IPP market is the lack of credible IPP and proper financial planning knowledge. This book is a must! When considering the income and fee potential generated from each IPP client, the "return on investment" (ROI) could be astronomical.

Today, accountants, financial planners, investment advisors and insurance agents have the unique opportunity to get into the IPP industry on the ground floor. The question is: How will they stake out their turf and make their mark in this lucrative new $6 billion annual IPP management fee market while it is still in its formative stages?

Notice to Reader

This book is strictly intended for education and informational use only. Every attempt has been made by the author and contributors to make the content as accurate as possible. In no way will the author, contributors and LexisNexis Canada be held liable for any actions that individuals reading this book may take in the future.

IPPs and the other complementary financial solutions mentioned in this book require specialties in areas such as accounting, actuary evaluation, investment management, pension legislation, employment law and employee benefit plan construction. Many financial professionals will need to seek educational and consulting services to aid them in the set-up, maintenance and wind-up stages of these solutions. Therefore, it is well worth the time and money to hire an executive and employee benefit consultant to assist in the design, implementation and maintenance of these solutions.

Peter J. Merrick
November 2006

ABOUT THE AUTHOR

Peter J. Merrick, B.A., FMA, CFP, FCSI is the President of Merrick-Wealth.com. Since the early 1990s, Peter has had an active career in the financial planning, investment, risk management, estate planning and executive benefit and pension fields. He has been retained for his executive benefit and financial planning expertise by some of Canada's largest financial institutions, and accounting and legal firms, to provide executive benefit consulting, succession and estate planning solutions to owner/managed businesses.

Peter is a Certified Financial Planner (CFP) registered with the Financial Planners Standards Council of Canada as well as a Financial Management Advisor (FMA). In the year 2000, Peter was awarded the prestigious Fellowship of the Canadian Securities Institute (FCSI), which is recognized as Canada's highest honour in the financial services industry.

Peter has appeared as a regular television guest on both ROBTV and CP24 in Toronto. Over the past decade, Peter has presented over 400 seminars and workshops to such organizations as the Canadian Institute of Chartered Accountants (CICA), the Human Resources Professionals Association of Ontario (HRPAO) and the Financial Planners Standards Council of Canada (FPSCC). He is a professional public speaker who has achieved the Distinguished Toastmaster's (DTM) designation, the highest level from Toastmasters International in the areas of public speaking and leadership. As well, Peter has taught at several post-secondary institutions in programs that lead to the Certified Financial Planning, Certified General Accountant, Certified Human Resources Professional and Certified Employee Benefits Specialist designations.

Peter is a professional financial writer, with 216 published articles to his credit. His articles have appeared in such magazines as *McLeans, CA Magazine, Ontario Dental Magazine, Accounting World, Benefit and Pension Monitor, Canadian MoneySaver, CSI Infocus*, the *Canadian Funeral Director Magazine, Canadian Auto Dealers, Dental Practice Management, Oral Health, Lawyers Weekly, The Bottom Line, MD Canada, The Bay Street Times, Canadian Business Franchise, HR Professional, Computer World, IT Ontario, Silicon Valley North, Forum, The Canadian Dental Association, Canadian HR Reporter* and numerous publications for LexisNexis Canada Inc. and CCH Canadian Ltd.

Peter is the author of the Canadian Securities Institute's course on Individual Pension Plans. This is his first published book.

CONTRIBUTORS

Ian E. Baker, FCIA, FSA, is a Principal and Consulting Actuary with Westcoast Actuaries Inc. and a Fellow of both the Canadian Institute of Actuaries and the Society of Actuaries. Mr. Baker specializes in Individual Pension Plans and has written many articles on this subject. Mr. Baker is a frequently requested speaker on the topic of IPPs. Mr. Baker is a co-creator of the *IPP Essentials* audio-visual CD. Mr. Baker has been qualified as an expert witness in both the Supreme Court of British Columbia and Alberta's Court of Queen's Bench. Mr. Baker is a member and former president of the Fraser Valley Estate Planning Council, and is an avid curler.

Gordon Berger has been in the financial services business since 1972. Gordon was admitted to the "Quarter Century Club", a division of the Million Dollar Round Table (MDRT), and is a life member of "Top of the Table", reserved for the top 400 insurance agents worldwide. Gordon has made numerous appearances on both television and radio on such programs as TV Ontario's *Money Blues*, *Money Talks* on CHFI Radio, and on CFRB. Gordon has participated as co-author of various books, such as *Power of Money* and *Turnaround, The Complete Canadian Guide*. Gordon is a co-author of the *Canadian Guide to Tax Planning, Benefits and Compensation for Executives and Managers*. Gordon has lectured at the University of Toronto, the Schulich School of Business, the Canadian Bar Association and CCH Canadian Limited.

Jordan Dolgin, LL.B., is a Partner and Chair of Wilson Vukelich LLP's Corporate Commercial Group based in Markham, Ontario. His practice focuses on domestic and cross-border mergers and acquisitions, private equity transactions, corporate reorganizations and technology-related commercial matters. He acts for many early-stage and well-established private and public enterprises across various industries and throughout all stages of the business life cycle. He also advises on commercial technology matters such as Web site and software development, software licensing and distribution, Internet and e-commerce transactions and technology joint ventures. Jordan believes in the importance of continuous professional development, is a frequent contributor to several industry publications and participates regularly in professional and client lecture series.

Kurt Dreger, B. Sc., ASA, CFP, has over 15 years of pension plan experience in Canada, working in many capacities. He has written many articles and spoken on the subject of executive retirement planning, in particular, Individual Pension Plans (IPPs) and Retirement Compensation Arrangements (RCAs). Kurt graduated in 1991 from the University of Western Ontario with a B. Sc. (Honours) in Actuarial Science. He became an Associate of the Society of Actuaries (ASA) in 1991 and a Certified Financial Planner (CFP) in 2000. From 1991-1998, Kurt worked as a Pension Consultant to Canada's largest pension plans. He continued in the pension field from 1998-2004 as Manager, Business Development, Standard Life. Since 2004, Kurt has been with the Group Pension department at Industrial Alliance Insurance and Financial Services Inc. as Business Development Manager. He is a member of, and plays active roles with, CPBI and ACPM.

Andrew Duckman, B.A., GBA Candidate, RIBO, is a seasoned corporate benefits consultant. He has over a decade of experience within the risk management, merchant banking and information technology sectors. His core competencies are employee benefit cost containment and executive and business owner benefit construction. Andrew began his career at Unum Provident developing unique financial solutions to serve the specialized needs of Canada's small and medium-sized businesses, and was responsible for integrating special risk solutions into the product lines of some of Canada's largest financial and insurance firms. In 2003, he joined one of Canada's leading Third Party Administrator and Brokerage firms, where he now serves as the Vice-President of Corporate Development.

Eugene Ellmen is Executive Director of the Social Investment Organization (SIO), Canada's association for socially responsible investment (SRI). He is widely regarded as one of Canada's leading authorities on SRI. He is the author of the critically acclaimed *Canadian Ethical Money Guide* (Toronto: Lorimer Press), published in five editions between 1988 and 1998. Before joining the SIO in 1999, Eugene had a varied career as business writer for Canadian Press, public affairs advisor for Credit Union Central of Ontario, communications advisor to a number of Ministers in the Ontario government and in private consulting on behalf of companies and non-profit organizations.

Bob Kirk, B.A., FLMI, ACS, is a partner of PanFinancial Insurance Agencies Ltd. who has worked in the financial services industry for over 26 years. He has held executive positions with PanFinancial, Transamerica Life, Unum Provident and ING Life/NN Financial, and management positions with MONY Life and North American Life. Bob's background is in Sales, Risk Management, Strategic Planning, Underwriting, Claims, Customer Service and Mergers. Bob has lectured at numerous industry and business functions, including the Schulich School of Business. His work has been published in a number of trade journals and he has served as a Canadian Editor of *On the Risk*, an insurance risk management magazine. Bob received his bachelor's degree from McMaster University, Ontario, and is a designated Fellow, Life Management Institute and Associate Customer Service.

David Leonhardt, CEO of The Happy Guy Marketing, a Canadian-based business that specializes in providing freelance writing, editing and Web site search engine ranking services. David was one of Canada's most interviewed spokespeople, often topping 500 media interviews a year, and helped to influence legislation and regulations across Canada. That expertise has since helped position his own business and those of his clients for success on the Internet and in the written word. David publishes *A Daily Dose of Happiness*, an ezine that is read by 40,000 people daily, and has been published in hundreds of books, newspapers, magazines and Web sites. He has also made cameo appearances with such luminaries as Zig Ziglar and Brian Tracy.

Cary List, CA, CFP is Acting President and CEO of Financial Planners Standards Council of Canada. Cary has spent the better part of the last two decades dedicated to the advancement of financial planning as a profession, and over the past four years he has overseen CFP certification in Canada. Under his leadership, CFP certification continues to be the gold standard for professional financial planning. Cary sits on the Council and the Certification Committee of the International Financial Planning Standards Board. He holds an honours mathematics degree from the University of Waterloo, is a Chartered Accountant and holds the Certified Financial Planner designation.

Gilles R. Marceau, CFP, CLU, RFP, PRP, is President of Gilles R. Marceau and Associates Inc. He is an accomplished Financial Planning, Retirement and Lifestyle Planning Consultant and Educator. Gilles has had a very successful 30-year career in the life insurance, banking and the investment and securities businesses. Gilles has held the positions of Director of Individual Insurance Marketing for one of Canada's leading life insurance companies; Regional Manager for a financial planning practice directed to high net worth individuals; Managing Partner, Marketing Development for what was Canada's largest trust company; and Managing Partner in a fee-based financial planning/employee benefit firm. He is currently the Chair of the Professional Retirement Planners designation accredited through the Canadian Association of Pre-Retirement Planners.

Trevor R. Parry, M.A., LL.B., is Executive Vice-President responsible for Sales and Marketing for Gordon B. Lang & Associates Inc. In addition to leading the consulting group for Lang's, Trevor works directly with clients, financial planners and advisors, accountants and lawyers in helping develop and implement advanced financial planning strategies. Trevor was called to the Ontario bar in 1996 and is a graduate of Queen's University Faculty of Law. Trevor also holds Masters and Undergraduate degrees in History from the University of Toronto. A dynamic public speaker, Trevor has presented at many conferences, including those presented by Advocis and the Canadian Bar Association. He has also been widely published in professional periodicals.

Kenneth C. Pope, **LL.B., TEP,** started his law practice in 1980. He travels the Province of Ontario to meet with clients and to present seminars on disabilities and estate planning issues. Ken is a Henson Trust specialist, providing financial security for families with a family member with disabilities or special needs. Ken has written dozens of articles on how guardians and parents of disabled children can financially and legally plan their affairs to protect the interest of their loved ones.

Ian Quigley, M.B.A., CFP, CIM, is an independent financial planner specializing in topics related to pension and small business tax planning. Ian holds an M.B.A. from the University of Alberta and is currently a candidate in the Chartered Business Valuator's program (CBV). He has his own consulting firm, Quigley Consulting Inc. Ian is the author of the highly acclaimed book *Compensation and Tax Strategies* (Toronto: Thomson Carswell, 2004). This book is widely used to teach accountants and financial planning professionals advanced solutions in executive compensation.

Stanley Risen, CA, is the VP of Sales and Consulting for Benecaid Health Benefit Solutions Inc., a Toronto-based financial services company. Benecaid is a leading provider of innovative health benefit solutions in Canada. Stanley is a Charter Accountant with 20 years of financial and managerial experience that has included senior positions at BDO Dunwoody as a senior audit manager, Pet-Pak Containers as the CFO and IMS Machining as the CFO.

Morden (Mort) Shapiro, B. Com., **FCA, CMC,** for over 25 years has consulted to accounting practices throughout Canada. Mort, a regular columnist in *The Bottom Line*, coaches accounting firms and frequently performs a Diagnostic Review of an Accounting Practice for practices of all sizes. A well-known teacher, author and facilitator of partners' retreats, he is also a frequent presenter of Professional Development courses and is available to address conferences and other professional meetings. Mort consults on a broad range of practice management issues, including: relationship management; partnership arrangements; succession planning; strategic planning; marketing; integration of technology; growth management; mergers; conflict resolution; and profit improvement strategies. He is available as an expert witness, arbitrator or mediator in professional negligence situations and partnership disputes. Mort offers expert guidance with respect to the federal *Personal Information Protection and Electronic Documents Act* (PIPEDA) and the Quality Control requirements for accounting practices.

Christopher P. Van Slyke, B.A., M.B.A., CFP®, is the Managing Director of Capital Financial Advisors, LLC, a fee-only wealth management firm in La Jolla, California. His expertise in comprehensive wealth management is reflected in the firm's emphasis on estate planning, asset protection, tax strategies, risk management, investment selection, business succession and retirement planning. A Certified Financial Planner practitioner, Christopher is also a financial planner member of the National Association of Personal Financial Advisors (NAPFA), an exclusive organization of fee-only planners. Christopher is a past member of the Board of Directors of the Financial Planning Association of San Diego and Los Angeles. He has been quoted or published in *The Wall Street Journal, The San Diego Union-Tribune, Financial Planning, Smart Money, Financial Advisor, Boomer Market Advisor, MSN Money, Wealth and Retirement Planner, thestreet.com, Bloomberg Wealth Manager*, the *Del Mar Times, Money Magazine* and *MorningstarAdvisor.com*.

INTRODUCTION

"We cannot solve problems with the same thinking we used when creating them."

"Definition of *Insanity*: Doing the same thing over and over, but expecting different results."

Albert Einstein (1879-1955)

In the early 1990s, at the beginning of my financial planning career, I was very fortunate to meet one of Canada's most successful businessmen.

He was in his late 50s and had much more life experience than me. He shared that 99.9% of the investment advisors he had met over the course of his career did not have the slightest idea of how to make money, nor did they understand what successful business people were looking for when they sought out professional advice.

He told me that when he took a risk, he got paid for it. He could buy a piece of property for a marginal amount, get it rezoned for a strip mall and then get franchises to sign letters of intent to lease for five years or more when the property was developed.

Once this was done, he would go off to the bank and borrow on the future revenue that would be generated from these highly profitable leases to develop his properties and create a residual income.

He knew that with his proven formula he could take his own money and make 100 times the amount with 1/10th the risk that any stockbroker could offer him, and he was right.

The vast majority of successful business owners are not looking for financial advisors to give them the life they want by making a killing in the stock market; these people have been able to create the life they want by themselves.

Successful business people want their financial advisors to show them ways to keep their wealth. In essence, successful people want their financial advisors to provide them with financial, tax, succession and estate planning holistic solutions. They don't need their advisors to sell them products such as stocks, mutual funds and life insurance to achieve their financial success. The point is that they are already successful.

Business people are looking for financial professionals who are positioned in the role of wealth manager. Someone who can see and understand the affluent and wealthy business owner's big-picture needs by constructing customized strategies to achieve their specific goals of wealth preservation, avoidance of unnecessary tax burdens, creditor protection, wealth accumulation and wealth distribution to themselves, their family, estate and charities.

Successful business owners have an understanding that a financial asset is something that puts money in their pockets, with minimum labour. They understand that a business can buy a car, but a car cannot buy a business! Liabilities are things that take money "out of one's pocket".

There are numerous advantages available to you if you own your own business, you take the risk and you have the creativity and fortitude to do something on your own. You are compensated for it. As an employee in Canada, your equation of earning an income goes like this:

- you earn;
- you're taxed;
- then you get to spend what is left over.

If you are a business owner and self-employed in Canada, our government allows you to adopt a much more favourable equation of earning an income:

- you earn;
- you spend, you income split, and you defer bonuses;
- then you are taxed on what is left over!

"Taxes are the price we pay for civilization."

Oliver Wendell Holmes, Jr.

Business owners are different from the rest of Canadians, if for no other reason than that the *Income Tax Act* favours people who work for themselves. The biggest expense business owners pay in a year is taxes. Reducing taxes legally is not only acceptable from a moral and ethical standpoint, it is also smart. In this country, there are three easy rules that keep money in your pocket and not in the government's:

1.   Find the right business structure for your business to pay less tax and protect what you have.

2.   Learn to make more money by using the tax strategies of the rich, such as implementing individual pension plans and retirement compensation arrangements; incorporate active businesses; create holding companies; create family trusts; make charitable donations; create health and welfare trusts; utilize corporately owned insurances; maximize executive and employee benefit plans; and

create employee profit-sharing plans, a succession plan and an estate freeze.

3.   Pay less tax legally and still sleep at night.

Those financial professionals who succeed in this new era will quickly identify their allies and recognize their enemies. They will build alliances with those professionals and organizations that will help them navigate the clear blue waters towards success. To succeed in this new era, financial professionals will have to place their focus on identifying and understanding a client's total financial life and create solutions that will solve a client's most important needs and goals.

Successful financial consultants in this new era, in addition to solving their clients' current problems, must correctly anticipate their clients' future problems and develop the necessary services to solve them. No longer will clients pay for services and products that only meet their past needs.

Successful financial consultants must make strategic bets on the services and capabilities that they must have if they want their current clients to continue to use their services in the future while attracting new clients.

The future looks bleak for financial practitioners who lack the resources, management skills or desire to change their business model to adopt services that will best serve their clients' needs. They should be always mindful of the old adage: "If you do what you have always done, you will get what you have always gotten."

A TRUE STORY

The seeds of this book were first planted on Tuesday, September 11, 2001. It was a perfect day in Toronto, not a cloud in the sky. I was driving to a meeting that was going to help me surpass my sales quota for the month.

I was listening to the radio when I heard at 8:50 A.M. that a plane had just crashed into the North Tower of the World Trade Center.

As I pulled into the parking lot a few minutes later in my client's office complex, a little after 9:00 A.M., I heard the radio announcer say that another plane had just hit the South Tower of the World Trade Center.

I knew something was up, but I did not have time to think much about it because I had to get to my very important appointment.

You see, that day, I was going to implement a new investment portfolio that involved "my" client buying $600,000 of mutual funds through me.

It was an important sales day!

For the first 25 minutes of the meeting, I had my client's full attention!

Then it happened. His wife called in around 9:40 A.M. to tell him that a third plane had just crashed into the Pentagon. Our meeting at that moment ended abruptly.

There was going to be no sale that day and no big payday.

As I drove home from that meeting, I came to the personal realization that the days of just selling product for the product's sake in the financial service industry were over for me.

If I were going to be successful in the financial advisory business going forward, I would need to learn how to present and implement solutions that were going to solve clients' most important needs. It was that realization that launched me on my journey to transform my practice from that of the transactional/commission-based business model I had operated prior to September 11, 2001, to that of the client centred/ solutions-based consulting practice model that I live today.

I discovered early on during the first days of my journey that the Individual Pension Plan would be a powerful ally in assisting me during this transition.

In this book you will be introduced to some of the most leading-edge financial planning concepts and best practices being applied to the financial planning consulting industry today and the insight from leading innovators successfully applying these concepts to the financial planning industry on both sides of the Canadian and U.S. border.

These experts have come together and provided their intellectual property and shared their wisdom throughout this text. I assure you that you will find as much true value in their contributions and insights as I have gained by their individual involvement in my own personal and professional journey.

THE BOOK

This book has been broken down into five distinct sections. Each section can be read individually or as a whole depending on your individual preferences.

Part I: IPP Essentials provides the essentials that a financial professional will be required to know and understand to offer holistic advice in the implementation, maintenance and winding-up of an Individual Pension Plan.

Part II: IPP Investment Considerations points out the restrictions that are placed on managing Individual Pension Plan assets in the current Canadian regulatory environment. This section explains how the adaptation and implementation of an asset allocation and rebalancing approach to managing a client's IPP and non-IPP portfolios is the best approach to gathering and managing client assets. It also explains how the outsourcing of the management of IPP and non-IPP assets to skilled money managers will free up a financial consultant's hands to provide efficient advice and to collect more assets under management. Lastly this section provides some insight into a major shift in regulations and thinking that is occurring today in the management of pension assets worldwide.

Part III: Advanced IPP Applications goes into great detail of some of the most advanced financial solutions that are being implemented hand in hand with the IPP solution by some of the leading minds in the financial professions today.

Part IV: The 21st Century Financial Consultant's IPP Concept Presentation Kit provides the tools and insights into what it will take to be a successful financial consultant in the 21st century.

The last section includes an epilogue and five appendices. If you, as a reader, have difficulty with some of the terminology used throughout the book, you will find Appendix E: Pension Speak particularly helpful because it is a comprehensive glossary of the terms used in the book.

This book will have achieved its primary purpose if you, the reader, have gained the required tools needed to allow you to transition your financial consulting practice effortlessly from that of a product-focused practice to that of a client solutions-focused financial planning practice — arming you, today's modern day financial professional, to prosper in this new, challenging and very exciting environment.

All the best in your pursuits!

PART I

IPP ESSENTIALS

CHAPTER 1

UNDERSTANDING THE INDIVIDUAL PENSION PLAN (IPP) HISTORY AND MARKET FORCES

Overview

This chapter presents the concept of the Individual Pension Plan (IPP). The chapter then describes the history of pensions and IPPs in Canada. It concludes by describing the market forces driving the growth of the IPP industry.

Learning Objectives

By the end of this chapter, you should be able to:

- explain what an Individual Pension Plan is;

- provide the historical background behind the Individual Pension Plan in Canada; and

- understand the market forces driving the Individual Pension Plan solution.

WHY READ THIS BOOK?

Incorporated businesses looking to add a benefit for their owners and top executives are beginning to learn about a little known tax deferral and tax minimization structure called the Individual Pension Plan (IPP). The IPP is what many in the financial industry are calling an "RRSP on Steroids", a "Super-Sized RRSP" or an "RRSP Upgrade". An Individual Pension Plan is a defined benefit pension plan for usually one person, a husband and wife, a small group of employees or a family. All members of an IPP need to be *bona fide* employees of companies that sponsor the plan.

IPPs are a successful person's answer to registered retirement savings plans. IPPs are sanctioned by the Canada Revenue Agency (CRA) and offer the best tax and retirement savings solution for individuals 40 years old and older who have a T4 income of more than $105,600, who work for an incorporated business and who historically have maximized their RRSPs and pension contributions.

IPPs offer significant amounts of additional tax-deferred income to be set aside for a business owner's and top executive's retirement. The IPP tax solution allows for hundreds of thousands of additional tax-deferred income dollars (from an incorporated business) to be invested into an IPP structure above and beyond the average Registered Retirement Savings Plan (RRSP) funding allotments. Thus, owners/executives are allowed non-taxable interest that compounds until retirement and the money is withdrawn from the plan.

In 2004, at the annual consultation held by CRA on Registered Pensions, a discussion ensued on "how Individual Pension Plans (IPPs) were a 'new' and uncommon type of pension plan some years ago, but now represent more than 1/3 (6,500 of 19,000) of the inventory (defined benefit pension plans). This type of plan design presents more compliance risk and the growth of this segment continues to increase. Although an IPP usually covers only one member, they require a disproportionate amount of attention when compared with plans covering hundreds of members. Consequently, a lot of audit activity has been focused on the IPP segment." As a result, the CRA Registered Plans Directorate intends to enhance its focus to monitor IPPs.

Advisors planning to enter the IPP market will need to acquire a basic understanding of tax laws, accounting, actuary evaluations, investment management, pension legislation, employment law and employee benefit plan construction as they begin to offer this specialized pension solution to their clients. Many employers and their financial advisors will need to seek educational services to aid them in the IPP set-up, maintenance and wind-up stages.

To be successful in the IPP arena today you need a lot of luck. "Luck" in this book has not been defined in the traditional sense of the word. "Luck" means when your preparation meets with opportunity. You need to be prepared to be able to identify and act upon every opportunity that presents itself to you, so you will create your own luck.

Pierre and Nicolas

As you journey through the pages of this book, be mindful of the tale of Pierre and Nicolas. Once there were two famous lumberjacks, named Pierre and Nicolas. No one knew who was the greatest lumberjack of them all. One day a promoter decided to host a competition between

Pierre and Nicolas to see who could cut down the most trees within a six-hour period. At the end the judges would count the cut trees and crown the winner with the title of the world's greatest lumberjack of them all.

The day of the competition was perfect, not a cloud in the sky. The judge officiating the event shot his starter pistol to begin the competition. Pierre and Nicolas started cutting feverishly. Fifty minutes into the event Pierre heard in the distance that Nicolas stopped cutting. Pierre kept cutting. Ten minutes later Pierre heard Nicolas resume. For the next five hours on the hour Pierre heard Nicolas stop cutting for ten minutes an hour.

At the end of six hours the judge again shot off his gun to signal to both lumberjacks that the competition was over. Pierre was sure that he would be declared the victor at the end of the count because he had heard every hour on the hour Nicolas stop cutting for ten minutes before beginning again. He was positive that the extra hour he had been cutting would assure him his crowning as the greatest lumberjack of them all.

The judges counted the cut down trees and recounted several times. Then they announced the winner, Nicolas. Nicolas had been crowned the greatest lumberjack of them all. Pierre was dumbfounded. How could this be possible? Pierre approached Nicolas and said: "It's impossible that you won. It could not be done. Every hour on the hour I heard in the distance that you stopped cutting for ten minutes. I cut for an extra hour than you."

Nicolas simply replied: "I did not stop once during our competition. I was sharpening my blade!"

IPP vs. RRSP

How good are IPPs vs. RRSPs? Imagine a 45-year-old owner/executive who has worked for the same company since 1991 and has averaged a T4 income of more than $100,000 a year. If she and her employer decide to "max-out" her IPP contribution room and RRSP going forward (using a yearly rate of return of 7.5%), she will accumulate $5,001,528 in registered retirement assets by the time she turns 69. Opting for this tax solution, this individual would have a registered retirement yearly benefit at age 69 of $378,044 fully indexed to the consumer price index.

In comparison, if this same owner/executive only utilizes her RRSP option from 45 years of age to 69, she would only accumulate $3,487,716 in registered retirement tax-sheltered assets. This amount of RRSP assets on an annual basis would generate $263,622 of retirement income from age 69 and beyond.

The decision is clear. The owner/executive who implements both the IPP and RRSP tax solutions as part of her retirement plan would have an additional $1,513,812 of tax-sheltered assets in her registered retirement plans and have an additional $114,422 in annual retirement income.

On the next page is a table that shows the accumulated dollar value for the business owner/executive with both an IPP and an RRSP. On the page following that is a table that shows the accumulated dollar value for the owner/executive with only an RRSP.

- based on
    cash flows

| | | With IPP | | | | | | | | | |
| Year | Age | IPP | | | | RRSP | | | | Total With IPP | Retirement Pension per Year |
		Beginning Balance	Contribution	Interest Income	Ending Balance	Beginning Balance	Contribution	Interest Income	Ending Balance		
2006	45	239,600	92,270	21,368	353,238	0	6,500	239	6,739	359,977	N/A
2007	46	353,238	22,242	27,312	402,792	6,739	600	528	7,867	410,659	N/A
2008	47	402,792	23,910	31,090	457,792	7,867	600	612	9,079	466,871	N/A
2009	48	457,792	25,703	35,281	518,776	9,079	600	703	10,382	529,158	N/A
2010	49	518,776	27,631	39,926	586,333	10,382	600	801	11,783	598,116	N/A
2011	50	586,333	29,703	45,069	661,105	11,783	600	906	13,289	674,394	36,712
2012	51	661,105	31,931	50,759	743,795	13,289	600	1,019	14,908	758,703	41,756
2013	52	743,795	34,326	57,049	835,170	14,908	600	1,140	16,648	851,818	47,429
2014	53	835,170	36,900	63,997	936,067	16,648	600	1,271	18,519	954,586	53,810
2015	54	936,067	39,668	71,666	1,047,401	18,519	600	1,411	20,530	1,067,931	60,955
2016	55	1,047,401	42,643	80,125	1,170,169	20,530	600	1,562	22,692	1,192,861	69,031
2017	56	1,170,169	45,841	89,451	1,305,461	22,692	600	1,724	25,016	1,330,477	78,034
2018	57	1,305,461	49,279	99,724	1,454,464	25,016	600	1,898	27,514	1,481,978	88,213
2019	58	1,454,464	52,975	111,035	1,618,474	27,514	600	2,086	30,200	1,648,674	99,678
2020	59	1,618,474	56,948	123,483	1,798,905	30,200	600	2,287	33,087	1,831,992	112,530
2021	60	1,798,905	61,219	137,172	1,997,296	33,087	600	2,504	36,191	2,033,487	127,014
2022	61	1,997,296	65,810	152,220	2,215,326	36,191	600	2,736	39,527	2,254,853	143,439
2023	62	2,215,326	70,746	168,754	2,454,826	39,527	600	2,987	43,114	2,497,940	161,784
2024	63	2,454,826	76,052	186,912	2,717,790	43,114	600	3,256	46,970	2,764,760	182,613
2025	64	2,717,790	81,756	206,845	3,006,391	46,970	600	3,545	51,115	3,057,506	206,031
2026	65	3,006,391	87,888	228,716	3,322,995	51,115	600	3,856	55,571	3,378,566	232,523
2027	66	3,322,995	94,480	252,704	3,670,179	55,571	600	4,190	60,361	3,730,540	262,529
2028	67	3,670,179	101,566	279,003	4,050,748	60,361	600	4,549	65,510	4,116,258	296,347
2029	68	4,050,748	109,183	307,826	4,467,757	65,510	600	4,935	71,045	4,538,802	334,720
2030	69	4,467,757	117,372	339,404	4,924,533	71,045	600	5,350	76,995	5,001,528	378,044

Note: Chart provided by West Coast Actuaries Inc. of British Columbia.

Year	Age	IPP Beginning Balance	IPP Contri- bution	IPP Interest Income	IPP Ending Balance	RRSP Beginning Balance	RRSP Contri- bution	RRSP Interest Income	RRSP Ending Balance	Total Without IPP	Retirement Pension per Year
2006	45	0	0	0	0	239,600	18,000	18,633	276,233	276,233	N/A
2007	46	0	0	0	0	276,233	18,000	21,380	315,613	315,613	N/A
2008	47	0	0	0	0	315,613	18,990	24,370	358,973	358,973	N/A
2009	48	0	0	0	0	358,973	20,035	27,661	406,669	406,669	N/A
2010	49	0	0	0	0	406,669	21,137	31,278	459,084	459,084	N/A
2011	50	0	0	0	0	459,084	22,299	35,252	516,635	516,635	28,124
2012	51	0	0	0	0	516,635	23,525	39,614	579,774	579,774	31,908
2013	52	0	0	0	0	579,774	24,819	44,397	648,990	648,990	36,135
2014	53	0	0	0	0	648,990	26,184	49,638	724,812	724,812	40,857
2015	54	0	0	0	0	724,812	27,625	55,378	807,815	807,815	46,108
2016	55	0	0	0	0	807,815	29,144	61,659	898,618	898,618	52,003
2017	56	0	0	0	0	898,618	30,747	68,529	997,894	997,894	58,528
2018	57	0	0	0	0	997,894	32,438	76,036	1,106,368	1,106,368	65,855
2019	58	0	0	0	0	1,106,368	34,222	84,238	1,224,828	1,224,828	74,052
2020	59	0	0	0	0	1,224,828	36,104	93,192	1,354,124	1,354,124	83,177
2021	60	0	0	0	0	1,354,124	38,090	102,962	1,495,176	1,495,176	93,390
2022	61	0	0	0	0	1,495,176	40,185	113,618	1,648,979	1,648,979	104,897
2023	62	0	0	0	0	1,648,979	42,395	125,234	1,816,608	1,816,608	117,656
2024	63	0	0	0	0	1,816,608	44,727	137,893	1,999,228	1,999,228	132,049
2025	64	0	0	0	0	1,999,228	47,187	151,680	2,198,095	2,198,095	148,120
2026	65	0	0	0	0	2,198,095	49,782	166,690	2,414,567	2,414,567	166,178
2027	66	0	0	0	0	2,414,567	52,520	183,026	2,650,113	2,650,113	186,496
2028	67	0	0	0	0	2,650,113	55,409	200,799	2,906,321	2,906,321	209,238
2029	68	0	0	0	0	2,906,321	58,457	220,127	3,184,905	3,184,905	234,875
2030	69	0	0	0	0	3,184,905	61,672	241,139	3,487,716	3,487,716	263,622

Note: Chart provided by West Coast Actuaries Inc. of British Columbia.

A LITTLE PENSION HISTORY — FROM YESTERDAY TO TODAY!

The legendary documentary filmmaker, Ken Burns, creator of the acclaimed mini-series: *The Civil War* (1990), *Baseball* (1994), and *JAZZ* (2001), once remarked during an interview, "that if we want to know where we are and where we are going, we first need to know where we have been." So let us begin by looking at an 87-year history of Canada's ever-changing tax, retirement and pension environment.

1919: The federal government, two years after the introduction of personal income tax, introduced legislation that allowed employees to make tax deductions for their contributions into pension plans.

1938: The federal government passed legislation that allowed employers to deduct their contributions to employee pension plans with no caps on the amount that could be deducted.

1941: The Canadian government during the Second World War placed strict wage freezes on the entire economy to control inflation during the war. Employers across Canada en masse started providing their people with pensions and other deferred income benefit plans that legally allowed them to work around the wage freeze and offer additional compensation to their employees without actually raising wages. In 1951, the Canadian government removed these wage freezes.

1947: The federal government placed limits on the amount of contributions that both employees and employers could make into pension plans.

1957: The federal government introduced Registered Retirement Savings Plans.

1971: The federal government placed limits on the amount of foreign property that pension funds and other registered tax-deferred retirement plans could hold within them to a maximum of 10%. The foreign content rules were introduced to ensure that a substantial proportion of tax-deferred retirement savings were invested in Canadian companies and to support the development of Canada's capital markets.

1972: The *Act to amend the Income Tax Act*, S.C. 1970-71-72, c. 63, was passed into legislation. The modern day *Income Tax Act* (ITA) was born. Before 1972 capital gains were not taxable in Canada.

1976: The federal government set defined benefit pension plan (DBPP) limits at $1,715 per year of service to a maximum of $60,025 promised annual defined pension retirement benefit. This remained the maximum until 1990. In 1976 the maximum defined benefit earnings was set at nine times the national wage at the time.

1984: The federal government's Marc Lalonde, then the Liberal federal Finance Minister proposed increasing RRSP contribution limits. In 1989, RRSP yearly contribution limits were to be increased to $15,500, which would put them in sync with the maximum benefit enjoyed by members of defined benefit pension plans. This proposed legislation to increase maximum RRSP contributions to $15,500 did not become a reality until 2004.

1987: The federal government knocked down the barriers separating the "four pillars" of the Canadian financial sector — banks, trust companies, insurance companies and investment dealers — and all these independent sectors were permitted to merge their services. With this convergence of financial institutions, one-stop shopping for financial services would be possible for each Canadian consumer.

1990: The federal government passed legislation amending the *Income Tax Act* which overhauled how the government grants taxed assistance for all pensions, RRSPs and other registered deferred income plans in Canada.

1990: The federal government set defined benefit pension plan limits at $1,722.22 per year of service to a maximum of $60,278 pension benefit per year for 35 years of employment service. This was considered to be enough to provide for a 70% pension for an individual earning a T4 income of $86,111. This limit remained until the 2002 federal budget.

1990: The federal government amended the *Income Tax Act* to include in section 147.1 designated plans to be created as of 1991 (S.C. 1990, c. 35, s. 16). A designated plan is a pension plan where more than 50% of the pension credits are for a specific person. These individuals are active members of a pension plan who may be a connected person to the employer of the plan and/or who earn two and one-half times the year's maximum pensionable earnings (YMPE).

A connected person is a person who owns directly or indirectly 10% or more of capital stock in a company or a related corporation. It also includes a person who does not deal at arm's length with a company. This includes a spouse or a common law partner. It should also be noted that if someone were a connected person at any time in the history of the employer who sponsors an IPP, CRA would always consider him or her a connected person. This amendment to the ITA gave birth to the Individual Pension Plan.

For example, if a business owner had sold 91% of his or her interest in his or her company in 1995 and only owns 9% of the IPP sponsoring company in 2006 at the time the IPP is set up for him or her, according to CRA rules this member will be considered for IPP purposes a connected person. Simply put: "Once a connected person, always a connected person!"

1990: Pension adjustments (PA) were first reported in that year to offset RRSP contribution limits for the first time in 1991. The PA is based on what is referred to as the Factor of 9. This is a pension credit formula used to determine the pension credit in a defined benefit pension plan. The federal government created the Factor of 9 to equalize the tax-assisted savings between all defined contribution plans and defined benefit plans. The Factor of 9 states that for every $1 of defined benefit pension benefit promised to a member the government considers that $9 of funding will be required to deliver that same benefit. However, this relationship is an average over a plan member's entire working career (later on in this book we will see how the Factor of 9 benefits older employees and puts younger employees at a disadvantage). It should be noted that the PA reported for defined contribution pension plans (DCPP) and deferred profit sharing plans (DPSP) are equal to the actual dollar amounts invested in those plans.

1990: RRSP maximum contribution limits for 1991 were set at $11,500 and were to increase to $15,500 by 1995 to put them at par with the maximum defined pensionable benefit.

1990: The foreign content limit for Registered Pension Plans and RRSPs were doubled in 1990 from 10% to 20%.

1990: The federal government instituted a policy that allowed for unused room in an RRSP to accumulate starting in 1991. Before this was introduced by the federal government, if an individual did not use his or her RRSP room in the year that it was granted he or she would lose the opportunity to contribute that amount in future years.

1991: The first modern Individual Pension Plans were registered with CRA and given pension registration numbers for reporting to CRA.

1992: RRSP maximum contribution limits of $15,500 for 1995 were pushed back to 1996.

1995: The maximum RRSP contributions for 1996 were frozen at $13,500. This maximum limit lasted for seven years.

1997: The federal government implemented Pension Adjustment Reversal (PAR) into the *Income Tax Act*. PAR restores *RRSP* contribution room for an employee who was terminated from a registered pension plan (RPP) or a *deferred profit sharing plan* (DPSP). PAR increases a former RPP and DPSP member's RRSP room by the difference between the total employee's PAs that were reported while a member of these plans and the actual pension transfer value to an RRSP. A PAR is calculated based on when membership in the plan is terminated. The RRSP room generated by PAR can be used by the individual to make RRSP contributions in the year of termination or it can be carried forward for use in future years. Before the federal government enacted PAR, when a member of a defined benefit pension plan left a plan, if he or she had lost RRSP room due to large pension adjustments that did not represent the actual amount vested within his or her DBPP, the former plan member would not have been able to recover the lost RRSP room.

2000: The federal government increased foreign content limits for Registered Pension Plans and RRSPs from 20% to 25% for 2000, and to 30% for 2001.

2003: The federal government increased yearly funding limits for RRSPs contributions, and pension benefit limits for all registered pension plans. The new limits for RRSPs were set at $14,500 for 2003, $15,500 for 2004, $16,500 for 2005 and $18,000 for 2006. Money purchase registered pension plans limits were set at $15,500 for 2003, $16,500 for 2004 and $18,000 for 2005. Defined benefit plan maximum pension benefit limits for accredited years of service were increased from $1,722.22 to $1,833 for 2004, and to $2,000 for 2005 for each year of employable service. When these plans reach their new maximum funding amounts as stated above, these amounts will increase with the average wage.

2004: The first of a series of Individual Pension Plan articles were published in *CA Magazine*, starting in the January 2004 issue. *CA Magazine* is a publication owned by the Canadian Institute of Chartered Accountants. These articles are accredited with launching the current boom in IPPs.

2005: RRSP and RPP limits were increased. Set limits for RRSP contributions were increased to $19,000 for 2007, $20,000 for 2008, $21,000 for 2009, and $22,000 for 2010. Set limits for defined contribution pension plans contributions were increased from $18,000 to $19,000 for 2006, $20,000 for 2007, $21,000 for 2008 and $22,000 for 2009. Set limits for defined benefit plan limits were increased to $2,111 for 2006, $2,222 for 2007, $2,333 for 2008 and $2,444 for 2009. All these limits are to be indexed to the average wage growth, starting in 2010 for defined contribution pension plans and defined benefit plans, and in 2011 for RRSPs.

2005: The foreign content limits for Registered Pension Plans and RRSPs were removed. This marked a fundamental change in the federal government's policy to direct moneys from Registered Pension Plans and RRSPs to support the Canadian capital markets.

2005: CRA's Registered Plans Directorate decided that it would shift its focus from an all-encompassing review of IPP documents when IPPs are first registered to a selective review of plan documents based on risk, and to more audits of IPPs on an ongoing basis.

For the first 14 years of the modern IPP history, CRA placed its focus on pre-registration review. Going forward, CRA's resources will be going towards audits of plans that are already registered. This means that the registration process of IPPs will be relaxed and made more quickly, but if an IPP is found not to be compliant with regulations, these pensions will be de-registered.

2005: CRA increased the amount of funds that needed to be transferred from RRSPs, DPSPs, DCPPs and other DBPPs, in a qualifying transfer to purchase IPP past service pension credits.

2006: In Ontario, a Risked-Based Pension Investment Monitoring Program and Investment Information Summary Form (IIS Form) was mandated to be submitted every year by sponsors of IPPs to the Financial Services Commission of Ontario (FSCO). It is believed that other provincial pension regulators will follow FSCO's lead and implement a similar risked-based pension investment monitoring process.

This form allows FSCO to reduce the risk that members of individual pension plans will not receive the benefits promised to them by their IPP sponsors due to poor investment performance and management within these plans.

- The IIS Form requests asset information, queries the status of the Statement of Investment Policies and Procedures (SIPP) and assesses compliance with the federal investment regulations and the SIPP.

- The plan administrator must certify as to the accuracy of the information on the IIS Form.

- Only the defined benefit component of a hybrid plan should be reported on the IIS.

Plans flagged by the automated assessment process will be subject to a further review. FSCO will follow up with the plan administrator if there is any non-compliance with the investment regulations or standards related to IPPs.

2007: The first formalized course provided on Individual Pension Plans in Canada was offered by the Canadian Securities Institute for financial consultants nationwide.

2007: The first book on Individual Pension Plans in Canada is published by LexisNexis Canada Inc.

MARKET FORCES DRIVING THE INDIVIDUAL PENSION PLAN SOLUTION

Similar to the adoption rate of RRSPs, which were first introduced in 1957 and did not become popularized in Canadian culture until the late 1970s when banks were allowed to sell RRSPs, IPPs are predicted by industry experts to become as commonplace for Canada's top earners in the next 15 years as RRSPs are today, as Canada's highest income earners trade in their RRSPs for the much more tax- and retirement-efficient IPP structure.

Let us look at some of the forces driving the growth of the IPP solution.

According to the Canadian Taxpayers Federation, in 2000, 22 million Canadians filed tax returns. Of those, 598,700 (2.7% of tax filers) earned more than $100,000 in T4 income. Potentially, an additional 600,000 business owners and executives have the ability to pay themselves T4 incomes of more than $100,000 if there is a tax incentive, such as the IPP, for them to do so.

The richest 10% of Canadian families have an average net worth of $980,903, accounting for 53% of national wealth in 1999. At that time, 72% of the $420 billion held in RRSPs were owned by the top 20% of affluent families. This 20% also owned 94% of the $92 billion invested in stocks outside RRSPs and 81% of the $80 billion invested in mutual and investment funds outside RRSPs.

According to the Canadian Federation of Independent Businesses, in the 1990s, there was an explosion of self-employment in this country. Currently there are 2.3 million self-employed Canadians and 1.1 million active incorporated businesses in Canada. With 75% of Canada's over 1 million businesses that employ fewer than five people, it can be assumed that most of the IPPs in this country will be created by owners of Canadian Controlled Private Corporations (CCPC) looking for a strategy to take money out of their corporations in a tax-effective way to help them prepare for retirement.

According to Statistics Canada, in the 2001 census, the median age of the average Canadian worker was 41.3 years old. Today 15% of working Canadians are within ten years of retirement. The creation of an IPP only makes sense for individuals aged 40 or older. The IPP maximum contribution for a 40-year-old is approximately $20,684 and will increase at a compound rate of 7.5% annually compared to the maximum RRSP 2007 contribution limit set at $19,000.

It is hypothesized that the IPP market will experience a growth similar to that of the mutual fund industry in Canada. The Investment Fund Institute of Canada reports that in 1990, the mutual fund industry was $24 billion. At the end of 2000, it had grown to $430 billion. The IPP market is on the verge of the same kind of explosive growth as more Canadians earn $100,000 and prepare to enter retirement en masse beginning in 2010.

In 2005, 230,000 Canadians were classified as millionaires, a growth of 7.2% from 2004, according to Merrill Lynch. High-net-worth Canadians were defined by Merrill Lynch as individuals who had financial assets over U.S. $1 million; this excluded their cars and homes. The majority of Canada's millionaires (70%) were older than 50 years of age.

According to the 10th annual World Wealth Report, the largest group (32%) of the wealthy in Canada earned their money through their employment. The next largest group was business owners (26%), followed by those who had inherited their wealth (16%).

Boomers are looking for both tax and investment solutions that will provide them with wealth preservation, CRA-sanctioned tax minimization and deferral capabilities, creditor protection, wealth accumulation and wealth distribution solutions, and the IPP delivers on all five of these criteria.

IPP specialists predict that over the next 15 years, if half of the people who currently earn $100,000-plus choose to upgrade their RRSPs to an IPP, there will be more than 300,000 of these DB pension plans in place across Canada. Currently, there are approximately 8,500 registered IPPs across Canada representing approximately $2 billion of total assets invested.

It is inevitable that the 20% of affluent Canadians who own 72% of the $420 billion in RRSPs will opt to migrate much of their RRSP assets into IPPs. If the average IPP accumulates $500,000, there will be more than $150 billion sitting in IPP assets or much, much more when additional voluntary contributions (which will be explained in Part III of this book) are added into the IPP asset mix. Given an average asset management fee of 2% per year, the assets held within IPPs will generate between $3 to $5 billion or more in recurring investment fees paid annually.

In addition, each IPP (to remain registered) will require actuarial and trustee administration, billing approximately $1,500 a year, generating approximately $450 million annually or more.

In real terms, an IPP will need to be accounted for on a company's corporate financial statement. The average cost for the total IPP new accounting services will roughly generate 2.4 million billable hours (IPP set-up) and also create 1.2 million in (ongoing) annual billable hours.

Lastly, the emerging IPP industry will create about $3 to $6 billion in new annual revenue for Canada's 68,000 Chartered Accountants, 35,000 Certified Management Accountants, 60,000 Certified General Accountants, 100,000-plus financial advisors and 2,600 actuaries which is not calculated into Canada's current gross domestic product formula, yet.

CHAPTER 2

IPP Features, Benefits and Limitations

Overview

This chapter begins by explaining the basic features and benefits of the Individual Pension Plan (IPP). It then goes on to detail the liabilities created by adopting the Individual Pension Plan solution. The chapter concludes by outlining the key differences between the Individual Pension Plan and the Registered Retirement Savings Plan (RRSP).

Learning Objectives

By the end of this chapter, you should be able to:

*   list the features and benefits of the Individual Pension Plan;
*   list the liabilities of the Individual Pension Plan; and
*   list the differences between an Individual Pension Plan and an RRSP.

IPP FEATURES, BENEFITS AND LIMITATIONS

In a nutshell, the IPP is essentially an RRSP upgrade, with three main differences: IPPs have significantly higher limits for contributions; they have creditor proofing; and they have restricted collapsibility options. In most provinces IPPs cannot be fully collapsed unless the plan holder is critically ill, severely disabled or has fallen on financial hardships. In essence, if the IPP is set up and maintained properly, effectively the IPP guarantees its member an income for retirement.

   Let us explore the features, benefits and limitations of an IPP in more detail.

Features and Benefits

Contribution for Current Service

Contributions to the IPP are far greater than what can be contributed into an RRSP for individuals over the age of 40. In essence the older a person is the greater the divide between what can be contributed into an IPP and what can be contributed into an RRSP on his or her behalf. In 2006, the maximum current service contributions that can be made into an IPP for an individual aged 69 could be as much as $42,462 compared to the maximum RRSP contribution of $18,000, a $24,462 difference in favour of the IPP.

Contributions for Past Service

For owners/executives, the IPP funding formula is more generous than the RRSP contribution limits. The plan normally allows companies to contribute for the pension plan member for years of service prior to the set-up of the plan going back to 1991 for connected persons. For non-connected persons, IPP funding contributions can go back further than 1991 to when the IPP member became an employee of the IPP sponsoring company.

If the first year of the set-up of an IPP is 2006, the past service and current service funding contribution/corporate deduction for a connected person could be as much as $241,800 for an individual who is 65 years old.

The table below shows the maximum corporate deduction a corporation may be permitted by Canada Revenue Agency (CRA) for a connected person based on the age of the plan member for 2006.

Table of Allowable IPP Contributions

(2006 Tax Deductibility for Corporations)

Age in 2005	Past Service from January 1, 1991	Current Service	Total Past and Current Service Corporate Contribution
40	$41,400	$18,900	**$60,300**
45	$68,300	$20,700	**$89,000**
50	$97,800	$22,800	**$120,600**

Age in 2005	Past Service from January 1, 1991	Current Service	Total Past and Current Service Corporate Contribution
55	$130,300	$25,000	**$155,300**
60	$165,900	$27,500	**$193,400**
65	$211,200	$30,600	**$241,800**

Note: The chart above was provided by GBL Inc. All assumptions in the table above are based on a 2006, $105,564 maximum annual pensionable income and an RRSP Qualifying Transfer of $231,600 into the IPP, for years of service going back to 1991.

A qualifying transfer is an amount that must be transferred from another registered plan such as an RRSP, unused RRSP room, defined benefit pension plan, money purchase plan, deferred profit sharing plan and/or a locked-in retirement account, before an IPP member can receive funding for past service in his or her IPP.

Depending on the actuarial firm used and its approved CRA Specimen Plan, which includes approved IPP text, funding formulas and documents by CRA, the maximum qualifying transfer amounts for a connected person for the example above could range from $231,600 to $260,000 for 2006. Throughout this book you will see different qualifying transfer amounts used by different actuaries and contributors.

Catch-up Contributions

Contributions that are not made into the IPP for a particular year can be made up in following years. If the IPP employer/plan sponsor makes a catch-up IPP contribution, this contribution will include an additional amount to compensate for the loss of income that would have been generated within the IPP based on a 7.5% rate of annual return. This additional contribution is a deduction for the employer and a non-taxable benefit for the IPP member.

Employees Earning Less Than $105,600 per Year and at Least 40 Years of Age

The age of a potential IPP member is the most crucial factor in determining if the IPP is a person's best retirement solution. IPP contributions for a member of at least 40 years of age and earning less than $105,600 per year will still produce a proportional advantage over RRSP contributions. Later in this book you will learn why contributions into an IPP for older plan members will always be greater than contributions into an RRSP for the same individual.

Luring Key People to Your Organization

By using an IPP as part of a total executive benefit package, a company can attract people who are currently employed and are members of a defined benefit pension plan. Traditionally such candidates may not have wanted to leave an employer or DB plan before retirement because tax rules prevented them from transferring the full value of their pension credits to a locked-in RRSP. Now a company can avoid such an obstacle by creating an IPP for these employees by transferring existing pension plan assets to the new IPP without tax implications. Opting to utilize this IPP benefit, the full commuted value from a previous employer's defined benefit pension plan can be transferred to the IPP at the new place of employment without a maximum transfer age value limit and triggering taxes to the IPP member.

Creditor Proofing

Creditors of the plan member or the incorporated business cannot seize assets held within the IPP in most situations provided that the IPP was created in good faith. However, all annual payments made to the retired employee are taxable earnings and could be seizable.

For plans that are not subject to provincial registration, as in Quebec for connected person plans, the funds under the non-registered IPP are not considered locked-in and could be considered as seizable. A legal expert should be consulted in this situation.

Extended Contribution Period

A company has 120 days after its year-end to make an IPP contribution which will be considered an expense for the company in the previous business fiscal year. Contributions into an RRSP that can be applied back to the previous calendar year need to be made within the first 60 days after the start of the New Year.

Ownership of Plan Assets

At retirement, the IPP member owns any actuarial surplus. It may be used to upgrade pension benefits, or the plan holder may pass it on to his or her spouse, heirs, or estate.

Greater Compounding on Interest on a Tax-Deferred Basis

Albert Einstein once remarked that one of the greatest human inventions was the creation of compound interest. The value of earning compound interest within the IPP in a tax-deferred way should never be understated. Let us look and see why it makes sense in the long run to save for retirement within a tax-deferred vehicle such as the IPP, where interest compounds tax-free until it is withdrawn.

Imagine you have a 55-year-old client, John Doe, who has owned an incorporated business since 1991, with a T4 income of more than $100,000 and a marginal tax rate in Ontario of 46.41%. This client is serious about saving for retirement and in the next ten years, when he reaches 65, he plans to retire. By creating an IPP for himself this year, your client will be able to defer $161,851 immediately from taxes from his company's and his personal income. This money will then compound tax-free. The next year John Doe will be able to contribute an additional $27,934 into his IPP, and the contribution into the IPP will increase by 7.5% annually until he retires (the investment chosen for this example earns 7.5% annually). When John Doe reaches 65, he will have accumulated $815,583 in his IPP.

If this client decides not to create an IPP for himself and instead chooses to take this same amount of money out of his business, after having paid the personal marginal tax rate of 46.41%, for the purpose of saving for retirement, then his financial situation becomes much different. The first year after taxes, John Doe will be left with $72,811 to invest. The following year, after taxes the $27,934 he takes out of his business, as personal income, will leave him with $13,925 to contribution to his non-IPP; and this annual contribution will grow at 7.5% (the investment chosen for this example earns 7.5% annually as well). At age 65, he will have an accumulated value in his non-IPP of $348,524.

Based on the stated assumptions, this particular client's IPP option will yield an additional $467,059 more than his non-IPP alternative. That is the power of tax-free compounding.

Guaranteed Lifetime Income to IPP Members, Their Spouses and Heirs

This pension plan offers a predictable retirement income. An actuary determines the current annual cost of the future retirement income. Spousal pension benefits may be upgraded to 100% at the time the member retires or at the plan member's death. Adult children with disabilities may also receive pension benefits after the IPP member's death. This will be further discussed in Chapter 18.

Terminal Funding

One of the most attractive features of the IPP is the possibility of terminal funding. The IPP member may elect to receive his or her pension benefit as early as age 50 without reducing the promised pension benefit.

While CRA restricts the benefits that can be pre-funded, the plan can be amended at retirement to provide the most generous terms possible. Some of these include full consumer price indexing and early retirement pension with no reduction as well as bridge benefits to compensate for CPP/QPP and Old Age Security (OAS) that IPP members will not receive until age 65.

Imagine an IPP has been created for a 49-year-old owner/manager. As of January 1, 2005, this owner/manager has T4 earnings of $100,000 and has maintained this level of income since 1991. It is safe to project that the owner/manager's income will remain at $100,000 annually adjusted to inflation until retirement. Assume that this IPP member will retire at age 60 on January 1, 2016, with 25 years of pensionable service (1991 to 2015). Before the retirement benefit begins to be paid out of the IPP, there is a window of opportunity for the company to make a one-time $251,000 terminal funding contribution to the IPP, in addition to regular IPP government-prescribed funding contributions and annual growth calculations when this IPP member retires.

Estate Planning

IPPs are the perfect vehicle to transfer assets from one family member to another in a tax effective way. With an RRSP on the death of a second spouse all assets within the RRSP become taxable. If an able adult child joins a business in which an IPP has been set up for the parent(s), the child can be added as a member of the IPP. Upon the death of the parent(s) any assets that have not been used to pay benefits to the retired parent(s) from the IPP can be transferred to the child, who is a member of the IPP, for the purpose of funding the promised pension benefit to the child without causing taxes to be triggered.

Another alternative is on the death of the IPP member the assets are available to be transferred to the spouse, to another beneficiary or to the member's estate.

Flexible Funding Options

Moneys can be used to fund the IPP that have accumulated in retained earnings of a company. Funding can come from outstanding bonuses owed to owners/executives by the employer making the employee's contributions into the IPP. Another option would be for the employer to obtain financing/loans from a financial institution. The business can access funds tax-effectively from a corporately owned Universal Life Policy by collateralizing the policy through loans from a bank using the cash value as the collateral, or shareholder loans. All interest on loans to fund an IPP in addition to all other IPP expenses are tax-deductible for the sponsor/employer and are a non-taxable benefit for the IPP member.

Limitations

Under the Age of 40 IPPs Are Ineffective and Detrimental for Tax-Efficient Retirement Savings

The value of defined benefit pension credits (the amount, determined actuarially, that is needed to be invested in a defined benefit pension plan to deliver the promised pension benefit) greatly varies depending on an IPP member's age. For individuals under the age of 40, his or her pension adjustment is over-valued, meaning that less money will actually be put aside tax-effectively within an IPP rather than if the individual utilized an RRSP or defined contribution pension plan. For individuals over the age of 40 the reverse happens. Their pension adjustment is under-valued, meaning that more money can be put away tax-effectively within an IPP than could be invested in either an RRSP or a defined contribution pension plan.

For example, if a 25-year-old earned $100,000 and is credited a $2,000 IPP benefit for this year's earning, his pension adjustment would be $18,000, giving him RRSP room of $600 due to the pension adjustment offset (multiply plan benefit by 9, then subtract the PA offset (9 × benefit − $600)). However, the true amount invested in his IPP to generate the promised benefit of $2,000 would only be approximately

$3,940 ($1.97 × benefit), not the $18,000 attributed to his pension adjustment for our 25-year-old.

On the other hand if a 69-year-old earned $100,000 and is credited the same $2,000 IPP benefit this year, his pension adjustment would be $18,000, giving him RRSP room of $600 once the pension adjustment offset is factored in as for our 25-year-old. But the actual amount invested in his IPP to generate the promised $2,000 pension benefit would be much greater, $42,462 ($21.23 × $2,000 pension benefit).

Pension adjustment offset is the minimum level of RRSP room that someone is given when they are participating in a defined benefit pension plan. Up until 1996, it was $1,000, and then from 1997 to the present, it is $600 per year for members of a defined benefit pension plan. The pension adjustment offset gives members of a defined benefit pension plan a minimum RRSP contribution room for any given year that they are members of DBPPs.

IPPs Are Expensive to Set Up and Maintain

The set-up fees for an IPP can range from $1,500 to $5,000 depending on the complexity of the plan. Annual administration fees range from $500 to $2,000. It should be remembered that the plan sponsor could write off these IPP fees. In comparison the cost for having a self-directed RRSP can range annually from $0 to $250, which cannot be written off at all by either the employer or the RRSP owner.

Before implementing the IPP solution, a cost-benefit analysis should always be completed for each situation. For example, in the case of an employer/business owner who is considering an IPP for himself or herself for 2006 with a set-up fee of $3,500, who is 40 years of age, who earns $200,000 annually with a marginal tax rate of 46.41% and who is not permitted to make any past service contributions into the plan, his or her corporation will be permitted to make a current service contribution of $19,600 this year into an IPP on the business owner's behalf. The business owner will also be given an RRSP contribution of $18,000 based on his or her last year's income for a combined corporate and personal tax deduction of $41,100 ($19,600 IPP contribution + $3,500 set-up costs + $18,000 RRSP contribution).

By creating an IPP, the business owner and corporation will have personal tax savings of $19,075 compared to only making his or her $18,000 RRSP contribution, which would provide a tax savings of $8,354. By completing a cost-benefit analysis for this business owner, it will be clearly illustrated that the IPP/RRSP option will deliver an additional $10,721 tax savings over and above the RRSP contribution only option.

IPPs Are Too Complex

IPPs are, first and foremost, defined benefit pension plans. Each IPP has to be approved by CRA, and in most instances IPPs need the approval of provincial pension regulators.

There is a need for annual filings and triennial actuarial reports filed with CRA to validate contributions into these plans. In addition there are special accounting procedures that must be completed on the corporate financial statements by IPP-sponsoring companies, along with investment restrictions for assets held within the IPP that are not required of ordinary RRSPs.

IPPs Are Contractual Employment Arrangements

The employer/IPP plan sponsor is required to make annual contributions into the plan. These mandatory contributions are not dependent on the sponsoring company showing a profit or loss on its books.

IPPs Have Withdrawal Restrictions

An RRSP can be collapsed at any time and the RRSP holder will then pay taxes on the proceeds withdrawn from his or her plan based on his or her marginal tax rate. IPP assets are usually locked-in and cannot be accessed by the plan member prematurely.

An IPP member can opt for several choices with the pension plan when his or her employment is terminated or when the plan member retires. At termination or retirement, pension plan funds may be used to pay out the plan benefit as promised. The IPP can also be transferred to or invested in the following financial instruments: Annuity (single or joint and last survivor); Locked-in Investment Retirement Account (LIRA); Life Income Fund (LIF) (in most provinces an LIF must purchase an annuity when its owner turns 80 years old); and Locked-in RRIF (LRIF) (where applicable, as some provinces do not require IPPs to be transferred to a locked-in plan at all). The pension plan can be transferred to a new employer pension if the new employer is willing to offer an IPP. If the IPP was registered in Quebec and the IPP member is a connected person, he or she has the option to transfer the assets from the plan to an RRSP and then take a lump-sum withdrawal, after applicable taxes have been withheld.

IPPs Restrict the Use of Spousal RRSPs

Contributions into an IPP can be made only into an employee's plan. Hence, income-splitting through contributing into a Spousal RRSP is extremely restricted to what is left over after the IPP member's PA has been subtracted from his or her RRSP contribution limit. Usually the RRSP amount left to invest into a Spousal RRSP is only the pension adjustment offset, which is $600 per annum.

IPP Surpluses

If the investments within an IPP do very well, delivering better than the actuarial investment return assumptions of 7.5%, a surplus will result in an IPP. A company/sponsor in this situation will not be permitted to make additional contributions into an IPP on behalf of the plan member until the surpluses have vanished. In the years that the plan runs surpluses a company/sponsor will not receive a deduction until contributions into the plan are permitted to resume.

In years that an IPP is running surpluses, where the IPP member is accruing pensionable credits, a pension adjustment will be generated, even though no funds are being contributed into the plan on the IPP member's behalf. The result: the IPP member's ability to contribute into an RRSP or any other registered plan will be deeply restricted to only the pension adjustment offset of $600 per annum.

IPP Underfunding

Depending on the province that an IPP is registered in, if a plan is underfunded based on actuarial assumptions and valuations, an employer/sponsor of an IPP may be mandated to make contributions into a plan, to make up for deficits in the plan. In some cases making up for deficiencies in funding into an IPP is desirable if a company has positive cash flow.

On the other hand mandatory IPP contributions may place a heavy burden on a business/IPP sponsor who might not have the ability to fully fund a promised IPP benefit at the time that contributions have been mandated to occur.

IPP Revocation of Plan Registration (Worst-Case Scenario)

If it is determined that an IPP is not in compliance with governing Pension Acts and CRA's Registered Plans Directorate's regulations, the registration of an IPP may be revoked at anytime. To remain registered by CRA, IPPs must at all times satisfy four criteria:

1. The IPP must comply with all laws and regulation governing Registered Pension Plans; all filings must be up to date.

2. The company/sponsor must be established for a reason other than to establish a pension plan prior to the plan being set up and/or the transferring of pension benefit assets from another defined benefit pension plan from another employer to the IPP.

3. The employee/employer must have a *bona fide* employment relationship between the plan member and his or her company.

4. If assets from another defined benefit pension plan have been transferred to an IPP, the member of the IPP needs to expect to have earnings at a similar level from the new employer as the member earned from the prior employer. The rule of thumb is that these earnings from the new employer should be similar to that of the old employer for three years.

The best-case scenario resulting from this worst-case scenario is that, when an IPP's status is revoked, the IPP immediately turns into a retirement compensation arrangement (RCA). The former registered IPP will have to then immediately forward 50% of all plan assets to CRA on behalf of the plan member. These funds will be refunded to the RCA plan member at a later date when money is withdrawn from the RCA.

In the very, very worst-case scenario CRA may not permit the assets from the IPP to be rolled over into an RCA. Thus taxes will be charged on all assets held in the former IPP. Heavy interest charges may be levied by CRA for overdue taxes owed by both the IPP sponsor and the member of the plan.

An RCA is a plan defined in subsection 248(1) of the *Income Tax Act*, R.S.C. 1985, c. 1 (5th Supp.), providing supplemental pension benefits to owners/managers and key employees of incorporated businesses. Contributions to an RCA are 100% tax deductible by the employer and are not taxable for the employee until the money is withdrawn from the RCA.

Money that is invested into an RCA through a trustee is divided equally between two accounts. The first account is called the RCA investment account. The second account is referred to as the refundable tax account, and this account is administered by CRA. Fifty per cent of the deposits into the RCA are forwarded to the refundable tax account, and 50% of the earnings earned within the RCA investment account are also forwarded to the refundable tax account every year. All funds in the refundable tax account are refundable to the recipient of the RCA when the recipient begins to withdraw his or her money. When money is withdrawn from an RCA, tax will be paid by the beneficiary of the RCA at his or her marginal tax rate. (RCAs will be further covered in Chapter 15.)

Note: Over the past several years CRA has been cracking down on registered IPPs, especially a Tailored Individual Pension Plan (TIPP). A TIPP is an IPP in which the pension adjustment is inappropriately low in relation to the benefit promised by the pension. CRA frowns upon TIPPs and on plan sponsors and members of plans that have been deemed TIPPs. Sponsors, plan members and advisors run the risk of having these pension plans deregistered and paying high interest and tax penalties to CRA.

Possible Heavy Fines and Penalties (Worst-Case Scenario)

It is important to understand that an IPP is a registered pension plan and because of this simple fact extra care must go into the set-up, maintenance and wind-up of these plans.

If for any reason an IPP is in violation of the federal government's *Pension Benefits Standards Act, 1985*, R.S.C. 1985, c. 82 (2nd Supp.), *Income Tax Act*, *Income Tax Regulations*, C.R.C., c. 945, or provincial Acts, an individual who contravenes any provision, or who avoids compliance, is guilty of an offence under these Acts. Individuals found liable for violating these Acts on their first conviction can be fined up to $100,000 or be imprisoned for a term not exceeding 12 months, or both. In addition a corporation/sponsor of an IPP that is convicted of violating these Acts and regulations may be fined up to $500,000.

IPP VS. RRSP

The following is a brief comparison between an IPP and an RRSP:

Quick Overview	RRSP	IPP
Contributions Limits	18% of individual's previous year overall T4 income.	Established by actuary according to CRA rules and both federal and provincial pension Acts. Contributions are based on the IPP member's current age and current income received from the IPP sponsor.

Quick Overview	RRSP	IPP
Contributions	Deducted by the individual.	Contributions and costs are deducted by the company and are not subjected to payroll taxes.
Creditor Protection	Most are not unless a part of an insurance contract.	Yes, expect in Quebec, the funds under the non-registered IPPs for connected persons could be considered as seizable.
Investment Risk	Lies with the individual.	Lies with the employer because if the performance is not up to the formula amount, the employer must make additional contributions.
Additional Contributions	If poor investment performance, no additional funds can be added to these plans.	If the investment performance is poor (less than 7.5% per annum), the company/sponsor in most jurisdictions has to make additional contributions to fund the plan.
Past Service	Taxpayer may have unused room that can be used to make further contributions.	Past service recognition, receive credit for previous years' income for funding retirement savings. IPPs can be funded back to 1991 for connected persons.
Current funding	Contributions can be made within 60 days after the end of the calendar year.	Contributions allowed 120 days after corporate year-end.
Transfer of Assets to other Family member upon death other than the spouse	No: On the death of an RRSP holder assets held within the RRSP can be transferred tax free to a surviving spouse or a dependent child. Upon the death of the spouse or the time a child is no longer deemed dependent all RRSP holdings are subjected to taxes of the deceased spouse's estate or former dependent child's marginal tax rate.	Yes: If other family members are placed on IPP as members of the existing plan, upon death of one of the members of the plan. Assets within the IPP can be transferred successfully without triggering taxes. IPP benefits can be transferred to a dependent child without triggering the assets within the IPP to be deregistered.

CHAPTER 3

ROLES AND RESPONSIBILITIES

Overview

This chapter introduces the roles and responsibilities of each party who is involved in the implementation, maintenance and wind-up processes of an Individual Pension Plan.

Learning Objectives

By the end of this chapter, you should be able to:

* list the roles and responsibilities of different parties involved in the IPP.

THE KEY PLAYERS

Who is involved in the set-up, maintenance and wind-up of an IPP? The key players that can be easily identified are the employer/sponsor of the plan, the administrator, the custodian, the trustee(s), actuary, investment manager/financial advisor and the IPP member. Each of these players must work within defined roles and follow sound IPP governance.

IPP Sponsor

The IPP sponsor is the company that creates an IPP for a *bona fide* employee. IPPs are usually only sponsored by incorporated businesses or incorporated professional corporations. The sponsor is responsible for providing continuous T4 income records to allow the actuary to properly determine the beneficiary IPP funding levels. Since an IPP is usually a pension for just one person, it is usually more cost effective that the sponsor of a plan also be the administrator of an IPP. From this point on in this chapter, the term sponsor and administrator will be interchangeable.

IPP Administrator

The IPP administrator as mentioned earlier is usually the employer/ sponsor of an IPP. For an IPP to become a registered pension plan it is required that an administrator has been appointed. The administrator is either a person or a group of people, or sponsoring company with the responsibility for the set-up, maintenance and winding-up of an IPP. It is a must that the IPP administrator resides within Canada.

The IPP administrator/sponsor is placed in a key position where it must decide that it will create an IPP compensation package for an owner, executive or a *bona fide* employee of the sponsoring company. After it has been decided that an IPP will be created, the administrator will appoint an investment manager/financial advisor to manage an IPP's assets. Even though an investment manager has been appointed the administrator still has fiduciary duties to make sure the IPP assets are properly managed according to the investment policy statement (IPS), and that the plan is fully funded. The administrator/sponsor is responsible for appointing the actuarial firm that will complete the needed actuarial calculations that are required by the Canada Revenue Agency (CRA) and the various provincial pension regulators for an IPP on an ongoing basis.

In the world of IPPs, it is usually the investment manager/financial advisor who works with the sponsor/administrator to select the actuarial firm. The administrator/sponsor is responsible for providing the needed financial data to the actuarial firm, so that an IPP quote can be produced by the actuary to show the financial benefits, liabilities and responsibilities of providing an IPP.

The administrator/sponsor will appoint a custodian who will actually hold the IPP assets. If the custodian is an insurance company, there may be no need to appoint a trustee, if certain conditions are met, which will be discussed later on in the trustee(s) section of this chapter. However, if the custodian of the assets of an IPP is a financial institution or financial firm, the administrator/sponsor will need to appoint a trustee(s) to manage/direct the investment manager on how to manage the funds in the IPP.

During the IPP set-up stage, the administrator/sponsor must decide what the amortization period to fund the past service contribution to the plan (1-15 years) will be. The administrator/sponsor then applies to CRA to register the IPP by completing Form T510, "Application to Register a Pension Plan", *and* Form T244, "Registered Pension Plan Annual Information Return". These forms will indicate whether or not a plan is a designated plan and if the plan member is a connected person. Once a plan has achieved designated plan status (IPP), it continues with this status unless CRA changes its status.

Other duties and responsibilities of an IPP administrator/sponsor include filing actuarial reports with CRA. Administrators must provide CRA and pension authorities with annual information returns and triennial actuarial evaluations. It is the IPP administrator/sponsor that applies to CRA for past service pension adjustment (PSPA) for IPP members. IPP administrators must make sure that PAs and PSPAs are produced and reported to CRA and the various provincial pension regulating bodies. IPP administrators are responsible to pay all registration fees for the IPP to both federal and provincial regulating bodies if these fees are applicable. IPP administrators will be responsible to pay pension benefits out to IPP members when these members are eligible to receive a pension benefit.

Lastly, IPP administrators are responsible for providing members information about their plans in a timely manner. This information includes:

Pension Plan Booklet: The administrator/sponsor of the IPP must provide this within 60 days after an individual has joined an IPP.

Annual Statement: The administrator/sponsor of the IPP must provide an annual statement of the plan to an IPP member within six months after the year-end of the plan.

Termination Statement: The administrator/sponsor of the IPP must provide this to an IPP member within 30 days after the member has retired from the sponsoring company. The administrator/sponsor of the IPP is responsible for advising the member within 60 days before retirement what his or her retirement options are.

Pension Adjustment Reversal (PAR): If the IPP plan member decides to transfer/cease being a member of the IPP and transfer his or her IPP funds to an RRSP or a DCPP, the plan administrator has to report a PAR that is greater than nil to both CRA and the employee by submitting a Form T10, "Pension Adjustment Reversal", to CRA on behalf of the former plan member. PAR restores RRSP contribution room for an employee that was terminated from a registered pension plan (RPP) or a deferred profit sharing plan (DPSP). PAR increases a former RPP and DPSP member's RRSP contribution room by the difference between the total employee's PAs that were reported while a member of these plans and the actual pension dollar transfer value to an RRSP.

Survivor Benefit Statement: The administrator must provide a survivor benefit statement within the first 30 days after the estate of an IPP member has provided a certified death notice of the plan member.

Custodian

The custodian is the entity that actually holds the assets inside the IPP. Either an insurance company or a financial institution or financial firm usually holds assets in an IPP. In the case where there has not been a contract of insurance to invest IPP assets in a "group insurance product", the administrator of an IPP will have to draw up a trust agreement and appoint as the custodian a corporate trustee or a three-party trustee to hold the assets within the IPP.

Trustee(s)

If an IPP invests its assets in anything other than in a group insurance product/insurance pension fund held by an insurance company, then the administrator/sponsor of the IPP must appoint a trustee(s) to administer the IPP assets while these funds remain registered in the IPP. A group insurance investment product should not be confused with individual segregated funds offered by insurance companies. IPPs that hold individual segregated funds need to have a trustee(s) appointed to administrate over the assets.

The reason why IPPs that hold group insurance investment products do not require a trustee(s) appointed to them is because these types of products have a built-in maturity date after the IPP member's 69th birthday. Pension law requires that a trustee(s) be appointed for RPPs with assets that do not have a maturity date after the pension plan member's 69th birthday. Regular investments and segregated funds do not have built-in maturity dates, so a trustee must be appointed on these types of IPPs to ensure that these plans do mature after the 69th birthday of the plan member.

A trustee(s) can be a trust company or at least three individuals who live in Canada, and who are charged to promote the financial security of a pension fund through sound investment policies and practices. If the trust for the IPP is set up using three trustees/individuals, at least one of these individuals needs to be completely independent from the corporation sponsoring the IPP and the IPP member.

What is expected of a trustee is something that has been considered by the courts over the years, and can now be found in the provincial

Trustee Acts. The rule has been expressed that the trustee must show ordinary care, skill and prudence, that he or she must act as a prudent person of discretion and intelligence would act in his or her own affairs.

The most popular method to date of setting up an IPP is by using the three-person trusteeship structure. Unfortunately many individuals accepting a trustee role in this type of IPP structure do not have a full comprehension of their responsibilities and duties. Trustees risk serious liabilities if they are in violation of the *Income Tax Act*, the *Income Tax Regulations*, the various Trustee Acts and Pension Acts and the common laws surrounding fiduciary responsibilities of trustees.

Before someone accepts the position as a trustee to an IPP, that person should have a firm understanding of the IPP itself and the information contained in all documents concerning the administration of the trust.

These duties include hiring and overseeing professional advisors and service providers in carrying out the responsibilities of the trust. IPP trust administration includes maintaining all trustee documentation and receiving and depositing all contributions into the IPP trust fund. The trustee(s) should know all the IPP's professional advisors and service providers and understand their roles. The trustee(s) should review the reports of each advisor. The trustee(s) should become familiar with the legal duties and responsibilities for a trustee and should be familiar with the assets held in the IPP and how these assets have been invested within the plan.

The trustee(s) is responsible in helping put together the information to file a T3P form to CRA. The T3P form is entitled "Employees Pension Plan Income Tax Return". The T3P form must be filed within 90 days after the year-end of the trust. If this form is late, CRA can impose penalties for filing late.

Prudent Trustee Investment Guidelines

Unless it has been specified in the trust documents, trustees must act unanimously on any decisions that are made concerning IPP trust assets. Some IPP trusts allow for the majority of the trustees to make decisions or for one of the trustees to act on behalf of all the trustees. If the trustees allow one of their members to manage and control IPP assets, all trustees are still responsible for what decisions are made and how IPP assets are cared for.

Beneficiaries of trusts should be able to expect an objective test of what is careful, skillful and prudent, and the trustee must document his or her conduct. Section 27 of the Ontario *Trustee Act*, R.S.O. 1990, c. T.23, is set out below as a representative example of the provincial Trustee Acts' investment guidelines that an appointed trustee to an IPP must follow.

Note: The investments guidelines within the Trustee Acts are complementary to the investment guidelines outlined in the various Pension Acts across Canada that are discussed in depth in Chapter 9 in Part II of this book.

Section 27 of the *Trustee Act* provides:

(1) *Investment standards* — In investing trust property, a trustee must exercise the care, skill, diligence and judgment that a prudent investor would exercise in making investments.

(2) *Authorized investments* — A trustee may invest trust property in any form of property in which a prudent investor might invest.

(3) *Mutual, pooled and segregated funds* — Any rule of law that prohibits a trustee from delegating powers or duties does not prevent the trustee from investing in mutual funds, pooled funds or segregated funds under variable insurance contracts, and sections 27.1 and 27.2 do not apply to the purchase of such funds.

(4) *Common trust funds* — If trust property is held by co-trustees and one of the co-trustees is a trust corporation as defined in the *Loan and Trust Corporations Act*, any rule of law that prohibits a trustee from delegating powers or duties does not prevent the co-trustee from investing in a common trust fund, as defined in that Act, that is maintained by the trust corporation and sections 27.1 and 27.2 do not apply.

(5) *Criteria* — A trustee must consider the following criteria in planning the investment of trust property, in addition to any others that are relevant to the circumstances:

1. General economic conditions.

2. The possible effect of inflation or deflation.

3. The expected tax consequences of investment decisions or strategies.

4. The role that each investment or course of action plays within the overall trust portfolio.

5. The expected total return from income and the appreciation of capital.

6. Needs for liquidity, regularity of income and preservation or appreciation of capital.

7. An asset's special relationship or special value, if any, to the purposes of the trust or to one or more of the beneficiaries.

(6) *Diversification* — A trustee must diversify the investment of trust property to an extent that is appropriate to do:

(a) the requirements of the trust; and

(b) general economic and investment market conditions.

(7) *Investment advice* — A trustee may obtain advice in relation to the investment of trust property.

(8) *Reliance on advice* — It is not a breach of trust for a trustee to rely on advice obtained under subsection (7) if a prudent investor would rely on the advice under comparable circumstances.

(9) *Terms of trust* — This section and section 27.1 do not authorize or require a trustee to act in a manner that is inconsistent with the terms of the trust.

(10) *Same* — For the purposes of subsection (9), the constating documents of a corporation that is deemed to be a trustee under subsection 1 (2) of the *Charities Accounting Act* form part of the terms of the trust.

Actuary

When an IPP is to be created, an administrator is required to appoint an actuary. An actuary is a person who is a Fellow of the Canadian Institute of Actuaries. Actuaries are business professionals who apply their knowledge of mathematics, probability, statistics, and risk theory, to real-life financial problems involving future uncertainty.

With the setting up, ongoing maintenance and wind-up of an IPP, actuaries are needed to complete the IPP's required valuation reports and to certify these reports that an IPP is properly funded to deliver the promised benefit for an IPP member. The other main responsibilities that are delegated to the actuary of an IPP are to draft the IPP plan documents, create board resolutions for the sponsoring company to sign, review insurance contracts or trust agreements where the IPP assets will reside and file with CRA and/or provincial regulators. Actuaries complete triennial valuations that must be submitted every three years to both CRA and, in some provinces, provincial pension regulators.

IPP Investment Manager/Financial Advisor

The IPP investment managers/financial advisors are appointed by plan sponsor/administrators and trustee(s) (if a trustee(s) has been appointed). They are charged with working with the IPP administrator and trustee(s) to develop a written investment policy statement (IPS). The IPS aim is to provide the IPP with guidelines for the long-term financial and investment decisions that will be made for assets within the plan. It generally includes investment objectives (return requirements and risk tolerance), constraints (cash requirements and timing issues) and guidelines for achieving the IPP's funding objectives.

IPP investment managers/financial advisors are charged with the responsibility of selecting and managing the investments that are invested in the IPP fund. Investment managers are responsible for making sure that the activities within the pension fund comply with the IPS and federal and provincial pension guidelines. Lastly, investment managers/ financial advisors are charged with the responsibility of reporting the activities within the IPP fund back to the administrator and trustee(s) (if a trustee(s) has been appointed) and actuary of the IPP.

IPP Member/Participant

The IPP member/participant is a designated employee of a company who is deemed or has been deemed to have contributions made to an IPP on his or her behalf. In most cases IPPs are set up for connected members of organizations.

In most situations, because IPPs are created for a connected member, these individuals are usually involved in making the decision to create IPPs for themselves. They may help in the selection of the IPP's administrator, investment manager, custodian, trustee and actuary. The member will provide past earning data and provide a complete list of current RRSP, DCPP, DPSP, Locked-in RRSP holdings and accumulated unused RRSP room amounts to assist in the first actuary evaluation. When an IPP is approved, the member will receive from CRA an approval notice that the member will have to provide to the custodian of the IPP. The member will also assist in transferring assets from his or her RRSP, unused RRSP room and/or other registered pension plans for the qualifying transfer that is required before the IPP can receive past service funding for prior years of service before the IPP was created.

The IPP member is also responsible for providing names of spouse, common law spouse or heirs to be beneficiaries in the event the member dies.

CHAPTER 4

INDIVIDUAL PENSION PLAN PROCESS

Overview

This chapter lays out the processes involved in the life cycle of an Individual Pension Plan, from the set-up, through to the ongoing maintenance and deregistration stages.

Learning Objectives

By the end of this chapter, you should be able to:

*   list the steps involved in the process of the implementation stage of the Individual Pension Plan solution;

*   list the steps involved in the process of the maintenance stage of the Individual Pension Plan solution; and

*   list the steps involved in the process of the winding-up stage of the Individual Pension Plan solution.

IPP PROCESS FOR NEW PLANS

The table below shows the life cycle of an Individual Pension Plan (IPP) through its set-up phase.

Step 1	A company/future administrator requests a quote to determine how much can be put into an IPP to fund a benefit for a potential IPP member. Information data such as date of birth and T4 earnings dating back to 1991 if earned by a connected person is gathered. If the individual is not a connected person, T4 earnings used to calculate pensionable benefits can be collected dating back to the time the employee began working for the sponsoring company.
	Determine IPP suitability by getting a quote from an actuary or a firm that specializes in setting up IPPs.

Step 2	The company/sponsor will need to review the quote to determine if the IPP is the best solution for the potential IPP member.
Step 3	The Plan sponsor decides to establish an Individual Pension Plan.
Step 4	The Plan sponsor appoints an administrator, a custodian, trustee(s) if needed, an actuary and an investment manager/financial advisor to design, register and manage the IPP.
Step 5	IPP documents such as the following are prepared: • Trust Agreement (if applicable) • Board of Directors Resolutions • Actuarial Valuation Report • Actuarial Information Summary/Cost Certificate (if applicable) • Application for PSPA (if applicable) • Application for Registration of Pension Plan CRA Form (T510) • Investment Objectives Guidelines • Locking-In Agreement (if applicable) • Letters to CRA and Provincial Authority (if applicable) • Past Service Pension Adjustment Certification Form T1004 (if applicable) • CRA Connected Person Information Return Form T1007 (if applicable) • Beneficiary Designations • Pension Plan Text A folder of all documents for the IPP sponsor's and IPP member's records are prepared.
Step 6	IPP documents are filed with CRA and provincial regulating authorities. The administrator pays fees for filing and registering IPP.
Step 7	CRA provides a temporary registration letter with a temporary seven-digit IPP registration number. Permanent IPP status has not been granted yet.
Step 8	Once CRA has provided a temporary IPP number, the sponsoring company can now make contributions for past service and current service. However, the qualifying transfer will not occur yet at this stage. The IPP must first receive final approval from CRA.

Step 9	If all filings are completed properly, CRA will give formal approval of the IPP by sending a registration letter to the sponsoring company and its appointed advisors.
Step 10	At this point, the IPP member must start the qualifying transfer process. These funds will originate from the IPP member's RRSP, RRSP's unused room, locked-in plans, DPSPs or pension plans or a combination thereof, and will be transferred to the IPP. CRA requires that the qualifying transfer process be completed within 90 days of the date that the IPP was formally registered by CRA.
Step 11	CRA's formal letter is sent to the sponsoring company of the IPP. This letter permits contributions to the IPP to be deducted as expenses off the sponsoring company's corporate tax return.

Note: Depending on the jurisdiction in which an IPP is registered, a cheque by the plan administrator for the IPP's registration will have to be paid directly to the regulatory pension authorities (see table below for these dollar amounts by jurisdiction).

PROVINCE	REGISTRATION FEE
Alberta	$70
British Columbia	$200
Federal	$10 per member
Manitoba	$100
New Brunswick	$100
Newfoundland	$500
Nova Scotia	$100
Ontario	$250
Prince Edward Island	N/A
Quebec (if non-connected person)	$500 + $7.15 per member
Saskatchewan	$100

ONGOING IPP ADMINISTRATION REQUIREMENTS AND PROCESS

The table below shows the life cycle of an IPP through its maintenance phase.

Step 1	The administrator/sponsor will need to provide the actuarial firm all T4 earnings of the IPP member for the current year of service. The member's pension adjustment (PA) is calculated based on the previous year's earnings, and this will be shown on the IPP member's T4. The sponsoring company is required to include a pension adjustment (PA) and the Plan's registration number for each IPP member on its T4 slip.
Step 2	A statement showing the IPP's assets for the previous year is required to be produced and forwarded to the IPP's actuary. In this statement the following must be provided: • Opening market and book value • Contributions • Transfers • Distributions • Closing market and book value *Note: The financial or insurance institution that holds the IPP assets will provide this information.* This information is required so the actuary, plan administrator and trustee can complete a T3P Employees' Pension Plan Income Tax Return if the IPP has been set up with a trust agreement with either a formal trustee or a three-person trustee arrangement. Also, what needs to be prepared for submission to keep the IPP registered are: • Financial Statements • Pension Statements • CRA Annual Information Return (Depending on the province of registration a Joint Annual Information Return may need to be filed with both CRA and the provincial regulators.) • Census of Trust Pension Fund (Statistics Canada may select the IPP at random to provide information regarding the assets in the IPP fund.)

Step 3	The Registered Pension Plan Annual Information Return is submitted to CRA on CRA Form T244 and, if needed, to the provincial regulators with the applicable fees for approval to keep the IPP registered.
Step 4	Sponsors of IPPs in Ontario are mandated to submit the Risked-Based Pension Investment Monitoring Program and Investment Information Summary Form (IIS Form) every year to the Financial Services Commission of Ontario (FSCO) to ensure that the assets held in the IPP are being properly managed and that the IPP will generate enough returns on investments to provide the promised benefit for the IPP member.
Step 5	Every three years a triennial valuation must be completed on behalf of the IPP. A triennial valuation is an actuarial valuation that reports on the strength of a registered IPP and that must be filed with CRA every three years. The valuation is used to set current service contributions for the next three years. It also determines if the IPP has a surplus or deficit in meeting its benefit obligations.

TERMINATION OF IPP MEMBER AND IPP WIND-UP

The table below shows the life cycle of an IPP through its winding-up phase.

Step 1	If an IPP member stops being a member of the IPP, or the plan winds up, he or she has transferring rights. The options available to a former member of an IPP include the following: 1. He or she can transfer the commuted value of the accumulated IPP to another registered pension plan. 2. He or she can transfer the commuted value of the accumulated IPP to an LIRA, LIF, or LRIF, or to an RRSP only in the Province of Quebec if the IPP member is a connected person. 3. He or she can transfer the commuted value of the accumulated IPP to purchase an annuity.
Step 2	A wind-up for purposes of an IPP is deemed to be in effect on the date determined by the sponsor of the plan.

	This date is referred to as the effective date. On the effective date, accrual IPP benefits for the member of the plan will end even though the member may continue working for the sponsoring company. In addition, on the effective date the member of the IPP is fully vested in the plan and all assets are the member's according to government formulas. IPP sponsors on wind-up of the plan must provide written notice to the IPP member of the proposed termination of the plan.
Step 3	An IPP will be considered to be wound up after the proper documentation has been filed with CRA and provincial regulators, and funding requirement have been met by the sponsoring company.
Step 4	If the IPP assets are not yet vested with the member of the IPP, Form T10 is filed with CRA. The T10 is a form that reports the pension adjustment reversal (PAR) to CRA on behalf of the former RPP member. The T10 restores the RRSP room that was reduced as a result of membership in a pension plan or DPSP, a portion of which the member is no longer entitled to as a result of termination from the plan. PAR increases a former RPP and DPSP member's RRSP room by the difference between the total employee's PAs that were reported while a member of these plans and the actual pension value transferred to an RRSP.

CHAPTER 5

APPLICABLE PENSION LAWS AND REGULATIONS

Overview

This chapter provides the foundation for understanding the applicable pension laws, regulations and industry standards that apply to the implementation, maintenance and wind-up of an IPP. The aim of this chapter is to unleash the key components of the Canadian pension sector that up till now have been known to only a few government officials, actuaries and employee benefit consultants.

Learning Objectives

By the end of this chapter, you should be able to:

*   understand pension laws governing Individual Pension Plans;

*   understand the tax laws and tax regulations governing Individual Pension Plans; and

*   understand the actuary formulas that are used to determine an Individual Pension Plan's funding requirements.

A thorough understanding of the basic legislative intent behind tax rules, Pension Acts and pension standards can assist in understanding the complexities behind the adopting of the IPP solution. Understanding the intent behind the various rules impacting IPPs should be the aim of every financial professional involved in recommending, implementing, maintaining and winding up IPPs. IPPs are built on several key foundations, and within this chapter we will address the cornerstones that make the IPP solution possible today.

FRAMEWORK FOR DEFINED BENEFIT PENSION PLANS REGISTERED UNDER THE DIFFERENT PENSION BENEFITS ACTS

Across Canada there are 11 legislative bodies that have authority to govern registered pension plans. The 11 jurisdictions and the names of the Acts regulating pensions are:

Federal: *Pension Benefits Standards Act, 1985*, R.S.C. 1985, c. 32 (2nd Supp.)

Alberta: *Employment Pension Plans Act*, R.S.A. 2000, c. E-8

British Columbia: *Pension Benefits Standards Act*, R.S.B.C. 1996, c. 352

Manitoba: *Pension Benefits Act*, C.C.S.M., c. P32

New Brunswick: *Pension Benefits Act*, S.N.B. 1987, c. P-5.1

Newfoundland and Labrador: *Pension Benefits Act, 1997*, S.N.L. 1996, c. P-4.01

Nova Scotia: *Pension Benefits Act*, R.S.N.S. 1989, c. 340

Ontario: *Pension Benefits Act*, R.S.O. 1990, c. P.8

Quebec: *Supplemental Pension Plans Act*, R.S.Q., c. R-15.1

Prince Edward Island: *Pension Benefits Act*, S.P.E.I. 1990, c. 41 (unproclaimed)

Saskatchewan: *Pension Benefits Act, 1992*, S.S. 1992, c. P-6.001

One of the main purposes of the federal and provincial Pension Benefits Acts is to set out minimum standards for registered pension plans to ensure that the rights and interests of pension plan members, retirees and their beneficiaries are protected. Pension standard legislation governs such matters as who is eligible for membership in a defined benefit plan, vesting and portability of the pension, death benefits and disclosure. The two basic tenets that are found in all the pension legislation across Canada are:

1.   Each Pension Benefit Act has far-reaching rules and guidelines regarding how pensions within their jurisdictions behave and function.

2.   Each Pension Benefit Act places the responsibility upon pension regulators to make sure all pensions within their jurisdictions comply with the rules and regulations and empowers these regulators with the authority to enforce rules, regulations and laws sanctioning them to fine violators and to take criminal action against such violators.

While setting up an IPP is voluntary in nature for an employer, once an IPP is registered, a pension sponsor has a legal obligation to follow all the pension rules that govern it, with no exception. IPPs must be registered federally with Canada Revenue Agency (CRA) and with every provincial pension regulatory body, with the exception of British Columbia, Manitoba and P.E.I. In Quebec, an IPP does not have to be registered with the provincial pension authorities if the IPP was created for a connected person. However, for all other members who are not connected persons to the IPP sponsor, these plans have to be registered with the Quebec provincial regulator.

As it applies to IPPs, federal and provincial Acts require registered pension plans promised benefits to be in accordance with standards set out in these Acts. Defined benefit pension plans must file actuarial valuations every three years, or more frequently, as required by these Acts. If these valuations show a pension plan's assets to be less than its liabilities, payments must be made into the plan to eliminate the deficiency over a prescribed period of time, provided that this has been legislated by the Pension Benefits Act and pension authority that the IPP is registered with. In addition, these Acts require that the administrators of these plans file an Annual Information Return (AIR).

Actuarial valuations for the purpose of defined benefit pension plans are conducted using two different sets of actuarial assumptions: "solvency valuations" use assumptions consistent with a plan being terminated, while "going-concern valuations" are based on the plan continuing in operation.

If a solvency valuation reveals a shortfall of plan assets to plan liabilities, the IPP usually requires its plan sponsor to make special payments into the IPP, sufficient to eliminate the deficiencies over a five-year period.

For example, if an IPP has been set up for both a husband and wife with an unfunded liability of $160,543, this IPP has a solvency deficiency of $121,121, which requires the company/sponsor to make special payments of $2,301 per month over a five-year period to eliminate this deficiency.

Where a deficiency exists on the basis of a going-concern valuation, these Pension Benefits Acts require special payments to eliminate the going-concern deficiency over 15 years. Using our example of an IPP being set up for both a husband and wife with an unfunded liability of $160,543, it will require the sponsoring company to make a minimum special payment of $1,461 per month over the next 15-year period to fund the liability of the going-concern deficiency.

In general, the payments that a plan sponsor must remit to a plan in a given year include the amount necessary to cover the ongoing current service costs associated with the plan, plus any "special payments" required in that year to pay down a funding deficiency over the relevant time period.

Again, using our example, the company/IPP sponsor for this husband and wife IPP will have to make a minimum IPP contribution equal to $2,301 per month to fund the solvency deficiency, and $1,461 per month for the underfunded liability.

Note: In the example above we are using an IPP set up in Ontario and are following rules that apply specifically to Ontario. If the company/sponsor makes the full $160,543 contribution into the IPP this year all solvency and underfunded liabilities requirements will have been met and this plan will be fully funded for the years of service credited to this husband and wife.

INCOME TAX ACT

It was not long ago when the federal government passed Bill C-52 into law in 1990 to amend the *Income Tax Act*, R.S.C. 1985, c. 1 (5th Supp.) (ITA) to include registered pension plans (RPP) formally as part of the Act. An RPP is a pension plan that has been set up by an employer, and registered by CRA, to provide a specified employee(s) with a pension when he or she retires. An RPP exists when there is a formal arrangement made by an employer (sponsor) to contribute on behalf of an employee (member) to a registered pension plan. RPPs and the definition of who can be a member of a plan are defined in section 147.1 of the ITA.

As of 1991, CRA allowed designated pension plans (DPP) to be registered. These types of plans are referred to as Individual Pension Plans. A designated pension plan is a pension plan where more than 50% of the pension credits are for a specific person. These individuals are active members of a pension plan who may be connected persons to the employer of the plan or who earn two and one-half times the year's maximum pensionable earnings (YMPE). The 2006 YMPE has been set at $42,100, so a designate plan applies to IPPs that have been set up for individuals who earn over $105,000 annually and are to receive a pension benefit at 65 for the 2006 year equal to 2% of his or her earnings for a maximum credited benefit of $2,111.

Other important areas that both the ITA and its supporting *Income Tax Regulations*, C.R.C., c. 945 (REG), cover are how an IPP sponsor needs to be engaged in an active business and the IPP member needs to be a *bona fide* employee who receives either a T4, T4A or T4PS for active income from the sponsoring business. Both the IPP sponsor and IPP member need to be separate legal entities from one another for an IPP to be allowed to be set up and maintained by a business/sponsor for a plan member.

For example, an unincorporated doctor cannot create an IPP for himself or herself because he or she would be both the IPP sponsor and IPP member. The unincorporated doctor could create an IPP for one of his or her employees because in this situation there would be two separate legal entities, the doctor (IPP sponsor) and the doctor's employee (IPP member). However, an IPP can be set up for a doctor who has an incorporated professional corporation because in this instance, there would be two separate legal entities: the incorporated practice (IPP sponsor) and the doctor (IPP member).

Also defined in both the ITA and REG are the guidelines for the types of investments that can be held within an IPP. The types of investments that can be held within an IPP will be covered in more detail in Chapter 9, in Part II of this book. Both the ITA and REG state that an actuary must show how contributions and assets amounts held in an IPP have been determined. Actuaries must certify all amounts that are invested into an IPP using an approved IPP funding formula. The ITA and REG outline the guidelines on how IPP benefits are to be paid out to a member of an IPP and what the available options are for an IPP member whose plan is winding up or if the members decide to transfer assets out of an IPP to another type of registered deferred income plan.

INCOME TAX REGULATIONS

The *Income Tax Regulations* are complements to the ITA. The REG specify the terms and conditions of applying the ITA. Since the IPP is classified as a designated plan, the amount of possible pensionable benefit earned per year of credited service for an IPP member is set within subsection 8500(1) of the REG. It states:

"defined benefit limit" for a calendar year means the greater of:

(a) $1,722.22, and

(b) 1/9 of the money purchase limit for the year;

A money purchase plan is also referred to as a defined contribution pension plan. This is a registered pension plan with CRA in which the contribution amounts are defined but the benefit of the pension received at retirement is not defined. Contributions limits for DCPPs are set for 2006 ($19,000); 2007 ($20,000); 2008 ($21,000); 2009 ($22,000); and 2010 (indexed to the average wage).

Based on the 1/9th formula, defined benefit maximum pension limits (per year of service) have been set as follows: 2006 ($2,111); 2007 ($2,222); 2008 ($2,333); 2009 ($2,444); and 2010 (indexed to the average wage).

Example

$19,000 DCPP contribution ÷ $9 = $2,111 DBPP pensionable service limit per each year of service up to 2006

Outlined in subsection 8515(7) of the REG are the assumptions and methodology that are to be used as guidelines by all actuaries across Canada in determining the maximum funding contributions permitted into an IPP based on the IPP member's age. The assumptions and methodology presented in this section include:

(a)   the projected accrued benefit method used to determine actuarial liabilities and current costs;

(b)   a valuation interest rate of 7.5% per year;

(c)   a salary increase rate of 5.5% per year;

(d)   a rate of increase in the Consumer Price Index of 4.0% per year;

(e)   retirement at age 65;

(f)   assumed continuous employment until retirement;

(g)   at retirement, member assumed to be married to a person who is the same age;

(h)   no pre-retirement mortality;

(i)   post-retirement mortality based upon the 1983 Group Annuity Mortality Table using 80% of the average of male and female rates; and

(j)   plan assets valued at their fair market value.

These actuarial assumptions and methodology are used to determine the contribution needed to produce a 2% IPP benefit for a person earning a T4 of $105,556 in 2006. This defined benefit pension formula produces a larger contribution amount made by an IPP sponsor for plan members older than 40 years of age than if this same IPP member/person made a maximum $18,000 RRSP 2006 contribution for the same year.

The table below compares the allowable maximum IPP contributions based on the member's age and the maximum RRSP contribution for 2006.

Age at January 1, 2006	IPP Contribution Rate of Income	IPP Contribution $	RRSP Contribution Rate of Income	RRSP Contribution $
40	18.6%	$19,633	18%	$18,000
45	20.4%	$21,533	18%	$18,000
50	22.4%	$23,644	18%	$18,000
55	24.6%	$25,966	18%	$18,000
60	27.0%	$28,500	18%	$18,000
65	30.1%	$31,772	18%	$18,000

Note: The above calculations may vary depending on the actuarial firm performing the IPP Quote and Valuation because how the actuary chooses to interpret subsection 8515(7) may be very different. To avoid problems with IPP registration, it is recommended that you contract an actuarial firm that has a pre-approved Specimen Plan Text.

CHAPTER 6

APPLICABLE PENSION INDUSTRY STANDARDS

Overview

This chapter addresses issues that are as diverse as accounting, actuary evaluation, pension legislation, employment law and marital and common law relationship breakdown.

Learning Objectives

By the end of this chapter, you should be able to:

- determine what jurisdiction an IPP should be registered in;

- understand pension adjustment and the Factor of 9 as they relate to an Individual Pension Plan;

- understand the role qualifying transfers play as it relates to funding a pension for past service;

- understand how the creation and maintenance of an IPP impacts on RRSP contributions in the first year of the plan and the years that follow the initial registration;

- understand how deficits, surpluses and excess surpluses are determined in the IPP funding formula;

- understand the differences between the career average formula and the final average as they apply to IPP calculations;

- understand how terminal funding works;

- understand how transferring IPP assets out of an IPP to a locked-in plan and Age Transfer Factor work;

- understand the significance of Accounting section 3461, Employee Future Benefits, in the Canadian Institute of Chartered Accountants (CICA) Handbook; and

- understand how IPPs are dealt with during a divorce or the ending of a common law partnership.

REGISTRATION WITH THE PROPER PENSION AUTHORITIES

Each IPP must be registered with the CRA Pension Directorate. However, where the IPP member shows up for work physically in Canada determines the provincial jurisdiction in which an IPP is registered and the pension authority under which an IPP will be governed. Currently, IPPs are not required to be registered in the Provinces of British Columbia and Quebec, if the participant is a significant shareholder of the corporation (connected person). If the IPP has been set up for a group of individuals, the registration of the plan will depend on where the majority of the plan members show up for work.

Suppose an IPP is set up for only one executive who lives in Ottawa, Ontario, but who works in an office in Hull, Quebec. This plan would fall under the jurisdiction of Quebec, not Ontario. If an IPP is set up for a husband, wife and their oldest son, who are all *bona fide* employees of a company where the husband and wife work in Ontario and the son works in Alberta, the IPP will be registered in Ontario and governed by the pension authority within Ontario.

FACTOR OF 9 (DETERMINING PENSION ADJUSTMENT)

Our entire Canadian private and corporate tax-assisted retirement saving system is based on what is referred to as the Factor of 9. The Factor of 9 is a pension credit formula used to determine the pension credit in a defined benefit pension plan for any given year. The federal government created the Factor of 9 to equalize the tax-assisted savings and benefits between all defined contribution pension plans (DCPP), deferred profit sharing plans (DPSP) and RRSPs to defined benefit pension plans (DBPP).

The Factor of 9 states that for every $1 of defined benefit pension benefit promised to a member, the government considers that the equivalent of $9 of funding would have to be invested in a defined contribution pension plan or RRSP to deliver the same end benefit. However, this relationship is an average over a plan member's entire working career.

The main assumptions that the Factor of 9 are based on are as follows:

- It assumes that the DBPP member will receive the maximum benefit that can accumulate in any year, which is 2% of the plan member's pre-retirement employment income per year according to the maximum pension benefit limits set by the federal government each year.

- It assumes that the DBPP member will not retire until he or she has accumulated 35 years of accredited pension service in the plan. It also assumes that RRSP and DCPP contributions would have been maximized during that 35-year period.

- The internal compound rate that the funds within a DBPP, DCPP, RRSP and DPSP are assumed to be growing at is a real rate of return of 3% per year.

- Upon retirement the member with the amount invested in a DBPP, DCPP and RRSP would have enough funds to be withdrawn for a 21.4-year period after retirement.

The Factor of 9 is used to come up with an IPP member's pension adjustment (PA). To calculate the PA, the yearly promised benefit that is earned by the member of a defined benefit plan is multiplied by 9. Whatever the amount calculated by the Factor of 9 is, even if all of the RRSP room is wiped out using this formula, the government will always give members of defined benefit pension plans a pension adjustment offset (PA offset). Up until 1996, the PA offset was $1,000, and then from 1997 to the present it was reduced to $600 per year for members of a DBPP.

Example

For 2006, a maximum IPP annual PA equals 2% for a maximum pension credit of $2,111.11 for a maximum income of $105,556 (where $2,111 × 9 = $19,000). This IPP member will be given RRSP room of $600 for this year.

In this case the PA would be $19,000, which is equal to the money purchase plan (DCPP) maximum contribution limit for 2006. However, due to the PA offset in this example, CRA will give this IPP member an RRSP contribution room of $600 for 2006. CRA automatically gives the PA offset to every plan member to make it simpler and fair because the PA/Factor of 9 formula is based on 2% of the income of a plan member based on a public sector government-defined benefit pension plan. While the majority of private sector-defined benefit pension plans are based on providing 1% of the member's income for pension per year for the plan member, these lower pension benefit plans require a lot less funding to provide promised benefits. The PA offset amount can be used to contribute into either an individual's RRSP or, if the plan member has a spouse, into a spousal RRSP.

All in all, for members of defined benefit pension plans who are younger than age 40, the actual amount needed to be invested into an IPP to produce the promised $1 of pension benefit at age 65 is less than the assumed $9 that the Factor of 9 uses; the actual amount needed to fund a defined benefit pension benefit in the future could be as low as a $1 to $3 contribution today for younger employees. For older IPP members (aged 40 to 69) the factor to deliver $1 of pension benefit tomorrow may be as high as $10 to $21.

The reason for the variance of the actual dollars needed to fund the same benefit is due to older members of a DBPP having less time value for the investments in their IPPs to compound in order to deliver the promised defined benefit; therefore, more money has to be invested into an older member's IPP to deliver the same benefit as a younger plan member's.

PAST SERVICE PENSION ADJUSTMENT (PSPA)

One of the main reasons the IPP funding formula is more generous than the RRSP limits is due to the fact that a company/sponsor can contribute into an IPP for the pension plan member for his or her years of service prior to the set-up of the plan going back to 1991 for a connected person, or, for a non-connected member, a company/sponsor can contribute into a DBPP/IPP going as far back as the date that the member was hired by the sponsoring company.

It is important to understand that when an employer contributes into an IPP for past service, this new contribution reduces an individual's RRSP deduction limit for any pension benefits earned in a year after 1990 for the following years through the reporting of a PA. Thus when past service credits are bought for an IPP member going back to 1990, a retroactive adjustment is required of the IPP member to give up some of the RRSP room he or she had in past years. This is referred to as past service pension adjustment (PSPA).

What does that mean, and are there any possible exceptions to the rule for funding an IPP for a connected person for employment years prior to 1991?

Imagine that we have a business owner (connected person) who has been working for his incorporated company for 26 years since 1980, and who decides that he wants his company to sponsor an IPP for himself. In this situation, his company would be restricted to funding his pension for only his years of service going back to 1991.

This restriction would not apply to non-connected persons. If this same business decided to create an IPP for a key executive who was a non-connected person who started working for this company at the same time in 1980, the company would be permitted to fully fund this key executive's pension benefit for the full 26 years of service since 1980.

The possible exception to the rule for a connected person to have an IPP funded by his or her company for prior years of service before 1991 would be for the company to also create an IPP for a non-connected member for the same years of credited service. So it is possible for the owner/connected person (this should be investigated with an actuary) to have his company fund his IPP for the full 26 years that he or she had received a T4 income since 1980 provided that the company also funded an IPP benefit for the same 26 years of service for its key executive (non-connected person).

It should be noted that funding of an IPP for pensionable service after 1990 is permitted by CRA in the form of one lump-sum contribution, and this is a fully deductible expense for the IPP sponsor in the year that the contribution is made. On the other hand, funding of the IPP for pre-1990 service, if permitted by CRA, cannot be fully deducted by the sponsor in the year that it is made. An IPP-sponsoring company is only permitted to spread out a pre-1990 contribution for the purposes of deductions over a number of years going forward after the IPP was registered with CRA.

2/3 Pensionable

It should be noted that for pre-1990 pensionable service recognized after June 7, 1990, the maximum pensionable benefit limit for pre-1990 pensionable service funding is $1,150.00 (2/3 of $1,722.22) for years up to and including 2003, and 2/3 (two-thirds) of the maximum pension limit for years after 2003. In the pension industry, this is referred to as 2/3 pensionable.

QUALIFYING TRANSFER

CRA's PSPA funding requirements for an IPP consist of two parts:

Part One: Direct deposits made by the employer only or by both the employer and employee for the purpose of buying past service pension credits.

Part Two: A qualifying transfer from the IPP member's RRSP, Deferred Profit Sharing Plan (DPSP), Locked-in RRSP, money purchase plan (DCPP) or the member's unused RRSP room.

Below is a chart that shows the maximum qualifying transfer amount needed by a connected person to receive a maximum pension benefit for each year of pensionable service, starting back from 1991 to 2005, that would be required by CRA to be transferred into his or her IPP.

Maximum Qualifying Transfer Calculation				
1991	$69,444 × 2% × 9	$1,000	=	$11,500
1992	$69,444 × 2% × 9	$1,000	=	$11,500
1993	$75,000 × 2% × 9	$1,000	=	$12,500
1994	$80,556 × 2% × 9	$1,000	=	$13,500
1995	$105,555 × 2% × 9	$1,000	=	$18,000
1996	$105,555 × 2% × 9	$1,000	=	$18,000
1997	$105,555 × 2% × 9	$600	=	$18,400
1998	$105,555 × 2% × 9	$600	=	$18,400
1999	$105,555 × 2% × 9	$600	=	$18,400
2000	$105,555 × 2% × 9	$600	=	$18,400
2001	$105,555 × 2% × 9	$600	=	$18,400
2002	$105,555 × 2% × 9	$600	=	$18,400
2003	$105,555 × 2% × 9	$600	=	$18,400
2004	$105,555 × 2% × 9	$600	=	$18,400
2005	$105,555 × 2% × 9	$600	=	$18,400
Sum of Pension Adjustments				$250,600
Past Service Pension Adjustment				($8,000)
Qualifying Transfer				**$242,600**

As it has been mentioned before, depending on the actuary completing the initial IPP valuation, the qualifying transfer amount may vary.

HOW PSPA AND QUALIFYING TRANSFERS WORK TOGETHER

Imagine we have a 50-year-old male owner/executive who has worked for the same company since 1991 to the present (2006) and he has averaged a T4 income of more than $105,564 a year during that same period. An IPP is set up for this individual this year, and a past service calculation has been performed by an actuary. It has been determined that the total liability for the IPP for past service (1991 to 2005) totals $341,950. Of this IPP's past service liability, the actuary has determined that $242,600 must be funded by a qualifying transfer. The IPP sponsor will make up the remaining $99,350 of unfunded liability for past service for the IPP.

Note: In our example, if the IPP member does not have enough funds in RRSPs, Deferred Profit Sharing Plans (DPSP), Locked-in RRSP, money purchase plans (DCPP) or unused RRSP room to make a qualifying transfer, the member will not be able to buy back past service credits going back to 1991 when the member received T4 income from the company.

IPP IMPACT ON RRSP CONTRIBUTIONS FOR THE FIRST YEAR OF THE PLAN

In the first year after an IPP has been registered with CRA, a connected person's RRSP contribution limit will be reduced by CRA by 18% according to a formula based on the member's T4 income in the 1990 tax year. The IPP member's RRSP contribution limit will be reduced by a maximum of $11,500, which was the maximum RRSP contribution limit for 1990.

This decrease in the IPP member's RRSP contribution limit for a connected person for the first year the IPP has been registered with CRA only pertains if the PA for 1990 was $0. If the IPP member who is a connected person had a PA reported for the year 1990, this reduction in RRSP deduction limits does not apply. In the second year after the IPP has been established with CRA, the plan member will only receive a PA offset of $600, which can be contributed to his or her RRSP, or to a spousal RRSP.

Example

Imagine that an IPP is registered in 2006 for a connected person who earns $100,000 for the same year, who has also received a T4 income from his or her company starting back in 1990, where the connected person did not get a PA for that year. Lastly, this connected person was eligible for the maximum RRSP contribution for 1990. This connected person's allowable RRSP contribution for 2006 would be $6,500 ($18,000 possible 2006 RRSP contribution without IPP − $11,500 maximum RRSP contribution for 1990 = $6,500 allowable 2006 RRSP contribution).

If the connected IPP member in this example did not work for the sponsoring company in 1990, he or she would receive the full $18,000 RRSP contribution limit for the first year of the plan.

The 1990 rule does not apply to IPP members who are not connected persons. Thus in the first year of an IPP's registration, the member's RRSP room for a non-connected member will not be reduced. Using our example from above, if a person was not a connected person and earned $100,000 and did not report a PA for 1990, this IPP member's maximum RRSP contribution limit for the first year of the plan would be the full 18% of his or her income or $18,000 for the first year of the plan.

In all of our scenarios listed above for both connected and non-connected members, every year following the first year of the plan, the member's contribution limit would be reduced to $600 per year thereafter until the plan is wound up or the member reached age 69.

The IPP Registration Effective Date

The effective date is the date that an IPP is considered to have been registered with CRA. This date is outlined in the IPP documents. This date cannot be before January 1st of the year that the application for registration of the IPP is made to CRA. When setting up an IPP, registration must be sent to CRA within 120 days of the corporate year-end. Additionally, it must occur within the same calendar year. Contributions must be made within 120 days of the corporate year-end, regardless of calendar year.

Thus, a company with a corporate year-end of March 31st has until July 31st to send the documents to CRA and make the contributions. A November 30th year-end will require documents to be submitted by December 31st (calendar year-end), but contributions do not have to be made until March 31st of the following year.

IPP DEFICITS, SURPLUSES AND EXCESS SURPLUSES

Deficits: The plan could be in a deficit position because the IPP fund returns were lower than anticipated due to the average industrial wage (AIW) rising faster than expected, or for any other reason such as a lower return of assets within the IPP. As a result, the actuary will require additional contributions to be injected into the plan in order to finance the deficit. Note that this deficit may be amortized over a maximum period of 15 years.

Surplus: The actuary will not require a contribution holiday or a decrease in contributions if the IPP surplus does not result in an excess surplus.

Excess Surplus: The actuary will require a contribution holiday or a decrease in contributions if the plan is in an excess surplus position. The excess surplus represents the lesser of 20% of the actuarial liabilities or the greater of 10% of the actuarial liabilities and two times the contributions for current service.

IPP RETIREMENT DATE AGE

All IPP members must begin taking pension benefits from the plan by December 31st in the year that the member turns 69 years old. This is similar to RRSP rules, which require that RRSPs be collapsed by the same date.

CAREER AVERAGE IPP VS. FINAL AVERAGE IPP

IPP final benefits that are promised to the member of the plan can vary depending on the status of the plan member (connected or non-connected person status) and the structure of the plan. The two main structures for determining the final IPP pension benefit are as follows:

Career Average Earnings IPPs

These IPPs are used to calculate the total annual pension benefit that a connected person can receive from his or her IPP. Career average earning IPP benefits are structured to pay out a pension benefit to a plan member based on the member's entire career during which he or she was eligible to acquire pension credits from the plan. Each year is treated equally in the weighting of the career average and capped at the CRA-prescribed pensionable amounts.

Career Average Formula

Annual Pension Benefit = Career Average of Pensionable Earnings × Years of Pensionable Service

Career Average IPP Example		
Year	**Earnings**	**Pension 2% of Earnings**
1998	$50,000	$1,000
1999	$50,000	$1,000
2000	$50,000	$1,000
2001	$50,000	$1,000
2002	$50,000	$1,000
2003	$75,000	$1,500
2004	$75,000	$1,500
2005	$100,000	$2,000
2006	$100,000	$2,000
2007	$100,000	$2,000
Annual Pension due at age 65		$14,000

Final/Best Average Earning Defined IPPs

These IPPs provide for the payout of pension benefits to the IPP member that are based on the member's pensionable length of service and the average earnings of the IPP member for a stated period of time. This formula can only be used for a non-connected person. Usually the best IPPs for non-connected members are based on an average of the top three earning years that are capped at the CRA-prescribed pensionable amounts.

Final/Best Average Formula

Annual Pension Benefit = Average of Final/Best Average Pensionable Earnings × Years of Pensionable Service

Final/Best Three-Year Average IPP Example		
Year	**Earnings**	**Pension 2% of Earnings**
1998	$50,000	$1,000
1999	$50,000	$1,000
2000	$50,000	$1,000
2001	$50,000	$1,000

Final/Best Three-Year Average IPP Example		
Year	**Earnings**	**Pension 2% of Earnings**
2002	$50,000	$1,000
2003	$75,000	$1,500
2004	$75,000	$1,500
2005	$100,000	$2,000
2006	$100,000	$2,000
2007	$100,000	$2,000
Annual Pension due at age 65		$20,000

TERMINAL FUNDING

IPPs allow for additional funding at retirement that in the IPP world is referred to as "Terminal Funding". Additional voluntary funding is allowed at retirement for the purpose of providing early retirement benefits/bridge benefits to supplement IPP members' incomes until they are eligible for full CPP and OAS benefits at age 65, full post-retirement CPI indexing and an unreduced pension benefit for a surviving spouse.

This amount is calculated by an actuary and includes unreduced early retirement benefits back to age 60, and 3% per annum prior to age 60 bridging benefits. Terminal funding creates another opportunity for additional tax-deductible contributions for employers and tax deferral for former employees that could be in the hundreds of thousands of dollars.

Example

Imagine that an IPP has been created for a 49-year-old owner/ manager. As of January 1, 2005, this owner/manager has T4 earnings of $100,000 and has maintained this level of income since 1991. It is safe to project that this income will remain at $100,000 annually, adjusted to inflation until retirement. Assume that this IPP member will retire at age 60 on January 1, 2016, with 25 years of pensionable service (1991 to 2015). Before the retirement benefit begins to be paid out of the IPP, there is a window of opportunity for the IPP-sponsoring company to make a one-time $251,000 terminal funding contribution to the IPP, in addition to regular IPP government prescribed funding contribution and annual growth calculations.

TRANSFERRING IPP ASSETS OUT TO A LOCKED-IN PLAN

For IPP members who want or need to wind up their IPPs, they have several options. They can purchase an annuity, a Life Income Fund (LIF), a Locked-in Retirement Account (LIRA) or a Locked-in Retirement Income Fund (LRIF).

In section 8517 of the *Income Tax Regulations*, C.R.C., c. 945, is a prescribed formula of how much money within an IPP can be transferred to another registered plan without triggering taxes on the amounts that are not allowed to be tax-sheltered. The dollar limits that are allowed to be tax-sheltered within an IPP in most cases are much greater than permitted when transferred to a LIRA, LIF or LRIF.

AGE TRANSFER FACTOR

In the pension industry there is a formula that is used to determine how much money can be transferred out of an IPP to another type of registered plan to avoid being taxed. This formula is based on the IPP member's age and is referred to as the "Age Transfer Factor".

The Age Transfer Factor formula is written out as follows:

Permitted Transfer Tax Deferral Assets = Promised Annual Pension × Age Transferred Factor

Example

Imagine that you have a client who is 50 years of age, and who had an IPP created for him or her. This client has 15 years of credited pension service to date. At age 60 this client decides to wind up his or her IPP and transfers as much as is permitted of the 25 years of pension credits to a LIRA. At the end of 2016, there will be $1,307,104 sitting in the IPP to fund a promised retirement pension benefit of $83,060 per year. This individual will only be permitted to transfer $955,190 into the LIRA ($83,060 × 11.5 Age Transfer Factor = $955,190). The remaining $351,914 ($1,307,104 − $955,190 = $351,914) cannot be transferred into a LIRA. This surplus money will become deregistered and become fully taxable at the client's top marginal tax rate. If the client lives in Ontario and has the top marginal tax bracket of 46%, the client will have to pay CRA $161,880 in taxes on this deregistered money.

The chart below shows the different Age Transfer Factors for the different ages used to determine the amount of money that is permitted to be moved from an IPP to a LIRA on a tax-deferral basis.

Age	Transfer Factor
Under 50	9.0
50	9.4
51	9.6
52	9.8
53	10.0
54	10.2
55	10.4
56	10.6
57	10.8
58	11.0
59	11.3
60	11.5
61	11.7
62	12.0
63	12.2
64	12.4
65	12.4
66	12.0
67	11.7
68	11.3
69	11.0

Retiring Allowance

Using the example above, if your client were terminated from employment at the time that he or she transferred moneys from his or her IPP to a LIRA, none of the $351,914 taxable funds that could not be transferred to the LIRA on the IPP termination would be eligible to be considered part of a retiring allowance, eligible to be put into an RRSP.

A retiring allowance is an amount of money that an employer pays to an employee in recognition of long service with a company or an amount paid for loss of employment or position. CRA may allow the taxpayer who receives a retiring allowance to defer part or all taxes on the amount by making payment into an RPP or LIRA if certain criteria are met. A retiring allowance must be paid directly from a former employer to a former employee. A retiring allowance cannot originate from the surplus taxable amounts that could not be transferred from an IPP to a LIRA.

Some rules that apply to retiring allowances include the following:

• An individual who is eligible for a retiring allowance can transfer the eligible part of that allowance into his or her RRSP or RPP within 60 days of December 31st.

• He or she can transfer $2,000 for each year or part year of service before 1996 in which he or she was employed.

• He or she can also transfer an extra $1,500 for each year or part year of service before 1989, as long as he or she was not entitled to receive any benefits earned under a pension plan or DPSP from contributions an employer made for each such year.

• These transfers do not reduce IPP or RRSP contribution room.

ACCOUNTING SECTION 3461, EMPLOYEE FUTURE BENEFITS, IN THE CICA HANDBOOK

The IPP is, first, a tax solution and then, second, a retirement strategy. What many experienced financial advisors who have successfully implemented the IPP solution know to be true is if a client's public accountant is not behind the IPP solution for his or her client, the IPP will not be implemented. It does not matter how much the investment advisor or actuary tries to convince the client to adopt the IPP solution, the IPP will not happen without the public accountant's support for the creation of an IPP.

Traditionally the big four accounting firms (Pricewaterhouse Coopers, Ernst & Young, Deloitte & Touche and KPMG) prepared financial statements for corporations offering large defined-benefit pension plans for hundreds of employees. Now with the emergence of the IPP, hundreds and even thousands of smaller public accounting firms and public accountant sole practitioners will be producing financial statements for incorporated businesses offering the IPP solutions to their key people. This is why it is important for financial advisors entering the IPP market to become familiar with the accounting standards that the Canadian Institute of Chartered Accountants (CICA) has adopted when showing IPPs on business clients' financial statements.

In the mid-1980s the CICA began to develop the accounting standards that would be applied to all retirement plans that employers promised to provide to their employees. These accounting procedures would pertain to both registered and non-registered plans, showing all current and future pension costs and obligations of sponsoring employers. The aim of these standards was to harmonize the accounting procedures for pension plans and their expenses, thus allowing for the comparability of pension expenses and liabilities between one sponsoring company to another.

In 1999, the CICA introduced into the CICA Handbook Section 3461, which required sponsors of DBPPs and IPPs to provide minimum disclosure on their financial statements that included the following components: the current service cost of the IPP, plus interest cost on the accrued benefit obligation, minus the expected return on plan assets, plus the amortization of any past service costs arising from a plan initiation or amendment, minus the amortization of any net actuarial gain or loss, plus any amount immediately recognized as a result of a temporary deviation from the plan, plus any increase or decrease in a valuation allowance, plus a gain or loss on a plan settlement or curtailment.

Note: Audited financial statements that meet Accounting Section 3461, "Employee Future Benefits", in the CICA Handbook and show an IPP's strength may need to be filed annually with pension regulators as well. However, under certain circumstances, filing certified statements of IPP strength by an actuary may suffice. Even though financial statements may not be required to be filed with IPP regulatory bodies, companies sponsoring IPPs will still have to account for these IPPs in their corporate books.

MARRIAGE AND COMMON LAW RELATIONSHIP BREAKDOWN AND THE IPP

According to Statistics Canada there are approximately 146,000 marriages each year. Of those, 38% of first marriages and 60% of second marriages will end in divorce. The story these numbers don't tell us is the one where a growing number of adults choose to live together.

Larry Lipiec, a lawyer and author of the book *I Had Dreams of a Happy House Now I'm a Former Spouse*, published by <helpmelarry.com>, challenges societal taboos by addressing the legal and financial realities of relationships in the 21st century.

He points out that marriage and common law cohabitation are not just personal relationships; under Canadian law, they are treated as business relationships/partnerships. One should be mindful that the rules that apply to the division of family assets also apply to the division of IPP assets and IPP pension benefits as well.

In regard to the division of IPP assets, assets will be divided according to provincial legislation and/or court orders if they exist. The recipient spouse of an IPP asset division is allowed to transfer the awarded IPP assets to his or her RRSP, avoiding paying taxes on the transfer.

IPP asset divisions after the end of a common law relationship or a marriage breakdown are valued using two methods:

The Value Added Method Formula: This formula for the division of IPP assets subtracts the value of the pension earned before the legal union of the couple from the value of the pension at the time of the official separation. Once that amount is determined, the split of the IPP assets occurs at the prescribed provincial and federal matrimonial asset division rates.

The Pro-Rata Method Formula: This formula for the division of IPP assets divides the value of the IPP assets on the date of legal separation based on how long the couple was married and the pension credits that were earned in the IPP. Once this amount is determined, assets are split between the divorcing spouses according to the prescribed provincial and federal matrimonial asset division rates.

How do these formulas work?

Imagine that a couple legally separates after ten years of marriage. The husband has been a member of an IPP for 15 years, 10 of which he was married. On the day of the couple's marriage, the IPP was valued at $150,000, and on the date of the legal separation, the IPP assets were valued at $500,000. This couple lives in a progressive family law province where all assets accumulated during a marriage are split evenly, 50/50, upon divorce.

Using the value added method to determine how much of the IPP assets would be legally the wife's, you will find that she would be entitled to $175,000 of the assets of the plan.

Formula

$175,000 transfer to spouse = $500,000 value of pension on date of separation − $150,000 value of pension on the date of marriage ÷ 50% division of matrimonial assets

Using the pro-rata method in our example above, you will find that the husband would be required to give his ex-spouse $166,500 of his IPP assets upon the date of their official separation.

Formula

$166,500 Transfer to spouse = $500,000 value of pension on date of separation × 10/15 or 66.6% of the time that the IPP was accumulating pension credits during the marriage ÷ 50% division of matrimonial assets

IPP members in Newfoundland & Labrador, Saskatchewan, Quebec, Ontario, Prince Edward Island and Alberta cannot transfer more than 50% of their IPP benefits that were accrued during the marriage to the other spouse upon divorce.

In British Columbia, there are no provisions in the provincial pension legislation for the splitting of pension plan assets or pension benefits. Divorcing spouses in British Columbia have to trade off other matrimonial assets, permitting the IPP member spouse to keep the full IPP.

IPP members who live in Manitoba are given a choice under their provincial legislation where they can either agree with their former spouse to split 50/50 the IPP assets or benefits that had accumulated while married or exchange assets, allowing the IPP member to keep the entire pension.

CHAPTER 7

IPP MISCELLANEOUS

Trevor R. Parry

Overview

This chapter begins by describing the options for companies making a final contribution to an IPP for its member. It continues by looking at the retirement options that an IPP member has available to receive a payout from the plan. It concludes by discussing the merits of having family IPPs and who best to name as beneficiaries of the IPP after the member has died.

Learning Objectives

By the end of this chapter, you should be able to:

- understand the value of an IPP sponsor making a final contribution into an IPP prior to an IPP member retiring;

- understand the options available for IPP members at retirement;

- understand the pros and cons of designating classes of beneficiaries for IPP assets after a plan member's death; and

- understand the recent IPP developments that could impact implementing the IPP solutions.

INTRODUCTION

We are all aware of the tax benefits that are afforded by the additional deductible contributions to IPPs over RRSPs. However, there are several other additional benefits to IPPs which often go overlooked. Most significant among these are: additional funding on retirement; investment expense deductibility; Employer Health Tax (EHT) savings; and creditor protection. It is critical to raise these issues with the companies that are considering establishing an IPP. While tax is a critical determinant, these other benefits are so significant that they must be weighed in the decision-making process.

The additional funding on retirement allows the company to make one large, final payment into the IPP. This amount varies by retirement age and length of service, but is frequently six figures, ranging up to over $1 million. This funding provides two significant benefit enhancements to the plan. The first is additional indexing. Many plans have a built-in indexing provision. Additional funding enhances this indexing level. Over the length of a plan member's retirement, this can have a significant impact on the total amount of pension received. The second benefit applies only to those plan members who retire prior to age 65. The additional funding provides a benefit-bridging provision for those who retire early. Enhancing both the reduced pension and Canada Pension Plan (CPP) benefits is a distinct advantage for the early retiree.

In order to take advantage of the additional funding, either the IPP must be maintained on retirement or the assets must be used to purchase an annuity. Rolling the assets into a Locked-in Retirement Account (LIRA)/Locked-in Retirement Income Fund (LRIF) will result in a surplus which will cause the assets to be taxable in the participant's hands in the retirement year.

The deductibility of investment expenses can provide a significant benefit to a business owner setting up an IPP for himself or herself. At age 69, an IPP participant could find himself or herself with $500,000 or more in the plan. A 3% management fee would result in a tax deduction of $15,000, meaning a savings of approximately $5,000 for that year alone, simply by having these assets held in an IPP.

In Ontario, an employer is required to pay a 1.95% EHT on all payrolls over $400,000. Contributions made to an IPP are not defined as income subject to this tax. This means that a company making $450,000 worth of contributions will save $8,775 over the life of the plan versus simply paying the money out as salary or bonus. The same holds true with the other provinces that maintain a payroll-based health tax. These provinces — Quebec, Manitoba and Newfoundland — all maintain health taxes on payroll in excess of 2%. In the case of Quebec, the tax escalates, and as such the savings realized by implementing the IPP for owners/managers has profound effects.

CREDITOR PROOFING ASSETS

Creditor proofing is something that anyone in business, or professional practice, should seek to implement. However, creditor proofing may be difficult for some. For instance, the lack of a uniform approach to professional corporation rules across Canada means that in some provinces the assets of the professional corporation can be creditor proofed through the use of a holding corporation, while in others that is impossible. Some business owners have utilized segregated funds to creditor proof invested assets. While this strategy has merit, it also has severe limitations and costs. Segregated funds carry higher management expense ratios (MERs) than other mutual funds and will erode capital over the accumulating years.

As a pension is a trust, with the plan member enjoying beneficial ownership, the assets of the pension are creditor proof. An IPP properly designed may also provide creditor protection for any plan surpluses that may arise. Therefore, traditional business owners and incorporated professionals alike may creditor proof substantial assets from personal and corporate creditors.

The IPP, however, will not provide protection from the results of marriage breakdown. The net family property (NFP) calculation, which will give rise to equalization payments, will include pension assets in that calculation. Including the employed spouse in the IPP from plan inception may mitigate the effects of an NFP calculation in the future.

RETIREMENT OPTIONS

On retirement, an IPP participant has three options on how to handle the assets in his or her plan: rolling the funds into an LIF, purchasing an annuity or drawing a pension directly from the IPP.

Rolling the funds into a LIRA discharges any further obligations to the plan. A wind-up is performed, and any surplus or deficit is calculated. Once any deficit is funded, the company no longer has any responsibilities to the pension. The subsequent pension will be based on the performance of the assets inside the plan and standard maximum/minimum withdrawal calculations for LIRAs. The additional funding on retirement is not available under this option.

While many individuals might consider the plan wind-up to be the most likely scenario for the eventual disposition of their IPP, the facts might be quite different. The parameters of a wind-up calculation are established by CRA, and the result is that too often a sizable surplus exists. A surplus of this nature must be paid out as income. This will result in considerable taxation in a single year. While the IPP may have provided considerable tax relief throughout its existence, no one likes to stomach a tax bill that can be in the hundreds of thousands of dollars.

Additional funding at retirement is also not permitted in the case of plan wind-up, which will further deprive the plan sponsor of considerable tax relief. While business owners may require plan wind-up for their non-connected employees, where possible, wind-up should be avoided for their own plans.

The purchase of an annuity will, like the plan wind-up, relieve the sponsoring company of any further obligations, but it will not result in the creation of a large taxable liability through a wind-up calculation. The pension will be based on the annuity rates at the time the annuity is purchased, and the entire asset may be used to purchase the annuity. This option will allow for an additional funding payment to be made on retirement. The annuity may be purchased at any time. If the plan was maintained beyond retirement as a formal pension plan, and in later years the plan sponsor wishes to dispense with the plan, the annuity is the only option. If, for instance, the company is sold after the IPP member reaches age 69, and no corporation exists to sponsor the plan, or age or infirmity makes continuance and maintenance of the plan too difficult, then the purchase of the annuity can make tremendous sense.

The final retirement option is to leave the plan intact and begin withdrawing a pension from it. This option still requires triennial valuations, and the sponsoring company is still responsible for funding any deficits. This plan allows for the additional funding on retirement, as well as an indexed pension with known annual payments. If the company is willing to maintain sponsorship, this is usually the preferred option for pension payouts.

IPPs provide several mechanisms to transfer assets from the plan participant to the beneficiary after the participant's death. By law, the spouse is always the primary beneficiary of an IPP. If the spouse has predeceased the participant, the assets will flow to the estate or surviving children based on the beneficiary designation.

DISPOSITION OF PENSION WITH A SINGLE PLAN MEMBER

On the death of the sole plan participant, the disposition of plan assets will depend on whether or not the plan participant has begun taking a pension. If the participant has not retired before death, the assets in the IPP will roll to the spouse in a tax-free transfer into either a LIRA or an RRSP, depending on the applicable provincial regulations. If the participant has retired, the disposition will depend on the election made at retirement. The most common practice is to have the pension pay a reduced pension benefit from the IPP (with 66 2/3% of the original amount) to the surviving spouse for the remainder of his or her life. When the spouse dies, any remaining assets will be paid to his or her designated beneficiary.

If there is no surviving spouse at the time of death, the plan assets will be paid in a lump sum to the designated beneficiaries: either the named children in equal installments or the deceased's estate.

DISPOSITION OF A PLAN WITH MULTIPLE MEMBERS

It is strongly advised that only spouses or parents and adult children be placed together in the same IPP plan. All members of the plan must be employees of the sponsoring company. If a deceased participant has a surviving spouse, and has not retired, the assets representing the commuted value of his or her pension will be dealt with as if he or she was the sole plan member, as described in the section above.

If there is no surviving spouse, but the participant has adult children who are part of the plan, and the participant has begun taking a pension, the situation changes. In this case, the assets in the IPP other than any of the remaining guaranteed benefit payout to pay the heirs of the deceased plan member or to the plan member's estate will remain in the plan and create a surplus for the remaining plan members. The company would then be required to take a contribution holiday until this has been utilized.

ASSIGNING MINOR CHILDREN AS BENEFICIARIES

When electing beneficiaries on an IPP, the participant and spouse should always select their estate if there are minor children. Depending on the applicable provincial regulations, there will be negative consequences for minor children if they inherit funds from a pension plan.

In Ontario, naming a minor child directly as a beneficiary will result in the intervention of the Children's Lawyer (Public Guardian), who will administer the pension assets until the child reaches age of majority. By designating the estate as the primary or contingent beneficiary, the intervention of this government agency will be precluded. While applicable probate and provincial taxes may attach to the pension asset, the individual will have far more control over those assets if the will is properly drafted. The executor or estate trustee will be able to invest and direct the pension assets according to the deceased's wishes.

This is particularly important in the case of incapacity of any minor beneficiaries. If a child is developmentally handicapped, the parent may wish to provide detailed and specialized terms regarding the distribution of assets and income from those assets. (Naming a disabled adult child to be the beneficiary of an IPP is further covered in Chapter 18 of this book.) The use of testamentary trusts, which can be quite detailed, is possible only through the use of a will, and the designation of the estate as the beneficiary of pension assets.

PAST SERVICE: WHEN TO SET UP THE PLAN

Since the IPP does, in most cases, generate significant tax relief to the sponsoring company because of the ability of that company to fund past service contribution, there has been some discussion as to when to put the pension plan in place. One position that has been advanced is that the sponsoring company should wait to establish the plan in order to maximize the past service contribution, and therefore enhance the tax relief. While technically correct in that waiting will generate larger contributions and deductions in the future, for many people, waiting may be impractical.

For instance, if a 45-year-old individual were to wait until age 65, he or she would be entitled to a past service contribution of $713,000. The question that this raises is simple: how many corporations have $713,000 on hand to fund past service? Waiting to maximize a past service contribution focuses purely on the tax relief represented by these initial contributions, and may in most cases make the IPP impossible to implement for the vast majority of corporations. Also, if a company were able to make this large, one-time contribution, how much of that contribution would offset corporate tax at the higher levels? It is quite likely that some of the $713,000 would be deductible at the small business tax rate, and, as such, the deduction would not be maximized.

In discussing IPPs with accountants, advisors and entrepreneurs alike, it is my experience that tax relief, while usually the primary reason for plan implementation, is not the only reason that leads to the IPP option. Financial planning concerns must be presented to the client. For instance, the ability to creditor proof assets is a significant benefit for many, particularly those whose businesses are in economic sectors with a higher risk of litigation, or professionals who are constantly concerned about defending claims of malpractice or professional negligence. By waiting to fund a larger past service contribution, in the future, the sponsoring company may be forced to retain significant assets for considerable periods of time, the result being that these assets could be at risk to creditors.

Both plan sponsors and members must also consider what the individual does in the interim period while he or she builds up the larger past service contribution. Invariably the individual will utilize his or her RRSP as the primary retirement funding vehicle. This in essence means that the individual by waiting to create a larger corporate deduction in the future, is forgoing considerable benefits for a considerable period of time. For instance, the ability to deduct investment management fees, which is a facet of the IPP and not available in the RRSP, must be considered. How many dollars could have been deducted by the sponsoring company in the 20-year wait?

CHANGE IN DIVIDEND TAX TREATMENT: REGISTERED PLANS IN JEOPARDY

In response to the wholesale conversion of corporations into income trusts, the federal government has moved forward in implementing changes introduced by the previous federal government, by changing the way in which dividends will be taxed. This has led some people to postulate that compensation strategies for owners/managers will change and that we will see a reduction in traditional T4 income in favour of dividend-based income. This argument is specious, as we are not aware of how these tax changes will manifest themselves.

Both plan sponsors and members must look at what "eligible dividends" will be subject to the new tax regime, especially since such dividends are those paid by Canadian public companies and not private corporations. While it may reduce the large shareholder bonuses paid in the past the dividend tax changes will not reduce the need to create *bona fide* deductions for companies, and this is very much what IPPs do.

There is a strategy espoused by some individuals for dividend payments to completely eclipse T4, but this is dangerous. Such a strategy would eliminate a business owner's involvement in many retirement savings programs. Participation in the Canada Pension Plan would cease, which might have negative effects on an individual's future retirement plans, and as dividend income is not earned income, the use of an RRSP would be eliminated. It would also not be illogical for CRA to seek redress through future tax changes if a wholesale conversion to dividend-based remuneration takes place. The tried and true saying that "pigs get fat and hogs get slaughtered" is something everyone should consider when examining "radical" strategies.

CONCLUSION

The tax relief provided by IPPs remains the primary reason for establishing a plan. Canadians are an overtaxed lot, and business owners are acutely aware of this fact. The advisor team owes a duty to the client to explore thoroughly all means of safe tax deferral and reduction, but it also owes a duty to explore other aspects of all strategies. The IPP presents the sponsoring company and plan member with significant benefits above and beyond pure tax relief. The ability to know with certainty the future income that will be provided by the IPP is of tremendous benefit in properly building a comprehensive retirement plan. Additional tax relief provided by deductibility of investment fees, actuarial fees and additional contributions to fund plan deficits must be considered. Creditor proofing is a must in our growingly litigious society. Estate planning benefits are also clear.

Demographics and economic and taxation realities will give rise to a significant increase in the use of IPPs, and, as professionals and advisors, we must always understand that thorough due diligence is the hallmark of service.

CHAPTER 8

ACTUARIAL CALCULATIONS FOR INDIVIDUAL PENSION PLANS

Ian E. Baker

Overview

This chapter goes into the workings of the formulas that are used by actuaries to perform the various actuarial calculations involved with the set-up, maintenance and wind-up of an IPP.

Learning Objectives

By the end of this chapter, you should be able to:

- understand what actuaries must calculate and certify for an IPP to be registered;

- understand pension limits and know the percentage of increases to these limits; and

- understand IPP pension plan governance.

INTRODUCTION

A defined benefit plan, like an Individual Pension Plan (IPP), defines the pension a member is to receive upon retirement via a formula. For a *connected person*,[1] the IPP formula is typically 2.0% of the member's *career average* indexed T4 earnings. The IPP formula for a *non-connected person* is usually 2.0% of the member's *highest three-year average* indexed T4 earnings.

---

[1] A person who owns directly or indirectly 10% or more of any class of shares of a company or who is not dealing at arm's length with such a person.

An *actuary*[2] is required by the *Income Tax Act*, R.S.C. 1985, c. 1 (5th Supp.) and by provincial pension regulators[3] to calculate and certify the contributions needed to properly fund this formulaic pension promise. The actuary is required to update his or her calculations at least every three years (triennial actuarial valuation) by provincial legislation and at least every four years by the *Income Tax Act*.

PENSION LIMITS

For many years, the largest dollar benefit available to a member of a defined benefit plan was $1,715 per year of pensionable service. This maximum pension limit (MPL) per year of pensionable service was changed in both the February 2003 and February 2005 federal budgets to the following:

TABLE 1		
Year Of Retirement	**Defined Benefit Dollar Limit $**	**Increase %**
2004	1,833.33	
2005	2,000.00	9.09
2006	2,111.11	5.55
2007	2,222.22	5.26
2008	2,333.33	5.00
2009	2,444.44	4.76
2010 +	Indexed to AIW*[4]	

* Average Industrial Wage index

---

[2]   A Fellow of the Canadian Institute of Actuaries.

[3]   Provincial pension regulators include the Office of the Superintendent of Financial Institutions (OSFI), which governs IPPs sponsored by federally registered companies.

[4]   The AIW Index has increased since 1990, as per the table below:

	Aggregate AIW Index 12 months ending each June 30th	**Increase %**
Year		
1990	6,206.66	
1991	6,507.68	4.85

PENSION PLAN GOVERNANCE

Pension plans are governed by the *Income Tax Act* and the *Income Tax Regulations*, C.R.C., c. 945, as well as provincial pension regulators.

Canada Revenue Agency (CRA) administers the *Income Tax Act* and its Regulations. CRA determines:

(a) whether the plan submitted for registration satisfies the primary test of a pension plan (the moneys contributed are to be used for pension purposes), whether the employer (plan sponsor) and the employee (member) have a *bona fide* relationship, whether the employer is an active company, whether the employee receives pension-eligible (*i.e.*, T4) income, *etc.*;

(b) the deductibility of employer contributions; and

(c) whether the plan maintains its formal registration status.

The provincial pension regulators (PPRs) administer their respective provincial Pension Benefits Acts. These Acts govern *minimum* plan provisions such as vesting, locking-in, minimum payments for current service contributions and solvency deficiencies. Provincial Pension Benefits Acts protect the member's rights to receive a properly funded pension.

IPPs are usually created for owner-employees and feature many *maximum* plan provisions (such as the formula pension and the post-retirement indexing of pension payments) to take full advantage of company deductions under the *Income Tax Act*. Given these circumstances, some PPRs have decided to exclude IPPs from almost all provincial pension regulation, as shown in the following table:

1992	6,751.07	3.74
1993	6,954.92	3.02
1994	7,051.57	1.39
1995	7,155.60	1.48
1996	7,239.76	1.18
1997	7,439.67	2.76
1998	7,541.09	1.36
1999	7,627.22	1.14
2000	7,775.85	1.95
2001	7,937.26	2.08
2002	8,088.31	1.90
2003	8,230.85	1.76
2004	8,379.91	1.81
2005	8,563.89	2.20

PROVINCE	EXCLUSION FOR CONNECTED	EXCLUSION FOR NON-CONNECTED
British Columbia	Yes	Yes
Alberta[5]	Yes	No
Manitoba	Yes	Yes
Quebec	Yes	No
Prince Edward Island[6]	Yes	Yes

The actuary in performing and reporting of actuarial calculations is subject to the professional standards promulgated by the Canadian Institute of Actuaries. These standards include:

(a) Consolidated Standards of Practice — General Standards (May 2002);

(b) Standard of Practice for Determining Pension Commuted Values (February 2005); and

(c) Statement of Principles on Revised Actuarial Standards of Practice for Reporting on Pension Plan Funding (March 2005).

ACTUARIAL VALUATIONS

Actuarial valuation reports will show three actuarial valuations — maximum funding, going concern and solvency. Maximum funding and going-concern valuations assume that the IPP will continue in active status. Solvency valuations assume that the IPP will be terminated as at the valuation date.

An actuarial valuation shows:

(a) the financial position of the plan; and

(b) employer's current service contributions for the member.

As at the valuation date, the financial position of the plan compares the actuarial value of assets to the actuarial liability. If assets exceed the liability, then the plan has an actuarial surplus. If the liability exceeds assets, then the plan has an unfunded liability.

---

[5] From August 2006, the Alberta pension regulator does not require the filing of documents, actuarial valuation reports and annual filings for IPPs for connected persons.

[6] As at this writing, Prince Edward Island has not promulgated any pension legislation. Therefore, all pension plans, including IPPs, are not subject to provincial pension legislation.

The actuarial liability measures the present value of pension benefits accrued by the member prior to the valuation date, *i.e.*, past service benefits. The current service contributions measures the present value of pension benefits expected to be accrued by the member in the following year(s).

ELIGIBILITY FOR PAST SERVICE BENEFITS

For calendar years 1990 and after, any pension benefit provided by the employer in a given year would reduce the pension plan member's RRSP deduction limit for the following year through the reporting of a pension adjustment (PA) on the member's T4.

Before an employer can provide past service pension benefits to, or make a past service pension contribution on behalf of, an IPP member, the *Income Tax Regulations* require that the IPP member satisfy the condition on "RRSP deduction limit lost". This condition must be satisfied through one or a combination of the following methods:

(a)   a reduction in the member's unused RRSP contribution room carried forward;

(b)   a withdrawal from the member's RRSP on a taxable basis so as to free up the necessary RRSP contribution room (This method is rarely used as the member makes a taxable withdrawal from an RRSP — defeating the purpose of setting up a new IPP, which is to achieve more tax sheltering.); and/or

(c)   transfer the amount on a tax-free basis from the member's existing RRSP account to the IPP (this most common method is referred to as a "qualifying transfer from RRSP to IPP"). *Note that only the member's own personal RRSP (i.e.,* the IPP member must be the annuitant of the RRSP) can be used. *Spousal RRSP (i.e.,* a plan under which the IPP member is the contributor but not the annuitant) funds *cannot be used* for this purpose.

If the "RRSP deduction limit lost" condition cannot be satisfied, the employer must either:

(a)   reduce the number of years of past service benefits being recognized; or

(b)   postpone the recognition of past service to a future date until the RRSP funds have accumulated to the required transfer amount.

Some individuals may wish to have a selected number of years recognized immediately and have other past years recognized only when remaining RRSP funds can accumulate to the required transfer amount.

Recognition of past years of pensionable service at IPP implementation is voluntary and at the discretion of the employer. Bear in mind that for a plan that is subject to PPRs, the employer must contribute a minimum amount based on the amount of current service contribution and the amortization of a deficit amount.

Recognition of additional years of past service for the IPP member would also result in an additional minimum funding obligation for the employer. The employer should take the mandatory minimum employer contribution into consideration to ensure that he or she is comfortable with the resulting mandatory minimum pension funding requirements.

For a new IPP effective on January 1, 2006, the maximum "RRSP deduction limit lost" for past service benefits from January 1, 1991 to December 31, 2005 is $250,600 calculated as follows:

Year	(1) T4 Income	(2) Benefit Entitlement	(3) RRSP Deduction Limit Lost
2005	≥ $105,556	$2,111.11	$18,400
2004	≥ $105,556	$2,111.11	$18,400
2003	≥ $105,556	$2,111.11	$18,400
2002	≥ $105,556	$2,111.11	$18,400
2001	≥ $105,556	$2,111.11	$18,400
2000	≥ $105,556	$2,111.11	$18,400
1999	≥ $105,556	$2,111.11	$18,400
1998	≥ $105,556	$2,111.11	$18,400
1997	≥ $105,556	$2,111.11	$18,400
1996	≥ $105,556	$2,111.11	$18,000
1995	≥ $105,556	$2,111.11	$18,000
1994	≥ $105,556	$2,111.11	$13,500
1993	≥ $105,556	$2,111.11	$12,500
1992	≥ $105,556	$2,111.11	$11,500
1991	≥ $105,556	$2,111.11	$11,500
Total			**$250,600**

$(2) = (1) \times 2.0\%$
$(3) = (2) \times 9.0 - \$600$ for years after 1996
$(3) = (2) \times 9.0 - \$1,000$ for years 1995 and 1996
(3) = years 1991 to 1994 had maximums based on lower T4 earnings

MAXIMUM FUNDING ACTUARIAL VALUATION

A maximum funding valuation, as its name implies, calculates the maximum deductible contributions allowed under the *Income Tax Act* and its Regulations.

Section 8515 of the *Income Tax Regulations* specifies that the assumptions to be used in a maximum funding valuation include:

(a)   actuarial liabilities and current service contributions are to be determined using the projected accrued benefit method;

(b)   valuation interest rate is 7.5% per year;

(c)   wage increase is 5.5% per year;

(d)   Consumer Price Index increases by 4.0% per year;

(e)   the member will survive to age 65;

(f)   the member will retire at age 65 (if the member is over age 65 as at the actuarial valuation date then the member is assumed to retire immediately);

(g)   the member's employment with the plan sponsor will continue until retirement;

(h)   at retirement, the member is married to a person who is the same age as the member;

(i)   post-retirement mortality rates are based upon 80% of the average of the male and female rates set forth in the 1983 Group Annuity Mortality Table;

(j)   the actuarial value of assets equals the fair market value of assets as at the valuation date;

(k)   pension payments are payable monthly in advance;

(l)   pension payments are increased each year by 1.0% less than the percentage increase in the Consumer Price Index; and

(m)   pension payments are guaranteed for five years, with 2/3 of the pension continuing to the member's surviving pension partner.[7]

Consider the January 1, 2006 actuarial valuation for a maximum-provision IPP for a connected person with the following characteristics:

(a)   date of birth: October 31, 1949;

(b)   1995 T4 earnings: $50,000 and had 12 months of service; and

---

[7]   Pension partner includes spouse, common law partner or same-sex partner as per applicable pension legislation.

(c)   2006 expected T4 earnings: $120,000.

To determine the actuarial liability in respect of 1995:

(a)   calculate the member's retirement date (first day of month coincident or following attainment of age 65): November 1, 2014;

(b)   calculate the duration from valuation date to assumed date of retirement: 8 years and 10 months;

(c)   determine the indexed T4 earnings as at the valuation date by multiplying 1995 T4 earnings by the AIW[8] in 2005 ($8,563.89) and dividing by the AIW in 1994 ($7,051.57), yielding $60,723.29;

(d)   determine the indexed T4 earnings as at the retirement date as $93,191.21 ($60,723.29 × 1.055 raised to the 8th power);

(e)   calculate the MPL in the year of retirement as $3,194.79 ($2,444.44 × 1.055 raised to the 5th power);

(f)   calculate the projected annual pension in the year of retirement as $1,863.82 ($93,191.21 × 2.0%);

(g)   choose the lesser of the result in (f) and the result in step (e) to arrive at the projected annual pension with respect to 1995 ($1,863.82);

(h)   determine the interest discount from the valuation date to the member's retirement date as 0.527910 (1.075 raised to the negative 8.833333th power);

(i)   calculate the annuity factor for a $1.00 per year pension payable monthly commencing at age 65 as $14.5263; and

(j)   multiply the result of (g) by the result of (h), and multiply that by the result of (i) to derive the actuarial liability in respect of 1995 to be $14,293 ($1,863.82 × 0.527910 × $14.5263).

To determine the current service contributions for 2006, 2007 and 2008:

(a)   calculate the member's retirement date (first day of month coincident or following attainment of age 65): November 1, 2014;

(b)   calculate the duration from valuation date to assumed date of retirement: 8 years and 10 months;

(c)   determine the indexed T4 earnings as at the retirement date as $184,162.38 ($120,000 × 1.055 raised to the 8th power);

---

8   See note 4, above, for details.

(d)   calculate the MPL in the year of retirement as $3,194.79 ($2,444.44 × 1.055 raised to the 5th power);

(e)   calculate the projected annual pension in the year of retirement as $3,683.25 ($184,162.38 × 2.0%);

(f)   choose the lesser of the result in (f) and the result in step (e) to arrive at the projected annual pension with respect to 1995 ($3,194.79);

(g)   determine the interest discount from the valuation date to the member's retirement date as 0.527910 (1.075 raised to the negative 8.833333th power);

(h)   calculate the annuity factor for a $1.00 per year pension payable monthly commencing at age 65 as $14.5263;[9] and

(i)   multiply the result of (g) by the result of (h) and multiply that by the result of (i), and multiply that by 1.075 raised to the 0.5th power[10] to derive the current service contributions for 2006 to be $25,402[11] ($3,194.79 × 0.527910 × $14.5263 × 1.036822). The 2007 current service cost would be $27,307 ($25,402 × 1.075). The 2008 current service cost would be $29,355 ($25,402 × 1.075 × 1.075).

---

[9]   A joint and survivor annuity (with the member aged 65 and the survivor aged 65), which pays the survivor $0.667 per year after the member's death, which is guaranteed for a period of 5 years and which is increased each year by 3.0% (1.0% less than the percentage increase in the Consumer Price Index).

[10]   Our company's practice (Westcoast Actuaries Inc.) is to assume that IPP current service contributions are to occur during the middle of a calendar year. Other actuarial firms may, for example, assume that current service contributions are made at the beginning of a year.

[11]   CRA requires that actuarial valuation reports express current service contributions for connected persons as a percentage of their T4 earnings up to a dollar maximum. In this example, the report would state that the 2006 current service contributions are 24.1% of T4 earnings up to $25,402. The percentage is derived by dividing $25,402 by the member's expected 2006 T4 earnings up to a maximum earnings level of $105,556 (the 2006 MPL of $2,111.11 divided by 2.0%).

CRA's reasoning is that because a connected person can control his or her own T4 earnings, it does want the employer contribution made after the member has received T4 earnings. In this case, if the member had $10,000 of T4 earnings in January 2006 and February 2006, *etc.*, then the employer should contribute $2,410 in February 2006 and $2,410 in March 2006, *etc.*, until the dollar maximum of $25,402 is attained. In other words, CRA does not want the employer to contribute $25,402 until the member has received at least $105,556 in T4 income for 2006. Of course, if, for example, the member received a bonus of $120,000 of T4 earnings in January 2006, then the employer could immediately thereafter contribute $25,402 in respect of the member's 2006 current service contributions.

GOING-CONCERN ACTUARIAL VALUATION

The purpose of a going-concern valuation is to provide appropriate funding for the benefits being accrued, assuming that the plan continues indefinitely.

The actuary sets the assumptions for the going-concern valuation. The main assumption would be the interest assumption. In the current economic environment, an appropriate interest rate would likely be in the range of 5.0% to 7.0%. The lower the interest rate, then the higher the actuarial liability and current service contributions.

The actuary could choose to employ an actuarial value of assets which smooths the past market value of assets rather than employing simply the market value of assets. As such, the actuarial value of assets would show less variance.

Other assumptions would be consistent with the provisions in the plan text and consistent with each other. For example, if the interest rate was 5.5% per year, then the wage increase rate would be 3.5% per year, and the increase in the Consumer Price Index would be 2.0% per year, etc.

The key point is that, most likely, the employer contributions calculated under the going-concern valuation would be higher than the employer contributions calculated under the maximum funding valuation.

SOLVENCY VALUATION

The purpose of a solvency valuation is to provide appropriate funding for the benefits being accrued, assuming the plan terminates as at the valuation date.

The method of calculating the solvency deficiency and special payments to amortize that deficiency is specified by the various provincial Pension Benefits Acts. Fortunately, the method of calculation is the same across all provinces.

If the solvency valuation reveals a solvency deficiency, additional funding by the employer is required to ensure such deficiency is eliminated in five years. Certain adjustments to be made to the solvency assets to determine the solvency excess or solvency deficiency are as follows:

(a)   Solvency assets equal the sum of:

   (i)   market value of investments; and

   (ii) any cash balances and accrued receivable income items less amounts payable (and wind-up expense allowance — assumed payable from the plan).

(b) Solvency asset adjustment equals the sum of:

(i) the impact of using an asset adjustment method which smooths out market gains/losses over a period of up to five years; and

(ii) the present value of the special payments that are scheduled for payment within five years after the valuation date.

The hypothetical wind-up method is not technically an actuarial cost method (which deals with the allocation of the costs of the plan to various periods) but rather a method of estimating the liabilities of the plan should the plan be terminated. The primary requirement of this method is to comply with provincial Pension Benefits Acts. The solvency liabilities have been calculated as the present value of accrued benefits (all of which would be vested upon plan termination) for all members, whether active, retired or entitled to a deferred pension.

Assets are valued at market value adjusted for any receivables or payables as at the date of valuation, reduced by expected plan wind-up expenses.

The accrued benefit cost method was used to determine the solvency liabilities. Under this method, for each member, the accrued actuarial liabilities are determined as the present value of all benefits earned to the valuation date.

Members who are eligible to retire as at the valuation date are assumed to retire immediately. All other members are assumed to retire at age 65.

The benefits reflected in the valuation were those in effect at the valuation date. No allowance was made for subsequent benefit increases.

Pensions in payment were valued for retired members. Deferred pensions commencing at age 65 were valued for deferred vested members.

Actuarial assumptions[12] as at January 1, 2006 include:

(a) During the deferral period prior to pension commencement, interest rates are 4.50% per year for the first ten (10) years followed by 4.75% per year thereafter. After pension commencement, interest rates used are 3.01% per year for the first ten (10) years followed by 3.26% per year thereafter.

---

[12] These assumptions are in accordance with the Canadian Institute of Actuaries Standard of Practice for Determining Pension Commuted Values, effective February 1, 2005.

(b) During the deferral period prior to pension commencement, the salary scale is 3.45% per year for the first ten (10) years, followed by 3.45% per year thereafter.

(c) After pension commencement, pensions in payment are indexed at 1.45% per year for the first ten (10) years, followed by 1.45% per year thereafter.

(d) A member eligible to retire at the valuation date is assumed to do so. Otherwise the member is assumed to be eligible for a deferred vested pension at age 65 based on accrued benefits as at the valuation date.

(e) The member is assumed to terminate as at the valuation date, with full vesting of accrued benefits.

(f) Gender-distinct mortality rates are taken from the UP-94 Table projected forward to the year 2015, using mortality projection Scale AA.

(g) Ninety per cent of members are assumed to have a pension partner. Female pension partners are assumed to be three years younger than male members. Male pension partners are assumed to be three years older than female members.

A sample calculation is shown below:

ITEM	$
Actuarial Value of Assets (a)	142,708
Solvency Expenses (b)	2,000
Solvency Assets (c) = (a) – (b)	140,708
Solvency Asset Adjustment (d)	35,440
Total Solvency Assets (e) = (c) + (d)	176,148
Solvency Liabilities (f)	273,103
New Solvency Excess (Deficiency) (g) = (e) – (f)	96,955
Solvency Ratio (h) = (c) / (f)	51.5%

EMPLOYER CONTRIBUTIONS

The employer should make contributions in the range of the minimum required contribution and the maximum deductible contribution specified in the actuarial valuation report.

In determining the employer contributions to be made for any year, consideration should be given to various items, including:

(a)   the estimated value of benefits being accrued in a year;

(b)   the funded ratio of the plan (actuarial value of assets divided by actuarial liability);

(c)   the anticipated cash flow required to provide plan benefits; and

(d)   external factors affecting the employer's cash management.

The maximum contribution limit for 2007 will depend on the level of employer contributions made in 2006 and a reasonable amount of interest. Similarly, the maximum employer contribution limit for 2008 will depend on the level of contributions made in 2006 and 2007, plus a reasonable amount of interest.

The above contribution levels do not anticipate changes to any of the following in the future:

(a)   changes to provision of the plan;

(b)   changes in actuarial basis or assumptions;

(c)   experience gains (or losses); or

(d)   a significant change in membership of the plan.

Should any of the above occur, a re-examination of the employer's contribution may be necessary.

Under subsection 147.2(1) of the *Income Tax Act*, an employer contribution to a registered defined benefit pension plan is deductible in computing the employer's income for a taxation year if:

(a)   it is paid in the fiscal year or within 120 days from the end of the fiscal year;

(b)   it was not deducted in the previous year; and

(c)   it is an eligible contribution under subsection 147.2(2) of the *Income Tax Act*.

Subsection 147.2(2) of the *Income Tax Act* defines an eligible contribution as one which:

(a)   is made on the recommendation of an actuary;

(b)   is approved in writing by the Minister;

(c)   is based on an actuarial valuation prepared as of a date that is not more than four years before the day on which the contribution is made; and

(d)   is not in excess of prescribed limits if the plan is a designated plan.

A designated plan is one in which the total pension credit for members who either are connected with the employer or earn more than two and one-half times the year's maximum pensionable earnings exceeds 50% of the total pension credit for all the members under the defined benefit provisions of the plan. The prescribed limits are determined by using actuarial assumptions set forth in subsection 8515(7) of the *Income Tax Regulations*.

CONCLUSION

Actuarial calculations for IPPs are complicated. The key is for the employer to make contributions between the minimum required under the various Pension Benefits Acts and the maximum deductible contribution allowed under the *Income Tax Act*.

Note that the maximum deductible contribution overrides the minimum required contribution. For example, consider an IPP with a surplus of $2,500 and with a $5,200 annual payment to amortize a solvency deficiency. The minimum required contribution is $5,200 plus the member's current service contributions. The maximum deductible contribution is the member's current service contributions. The employer should make contributions equal to the member's current service contributions.

PART II

IPP INVESTMENT CONSIDERATIONS

CHAPTER 9

IPP REGULATOR INVESTMENT RESTRAINTS

Overview

This chapter provides a general outline of the restraints that are placed on investment managers/financial advisors managing IPP assets by regulating bodies.

Learning Objectives

By the end of this chapter, you should be able to:

- list the regulatory constraints placed on the management of assets held within an Individual Pension Plan;

- list and describe the main types of investments held within an Individual Pension Plan.

REGULATORY ENVIRONMENT

IPPs are highly regulated, and they must always comply with the investment rules that are found within the *Income Tax Act*, R.S.C. 1985, c. 1 (5th Supp.) (ITA), *Income Tax Regulations*, C.R.C, c. 945 (REG), Canada Revenue Agency's (CRA) Registered Plans Directorate and federal and provincial Pension Benefits Acts under which IPPs are governed. The trustee(s), custodian, administrator, investment manager and other appointed advisors to the IPP have a fiduciary duty to the beneficiary of the IPP to ensure that these plans' assets are invested properly to deliver the promised benefits to their beneficiaries.

When investing IPP assets, all parties involved must follow the prudent person rule, which means restricting the discretion in the IPP account to investments that a prudent person seeking reasonable income and preservation of capital might buy for his or her own portfolio. Lastly, investment risk for the overall asset mix within an IPP should be well diversified.

All IPPs in Canada are required by law to have a formalized Investment Policy Statement (IPS) that states the procedures and goals for the assets held within the IPP and its position on loans.

When an investment manager/financial advisor is developing the Investment Policy Statement for an IPP and investing IPP assets, the investment manager/financial advisor must always take the restraints placed on defined benefit pension plans into account.

If the investments within an IPP do very well, delivering better than the actuarial investment return assumptions of 7.5%, a surplus will result in an IPP. A company/sponsor in this situation will not be permitted to make additional contributions into an IPP on behalf of the plan member until the surpluses have vanished and a new actuarial evaluation stating that there are no surpluses left in the IPP has been filed with the proper regulators.

In the years that the plan runs surpluses, a company/sponsor will not receive a deduction until contributions into the plan are permitted to resume. In years that an IPP is running surpluses, where the IPP member is accruing pensionable credits, a pension adjustment will be generated, even though no funds are being contributed into the plan on his or her behalf. This results in the IPP member not having the ability to contribute into an RRSP or any other registered plan except his or her allowable pension adjustment offset amount of $600 per year.

Depending on the province in which an IPP is registered, if a plan is underfunded based on actuarial assumptions and valuations, an employer/sponsor of an IPP may be mandated to make contributions into a plan in order to make up for deficits in the plan. In some cases making up for deficiencies in funding in an IPP is a positive if a company has a positive cash flow. On the other hand, mandatory IPP contributions may place a heavy burden on a business/IPP sponsor's cash flow, and the business/IPP sponsor might not have the ability to fully fund a promised IPP benefit at the time that contributions have been mandated.

INVESTMENT

In paragraph 8502(*h*) of the *Income Tax Regulations* are the directives of investments permitted into registered pension plans and their restrictions. Note: In addition, it is important to investigate the investment restrictions that are mandated by the federal and provincial Pension Benefits Acts.

Permitted Investments Within IPPs and Other Defined Benefit Pension Plans

The following is a list of investments that are permitted within IPPs and other plans:

(a) bonds, debentures, notes, coupons, term deposits, guaranteed investment certificates, insurance contracts, and mortgages;

(b) shares listed on a recognized stock exchange by Canadian regulators;

(c) derivatives, which could be used for hedging a portfolio risk;

(d) real estate holdings;

(e) mutual funds and other managed money products.

As of the end of 2005, there are no longer any foreign content restrictions placed on Registered Pension Plans or RRSPs.

Prohibited Investments Within IPPs and Other Defined Benefit Pensions

The following is a list of IPP limitations:

(a) An IPP is limited to holding up to 10% of its entire book value in any one entity, affiliates and associates. The only exception to this rule is holdings in government guaranteed issues.

(b) An IPP is limited to holding up to 5% of book value of any parcel of real estate up to 25% total book value of assets in real estate holdings.

(c) An IPP is limited to holding up to 15% of book value of any resource property up to 25% total book value of assets. Resource property types of assets are grouped in with real estate holdings.

(d) An IPP may not hold property that is a share of the capital stock of, or a debt of, an employer who is sponsoring the IPP.

(e) An IPP may not hold property that is a share of the capital stock of, or a debt of, a person who is connected with the employer who is sponsoring the IPP.

(f) An IPP may not hold property that is a share of the capital stock of, or a debt of, a person or partnership that controls indirectly or directly the employer who is sponsoring the IPP.

(g) An IPP may not hold property that is a share of the capital stock of, or a debt of, a member of the IPP.

(h)　An IPP may not hold property that is a share of the capital stock of, or a debt of, a person or partnership that is not at arm's length from the employer, a person who is connected to the employer, a plan member or a partnership to the IPP.

It is important that all investments held within an IPP first go through an in-depth screening process to ensure that they meet the guidelines placed on pension assets by CRA and provincial pension regulators.

Currently, most assets held in IPPs today have not gone through a proper screening process to determine their appropriateness for these plans. CRA and pension regulators across Canada have initiated an aggressive audit process of assets held in IPPs over the last few years. If IPP portfolios are found to be offside of the pension investment guidelines, pension plan sponsors, administrators, trustees and investment managers risk fines and penalties, and offside IPPs risk being deregistered.

CHAPTER 10

INVESTMENT PHILOSOPHY 101

Christopher P. Van Slyke
Peter J. Merrick

Overview

This chapter discusses arguably the most advanced investment strategies and management for IPP portfolios around today. It combines several methodologies that include Modern Portfolio Theory, the three-factor model and fixed-income strategies.

Learning Objectives

By the end of this chapter, you should be able to:

- understand the basics of Modern Portfolio Theory;
- understand the basics of the three-factor model;
- understand the basics of fixed-income strategies.

MODERN PORTFOLIO THEORY

In 1990, Harry Markowitz, William Sharpe and Merton Miller, three noted financial economists, won the Nobel Memorial Prize for Economics for their work in developing Modern Portfolio Theory as a portfolio management technique. Modern Portfolio Theory has been used to develop and manage investment portfolios for large institutions, as well as for individual investors. There are four components to Modern Portfolio Theory.

Investors Inherently Avoid Risk

Investors are often more concerned with risk than they are with reward. Rational investors are not willing to accept risk unless the level of return compensates them for it.

Securities Markets Are Efficient

The "efficient market hypothesis" states that while the returns of different securities may vary as new information becomes available, these variations are inherently random and unpredictable. Assets are repriced every minute of the day according to what news comes out. As new information enters the market, it is quickly absorbed into the prices of securities, and thus hard to capitalize on. In fact, advancing information technology and increased sophistication on the part of investors are causing the markets to become even more efficient.

The implications of the efficient market hypothesis are far-reaching for investors. It implies that one should be deeply skeptical of anyone who claims to know how to "beat the market". One cannot expect to consistently beat the market by picking individual securities or by "timing the market".

Focus on the Portfolio as a Whole and Not on Individual Securities

The risk and reward characteristics of all of the portfolio's holdings should be analyzed as one, not separately. An efficient allocation of capital to specific asset classes is far more important than selecting the individual investments.

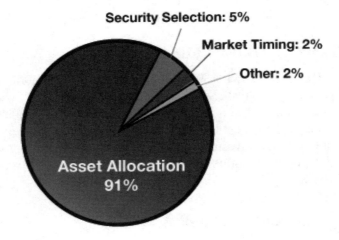

Determinants of Portfolio Performance

Security Selection: 5%

Market Timing: 2%

Other: 2%

Asset Allocation 91%

Source: "Determinants of Portfolio Performance" published in the Financial Analysts Journal (August 1986) by Gary P. Brinson, L. Randolph Hood and Gilbert Beebower.

As the pie chart shows, your asset allocation can determine over 91% of the performance variation of an investment portfolio. How the investment dollars are allocated far outweighs the potential effects of individual security selection and market timing. This will be further explored in Chapter 11.

Every Risk Level Has a Corresponding Optimal Combination of Asset Classes That Maximizes Returns

This is called the "efficient frontier". Portfolio diversification is not so much a function of how many individual stocks or bonds are involved, but the relationship of one asset to another. This relationship is referred to in the investment world as "correlation". The higher a correlation between two investments, the more likely they are to move in the same direction.

The efficient frontier represents the range of hypothetical portfolios that offer the maximum return for any given level of risk. Portfolios positioned above the range are unachievable on a consistent basis. Portfolios below the efficient frontier are inefficient portfolios (too much risk, not enough reward). The ideal portfolio exists somewhere along the efficient frontier.

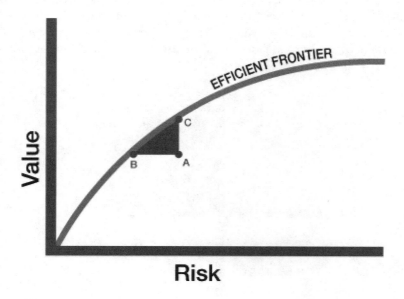

The portfolio represented by point A is inefficient because portfolios exist with the same value but less risk (Portfolio B); portfolios exist with the same risk but more value (Portfolio C); and there are portfolios with a combination of these two conditions. The efficient frontier, as originally defined in Modern Portfolio Theory, is a line that represents the continuum of all efficient portfolios.

THE THREE-FACTOR MODEL

Most finance academics and investment professionals acknowledge that there are three primary factors influencing equity portfolio returns:

(1) **Exposure to the overall market (beta).** The term beta refers to a measure of an investment's volatility, relative to an appropriate asset class or the overall market.

(2) **The percentage invested in large company stocks versus small company stocks.** Over time, small company stocks have higher expected returns than large company stocks. This is because stocks of small companies are riskier than those of large companies, and investors demand a premium for this risk.

(3) **The percentage invested in growth stocks versus value stocks.** Over time, value stocks have higher expected returns than growth stocks. Value stocks are those that sell at lower prices relative to their earnings and book values. They are perceived by investors to be riskier than growth stocks, and investors demand a premium for this risk as well.

FIXED INCOME

The role of fixed income in a portfolio is not only to produce income, but also to reduce volatility. The best way to accomplish this is to employ the following strategies:

- use shorter maturities (maturities under five years);
- use high quality issues;
- use a variable maturity approach;
- use a diversified global approach while hedging all currencies.

Together, Modern Portfolio Theory, the three-factor model, and fixed-income strategies along with the institutional approach that will be discussed in Chapter 11 can help form an overall investment philosophy for the management of IPP portfolios.

One of the main fiduciary responsibilities of the traditional defined benefit pension plan sponsor is choosing outside investment management for the plan that would meet the mandate of the plan that has been outlined in the IPP's investment policy statement.

IPP: ASSET ALLOCATION AND REGULAR REBALANCING OF PORTFOLIOS

Overview

This chapter discusses the benefits of adopting an allocation approach towards the management of Individual Pension Plan assets to achieve the fulfillment of an IPP's promised benefit for its member. Then it evaluates the different types of asset management vehicles that are most commonly used by IPPs today. The chapter concludes by making the case for using money management products to manage IPP money.

Learning Objectives

By the end of this chapter, you should be able to:

- describe what asset allocation is and the value of applying its principles to managing IPP assets;
- describe regular rebalancing of IPP portfolios and the value of applying its principles to managing IPP assets;
- list the five-step process of proper IPP portfolio management;
- understand the basics of the institutional approach;
- list the main types of money-managed products that are held in IPPs today;
- understand the argument for using money managers to manage IPP assets.

IPP: ASSET ALLOCATION

The type of investment planning this chapter addresses is referred to as asset allocation. This means that as an investor, an individual allocates proportions of his or her liquid assets within his or her IPP portfolio into different asset classes. In asset allocation, an individual or, in our case, an IPP investment portfolio can be in one or a combination of three main categories:

(1)   equities — ownership in companies;

(2)   fixed income — money invested in GICs, bonds, and mortgages; or

(3)   cash — that is money invested in T-bills, and in chequing and savings accounts.

Studies have shown that asset allocation is the single greatest determinant of investment performance. It has been shown that approximately 91% of the total long-term return of an investment portfolio is due to the asset allocation.

Unaware of this, many people blindly sink money into this or that investment without ever formulating an asset allocation model that is in sync with their financial goals and investment personality.

Once a client's investment objective for his or her IPP portfolio has been determined, an advisor helps the client formulate an investment policy statement for his or her portfolio. The target annual investment return for an IPP while the client is accumulating pension credits is the defined benefit pension plan proscribed return of 7.5% so the plan will be found to be either over- or underfunded. As a rule of thumb, it is wise to allocate current and future IPP investment assets in a well-balanced portfolio that includes equities, fixed income and cash. Designing this type of portfolio is like keeping your money in separate pockets and in a separate pair of pants.

All asset classes move in cycles, and each asset class has its own cycle. Typically, when one or two asset classes are performing well, the other asset classes may not be performing as well. By having a well-defined asset allocation strategy in place, the financial ride is much smoother to achieve the capital requirements to deliver the promised benefit to the IPP member.

Let's go through an example of asset allocation diversification and how this can work for the typical investor. Let's imagine a set of twins, Gwen and Joan. Both are 40 years of age.

Gwen invests $1 million in a 7% bond, which matures in 20 years. Joan also invests $1 million for 20 years but separates the money into five $200,000 investments. The first investment loses everything, the second earns nothing, the third earns 4%, the fourth earns 7%, and the fifth earns 15%. At age 60, Gwen's investment has grown to $3,869,700, while Joan, who has practised asset allocation, has grown her initial investment to $4,685,300. Joan's practice of asset allocation has yielded her an additional $815,600 over Gwen's strategy of placing all her money in one asset class. This is the true power of asset allocation.

Let's imagine that an IPP sponsor/owner of a business decided to put all of his or her IPP assets into a technology portfolio at the end of the bull market of the 1990s. Then in the middle of 2000, the very foundations of the technology sector in the stock market began to crumble, free falling into negative territory. This IPP sponsor could now be hurting. Depending on the province the IPP was registered in, the IPP sponsor would be on the hook to make additional contributions into the IPP to make sure there was enough capital available to deliver the promised pension benefit. What if the plan sponsor did not have the funds in his or her company to make new contributions into the IPP? Then what? With asset allocation it does not need to be this way.

IPP: REGULAR REBALANCING OF PORTFOLIO

Along with asset allocation, regular rebalancing of an IPP portfolio is an essential element of long-term investment success. Rebalancing is a fundamental part of the process of reaching an IPP's financial goals in the most effective way while lessening the overall instability of the total IPP investment portfolio.

An example of how effective rebalancing can be is illustrated in a study conducted by T. Rowe Price of Baltimore, Maryland, a top investment manager. What T. Rowe Price did was construct two $10,000 model portfolios made up of 60% equity, 30% fixed income and 10% cash.

Using historical data spanning a 25-year period from the end of 1969 to September 1995, T. Rowe Price invested one portfolio using the original mix and never rebalanced at all.

The identical portfolio invested at the same time was rebalanced every three months to the original target allocation of 60% equity, 30% fixed income and 10% cash.

At the end of the 25-year and nine-month period, the rebalanced portfolio grew from $10,000 to about $145,000; the untouched portfolio grew to $141,000. By following a disciplined rebalancing asset allocation approach to investing, IPP clients are joining the ranks of the world's greatest investors by buying low and selling high. You do this by constantly trimming the asset classes that have done well and replenishing the asset classes that have decreased in value.

From time to time, as IPP members' lives change, and as do laws and regulations governing IPPs, it is very important to re-evaluate the asset allocation mix within IPP portfolios and modify and change the IPP's investment policy statement.

What makes the asset allocation approach the approach for long-term IPP investing is that it eases the turbulence that happens while investing, and empowers both the IPP sponsor and IPP member to stay the course to achieve the desired outcome of the IPP, that is, larger amounts of money saved in a tax-deferred way for retirement.

THE FIVE-STEP PROCESS TO PROPER IPP PORTFOLIO MANAGEMENT[*]

Step One

Determine the amount of equity and fixed income exposure that will be in the IPP portfolio. This primarily depends on the IPP sponsor's and IPP member's goals, resources, time horizon, and risk capacity and tolerance. Just as an example, many pension managers recommend a blend of 60% equities and 40% fixed income. This is referred to as a "60-40" balanced portfolio.

Step Two

Add asset classes to increase expected return and decrease volatility. Securities are grouped together according to similar risk and return characteristic called "asset classes". After establishing the equity-to-fixed income ratio, begin adding other asset classes for two reasons. Either they increase the expected return, or they help lower volatility. As mentioned in the previous chapter, there is a vast amount of research available today that demonstrates that portfolio returns over time are influenced by three primary factors:

- the amount invested in equities versus fixed income;
- the amount invested in large company stocks versus small company stocks; and
- the amount invested in growth companies versus value companies.

---

[*] Christopher P. Van Slyke, B.A., M.B.A., CFP, whom you were introduced to in the previous chapter, is the managing director of Capital Financial Advisors, LLC, in La Jolla, California. His firm has developed a very useful five-step process for selecting investments and managing a wealthy client's IPP and other investment portfolios. This methodology is very helpful for advisors who plan to or are currently managing clients' IPP and other moneys. The process has been provided for your information.

When it comes to diversification, the number of investments owned in the IPP portfolio is not what is important. How effective these assets are diversified in the portfolio is what really matters. If most of the funds in an IPP portfolio are invested in the large cap growth asset class, then the portfolio does not have proper diversification. These investments will probably move up and down together, not independent of each other.

Step Three

Adjust the portfolio for constraints. Once the "model" IPP portfolio has been developed and agreed upon by the IPP sponsor and IPP member, it is time to turn the attention to implementing the IPP investment strategy. This step requires the reviewing of the IPP portfolio for portfolio constraints to adjust asset weighing accordingly. A constraint may be a limitation of the percentage of one holding within the IPP portfolio, a stock that the IPP member just cannot part with, illiquid positions or regulatory restrictions. The model IPP portfolio is then tweaked to accommodate these particular constraints.

Step Four

Choose the correct investment vehicle for each asset class. The final step of implementation is selecting the best investment(s) for each asset class. For diversification and better risk/reward ratios, pension experts generally prefer institutional managed money products.

Step Five

Review, monitor and adjust. IPP portfolio management is not something that is set once and forgotten about. Markets change everyday, and so does the IPP sponsor's and IPP member's tax planning and retirement needs. An IPP portfolio needs to be frequently reviewed, monitored and, if needed, adjusted to restore the IPP portfolio to its desired asset allocation. This could be the most important step of all.

INSTITUTIONAL APPROACH

Institutions managing pension assets have long out-performed the average investor for a variety of reasons as shown below.

Retail:		Institutional:
Looks at individual positions		Looks at portfolio as a whole
Has concentrated positions		Seeks broad diversification
Is short-term performance-oriented		Prefers risk management
Prefers active management	**VS**	Prefers asset-class management
Looks at short-term measures		Looks at long-term measures
Sells on dips		Buys on dips
Incurs high turnover		Has lower turnover
Higher cost		Lower cost
Higher taxes		Lower taxes
Emotional mentality		Rational mentality

Chart above provided by Capital Financial Advisors, LLC of La Jolla, California.

There are several sound types of investment management vehicles that an investment manager operating under the direction of an administrator or trustee(s) of an IPP can use. These are as follows:

- IPP assets could be invested in pooled funds. The fees are much lower than mutual funds and they can all be written off.

- Assets in an IPP can be invested in pension funds; with these types of investments, there is no need to have a corporate trustee or a three-party trustee because the maturity dates of these funds occur after the 69th birthday of the IPP member.

- IPP assets can be invested in either mutual funds or insurance segregated funds.

- Lastly, assets within the IPP can be invested in a discretionary investment account where the investment manager will choose the types of holdings placed in the IPP fund.

Overall, the best strategy for managing assets is to have designed a well-balanced portfolio to meet both IPP regulatory and IPP pension benefit needs and to monitor and review this strategy regularly.

THE CASE FOR MONEY MANAGEMENT

Many people in the media have objected to managed money products because they say it adds another layer of people who charge fees.

Successful investors like Warren Buffett believe markets are not always efficient. According to pundits of the efficient market theory, the price of a stock reflects a company's true underlining value. Those that believe in the efficient market theory believe that no single entity can affect the prices of stocks or bonds.

In reality, the managers of Canada's largest mutual fund companies and pension management firms can buy a significant percentage of a Canadian company's stock, causing the price of that stock to go up, as other buyers follow in the wake of these mutual fund companies' and pension management firms' purchases.

Those who buy Canadian shares from full service or discount brokerages usually have no idea when the buying began.

So what are mutual funds, money managed accounts and pool funds? They are a collective of sorts, where people have pooled their financial resources together, under one roof, and hired the same professional management.

These managers claim that an individual investor may be able to buy the same stocks cheaper on his or her own, but he or she would not have bought the same stocks at the same time with the same knowledge.

If markets were perfectly efficient, and research did not make a difference, then relative fund performance would be based on chance.

If it were that easy to make money from investing in stocks, individual investors would only need to watch business news programs. But information in an efficient market is disseminated randomly.

From experience, it can be argued that although information may be random at its outset, its development is sequential. Stories have a beginning, middle and end. Sometimes hearing the news and acting on it first provides an advantage.

Sometimes having the wisdom not to react will prove more successful. Sometimes it helps to know the people releasing the information in the first place.

Wisdom comes from making mistakes and then learning from those mistakes. These lessons can be expensive, especially for someone using his or her own money, such as a hobbyist.

Money managers are people, like you and me. Maybe they are no smarter than anyone else, but they have the time and money to find that garage in Richmond Hill, Ontario's Silicon Valley North, where two recent grads from Waterloo University are working on the next Internet breakthrough.

Pension and mutual fund managers are more likely to find out which companies in India or China will grow and which national government is about to fall. Efficient markets require that access to information be, if not free, at least equal.

Fund managers claim that their information is not random, but the result of well-developed methodologies and access to information, which, although public enough to avoid security violations, is too fresh to be widely disseminated.

In the Canadian Securities Course text (note that every registered Investment Dealer Association stockbroker is required to take the Canadian Securities Course before he or she can become licensed), it states that for a portfolio to be well diversified, it would need to hold between 15 to 30 stocks to avoid a single company's risk, that is, the risk that a company's management team might do something stupid.

Some people can afford the time and the money to design their own portfolios. Owning this many companies in a portfolio requires multiple costs for transactions and time for tracking, following and measuring performance. This all leads us back to the initial question.

If someone believes in perfectly efficient markets, that there is no truth to the herd mentality, that research does not matter, and that there is no value in delegating his or her investing, then there is no reason for these individuals to buy money management products.

The financial industry has gone through a fundamental change from being transactional based — buying and selling — to one focused on fees and the gathering of assets. By placing IPP clients into money-managed products, advisors will be able to focus on providing solutions to solve clients' very real needs instead of getting caught up in the day-to-day administration of choosing what stock or bond to buy or sell.

I would like to leave you with what I believe are the best criteria for picking an excellent money manager to run an IPP portfolio:

• Make sure that the money manager has done better than the average of the money manager's peers for a meaningful period of time, say ten years.

- Make sure that the money manager has been running money for a while and has some combat experience, meaning managing money in both the boom years of the late 1990s and the bust years of the early part of the 21st century.

- Make sure that the money manager is a long-term investor. The money manager should be an owner of stocks and bonds. The money manager should not rent them.

The IPP solution is on the verge of an explosive growth, and using money management products that are designed to meet an IPP's funding objectives will free up much of the IPP clients' and their advisors' time.

CHAPTER 12

SOCIALLY RESPONSIBLE INVESTING: A NEW TREND IN PENSION INVESTING

Peter J. Merrick
Eugene Ellmen

Overview

This chapter lays out the case for socially responsible investing (SRI) for both IPP portfolios and other non-IPP portfolios for today's modern investor.

Learning Objectives

By the end of this chapter, you should be able to:

- understand what socially responsible investing is;
- understand the emerging influence of "cultural creatives" subculture in the developed world;
- learn about the new trend of socially responsible investing occurring in the Canadian institutional marketplace;
- understand how you can make a difference when investing assets within IPP portfolios and other non-IPP portfolios.

"We do not inherit this land from our ancestors; we borrow it from our children."

Haida Indian Proverb

WHAT IS SOCIALLY RESPONSIBLE INVESTING?

Over the last decade, we have worked with hundreds of corporations, non-government organizations, families and individuals to help them to invest their money so they can create a better future. Collectively, we have learned through experience that in reality, money is something we have chosen to trade our life energy for. In the last 50 years, money has dematerialized from paper into electrical pulses of 0s and 1s, with trillions of dollars swirling around the world every minute. The truth is, when we invest our money, we are really casting a vote on the type of future we want to create. When North Americans poured billions of dollars into the Asian markets in the early 1990s, world attention focused on the potential of the Asian tiger.

In the late 1990s, technology was the focus. Perhaps the reason for the collapse of both these investing fads was that they were based on greed and fear, not long-term sustainable financial growth.

We are living in the most exciting, challenging and critical time in human history. Never before has so much been possible, and never before has so much been at stake. Around us are environmental, social and economic crises, along with extreme geopolitical tensions. It is evident that the roots of these crises lie within us: our materialism, our yearning for power, our love of money and our fear of each other.

In the 21st century, many investors have come to believe that we can do good for society with our investments and do well financially at the same time. Most of us would prefer to invest in companies that share the same values we do; if only we could outpace the S&P 500 or TSX at the same time. Now that goal has become more than an ephemeral New Year's resolution.

Yet the fact is, investing that reflects investors' values are both possible and profitable. Socially responsible investing, once largely dismissed as a novelty for the politically correct, is now considered a smart and lucrative way to make money in the long run.

If you feel this way, you are not alone. Toronto-born Paul Ray, a sociologist, and his wife, Sherry Anderson, a psychologist, now living in California, drew upon 13 years of survey research studies on 100,000 adults to find that as of the year 2000, there were 50 million people in the United States and 90 million in the European Union who would identify themselves as cultural creatives (*The Cultural Creatives: How 50 Million People Are Changing the World* (New York: Three Rivers Press, 2001)). According to Ray and Anderson, what makes someone so is being an "individual who cares deeply about ecology and saving the planet, about relationships, peace, social justice, and self-actualization, spirituality and self-expression". Such individuals have a burning desire to have their values reflected in their careers, investments and community.

The ranks of cultural creatives have been growing by leaps and bounds over the last 50 years. They want their money manager and financial advisor investment processes to be rigorous and demanding. But they want one more element put into the mix. They want to invest in responsible companies.

Socially responsible investing is about striking an appropriate balance: finding that golden meaning between a life that neither bows down to money nor neglects financial responsibilities, getting a good return for yourself without forgetting about others.

The overall amount of money (or assets under management (AUM)) invested in one or more of the three main SRI strategies (screening, shareholder advocacy and community investing) grew to $2.29 trillion in 2005. Nearly one in ten dollars is now invested in SRI (9.4% of the $24.4 trillion) in total assets under professional management in the United States, according to the U.S. Social Investment Forum. According to this report SRI assets have grown by 258% within one decade, outpacing the growth of the overall market.

A PERSPECTIVE ON CANADIAN AND INTERNATIONAL PENSION PLANS

This growth in socially responsible investment is being reflected in new approaches to pension management in Canada and Europe.

Across the Atlantic, large and very influential pension fund managers in the United Kingdom and Europe are banding together to conduct research into the impact of social and environmental analysis on pension returns. These fund managers believe that investment in socially responsible and sustainable companies with good governance structures will pay off in long-term value and lower long-term risk.

A group of European pension fund managers and asset firms managing hundreds of billions of euros has established the Enhanced Analytics Initiative, a process to establish incentives for investment brokers to begin analyzing non-financial factors. In addition, institutions such as the giant ABP pension fund and asset manager in the Netherlands (the second largest pension fund manager in the world), the Norwegian Government Pension Fund and the Fonds de Reserve (the state pension managers in France) are all using social and environmental analysis as part of their investment selection and management.

In Canada, several large pension managers have signed the United Nations' Principles on Responsible Investment (UNPRI). The Canada Pension Plan Investment Board, the British Columbia Investment

Management Corp. and the Caisse de depot et placement du Québec are among the largest pension fund managers in Canada. They have also signed the UNPRI treaty, pledging to look into socially responsible investment strategies and analysis.

Not only is pension management an issue, but so too is the topic of shareholder voting. As fiduciaries responsible for the investment of billions of dollars worth of assets, Canadian pension managers are in a position of owning shares in every major company in Canada, as well as the largest international corporations. With this ownership comes responsibility for the voting of shares in these companies. Every year, shareholders raise important issues of social responsibility, environmental well-being and corporate governance with major Canadian and international companies. Pension plan managers have a responsibility to cast their votes on these issues with care, and with the pension plan members' interests in mind.

Pension regulation is one of the drivers of these new approaches. The United Kingdom, Germany, France and other countries now require pension fund managers to disclose the extent to which they take social and environmental factors into account in their investment decision-making. By providing regular information on these issues to plan members, European pension fund managers are providing their members with an additional level of knowledge about their investment policies. These disclosures answer important questions from plan members about the social responsibility of their pension asset managers. Such a proactive approach heads off costly and divisive stakeholder debates over questions like tobacco or military investments.

In Canada, mutual fund managers are now required by Canadian securities commissions to reveal how they vote on such issues, disclosing their voting policies and showing exactly how they vote on shareholder resolutions. The requirement follows similar rules in the United States, driven by the belief that mutual fund managers were asleep at the switch when executives were raiding corporate coffers at Enron, WorldCom and other companies. More vigorous attention to voting would have placed management under greater scrutiny, reducing losses to investors. It is only a matter of time until pension fund managers are brought under similar shareholder voting disclosure rules.

The debate about pension funds during the last few years has centred on the issue of pension deficits. Rich benefit packages and accounting rules encouraging fund managers to overestimate future returns combined with lower stock values and bond yields have led to a crisis in the funding of many of Canada's largest defined benefit pension plans.

There is no doubt that significant reform is needed to put the funding of these pensions back in order.

But pension fund managers are also going to have to answer the questions of how social responsibility, sustainability, corporate governance and proxy voting fit into their long-term investment vision. The short-term funding issues are only a part of the puzzle of the pension problem. Equally important is the need to reform investment policies to take account of the long-term issues of responsible and sustainable business. As major investors in Canadian business, pension fund managers will need to look carefully into these issues. Not every pension plan manager will answer these questions in the same way. But now that these questions have been asked, they will need to be answered, and disclosure to plan members is the best way to ensure that plan members get the information they need.

WHERE TO FIND GOOD INFORMATION TO INVEST IPP ASSETS

Established in 1989, the Social Investment Organization (SIO) is the national non-profit association for the socially responsible investment (SRI) industry in Canada. The SIO has more than 400 members across Canada, representing SRI mutual fund managers, financial institutions, investment advisors, asset managers, institutional investors, individual investors and non-profit organizations with an interest in responsible investment. Its members serve more than half a million depositors and investors in Canada.

The mandate of the SIO is to take a leadership role in furthering the use of social and environmental criteria within the investment community; to raise public awareness of socially responsible investment; to establish the case for environmental/social analysis with other investment organizations; and to provide a forum and information source on socially responsible investment for its members and the public.

The SIO defines SRI as the process of selecting or managing investments according to social or environmental criteria The SIO estimates that there is approximately $65.5 billion in socially responsible investment assets under management in Canada.

MAKE A DIFFERENCE

In November 1992, 1,700 of the world's leading scientists, including the majority of Nobel laureates in the Sciences, issued the greatest appeal to the human residents of this planet by publishing a warning to humanity that stated:

"Human beings and the natural world are on a collision course."

It is not too late to make a difference. On May 2, 2005, Bob Hunter, one of the founders of Greenpeace and one of our mentors, died of cancer at the age of 63. You might remember Bob as the quirky guy who used to read the newspaper in his bathrobe every weekday on Toronto's City TV *Breakfast Television*. Bob's indomitable spirit fired the direct action mode of the environment protection movement and created Greenpeace. In Bob's last book, *Thermageddon: Countdown to 2030* (New York: Arcade Publishing, 2003), Bob persuasively argued that around 2030, the climate change for our planet would be irreversible, what he called "Thermageddon", and he reviewed the scientific evidence to support this theory. Included in his discussion was the role each North American citizen plays in contributing towards global warming patterns in the world. Throughout his book, he expressed grave concern for the world that his generation was leaving his grandchildren and the grandchildren of the world. His lasting challenge was for each of us to do his and her part to make this a better world after we depart it than how we found it.

One of Bob's most admirable traits was that he was not just a man of the spoken and written word, he was a man of action. On a very cold day in March 1976, Bob and Paul Watson, co-founder of Greenpeace, stood on an ice floe off the coast of Labrador, Canada as a large sealing ship approached them. The ice cracked and split beneath their feet as Watson said to Bob, "When it splits, I'll jump to the left and you to the right." Bob looked straight ahead and calmly said, "I'm not going anywhere." Because Bob stayed, Watson stayed, and the two of them brought that seal killing ship to a dead stop.

Bob Hunter's life proves that each and every one of us can make a difference. It is a moving call for action backed by deeds and facts. One way we can do our part is by acting on the belief that there is absolutely no conflict in doing what is right by investing both IPP and non-IPP portfolios in companies that respect the environment, treat their employees well and conduct their businesses ethically while earning a good solid return. Plus, this type of investing just feels good because it is good!

Remember: Act locally today by investing your money in SRI, and think globally about how we will all be doing our part in making this a better world for our grandchildren's tomorrows!

PART III

ADVANCED IPP APPLICATIONS

CHAPTER 13

MAXIMIZING IPPS WITH IMFS AND AVCS — A POWER-CHARGED OPTION

Kurt Dregar

Overview

This chapter introduces the concept of utilizing Investment Management Fees (IMF) and additional voluntary contributions (AVC) in conjunction with an IPP to maximize retirement savings for both IPP sponsors and IPP members.

Learning Objectives

By the end of this chapter, you should be able to:

* describe what IMFs and AVCs are;
* understand the long-term benefits of utilizing IMF and AVC in conjunction with an IPP to maximize retirement savings for both IPP sponsors and IPP members.

IMFs AND AVCs

So far within the pages of this book we have covered many concepts related to getting the most out of an IPP. In this chapter you will discover the power behind applying two new concepts — the investment management fees (IMF) and additional voluntary contributions (AVC) in conjunction with an IPP to create maximum tax relief and retirement savings for the IPP member.

An IMF is the fees that someone pays a financial institution to manage their investment/retirement assets. An AVC is the additional funds that can be invested within an RPP in addition to the prescribed amounts set out in the RPP plan text. The unique value proposition of an AVC is that it is not subject to the locking-in provisions found in Registered Pension Plans.

What is important to understand is that funds held within an IPP are usually held at a financial institution of some kind, and these institutions charge some kind of IMF to manage these IPP funds.

As stated in the second chapter of this book, IMFs as they relate to IPPs are a deductible expense to the IPP sponsoring company. As an example, consider that ABC Company (client) sets up a 2006 IPP for the 50-year owner named Mr. Owner (plan member). To fund the past service, Mr. Owner was required to transfer $250,000 from his personal RRSPs into the IPP, and ABC Company contributed $100,000 for remaining past service contribution. As well, ABC Company makes a $24,000 contribution for 2006 service.

If we assume an IMF of 2% and a net rate of return of 5.5%, the IMF for 2006 would be $7,878. An invoice would be produced in early 2007 and sent to ABC Company. This would continue each year until the IPP is wound up. Each year, the IMF invoice amount would be fully tax deductible to ABC Company. There is no taxable benefit to Mr. Owner. As you can see from Figure 1, below, the IMF invoice grows each year and represents one third of the IPP payments up to age 65. These are significant dollars not to be ignored.

Figure 1: Impact of Invoicing the IMFs

Assumptions

IMF	2.00%
Net Rate of Return	5.50%
Gross Rate of Return	7.50%
RRSP Transfer	250,000
Past Service Contribution	100,000

Age	IPP Current Service Contribution	IPP IMF Invoice	Total IPP Payment	IPP Fund End of Year
50	24,000	0	24,000	393,910
51	25,800	7,878	33,678	450,179
52	27,735	9,004	36,739	512,688
53	29,815	10,254	40,069	582,057
54	32,051	11,641	43,692	658,964
55	34,455	13,179	47,634	744,151
56	37,039	14,883	51,922	838,430
57	39,817	16,769	56,586	942,685

Age	IPP Current Service Contribution	IPP IMF Invoice	Total IPP Payment	IPP Fund End of Year
58	42,803	18,854	61,657	1,057,886
59	46,014	21,158	67,171	1,185,088
60	49,465	23,702	73,167	1,325,446
61	53,175	26,509	79,684	1,480,221
62	57,163	29,604	86,767	1,650,786
63	61,450	33,016	94,466	1,838,643
64	66,059	36,773	102,832	2,045,428
65	0	40,909	40,909	2,196,721
Total	**626,841**	**314,133**	**940,973**	

One note of consideration when invoicing the IMF is the effect on the funded position of the IPP at the time of the actuarial valuation. By paying the IMF, the IPP has basically provided itself with a gross rate of return which will provide a better funded position than a net rate of return.

Had the IPP been in a deficit position with a net rate of return, there would have been additional contributions to fund the deficit. This would have similar effects of paying for the IMF.

As well, should the IPP investments perform exceedingly well, the IPP may be in an excess surplus position, thus eliminating some future employer contributions. Paying for the IMF can contribute to IPPs getting to an excess surplus position earlier.

As you can see, invoicing the IMF in an IPP is a feature that should be considered for an IPP sponsor and IPP member.

NEXT STEP

Consider the same IPP client from above and also consider that Mr. Owner has an additional $500,000 in his RRSPs. He is either paying management expense ratios (MERs) or IMFs or some sort of management fee for his RRSP assets, and these fees cannot be tax deductible to ABC Company.

However, Mr. Owner can transfer this $500,000 of RRSPs into the IPP. Since he has already transferred $250,000 of his RRSP assets into the IPP to fund the past service, the remaining $500,000 of transfer will be deemed as AVCs.

The IPP now has essentially two sub-accounts: regular contributions and AVCs. The regular contributions are the sums of the current service costs and total past service funding going into the IPP. The AVC is the RRSP transfer not associated with the past service funding. Now the IMF on IPP and AVC assets is a deductible expense to ABC Company.

If we assume an IMF of 2% and the net rate of return of 5.5%, the IMF for 2006 would be $18,428 when you include Mr. Owner's AVCs. An invoice would be produced in early 2007 and sent to ABC Company. This invoice is almost equal to Mr. Owner's 2007 IPP current service contribution and is almost greater than the 2007 RRSP limit. As you can see from Figure 2, below, the IMF invoice grows each year and represents almost one half of the IPP payments up to age 65 when we consider the AVCs. This is a significant tax-sheltering opportunity not to be ignored.

Figure 2: Impact of Invoicing the IMFs with AVCs

Assumptions

IMF	2.00%
Net Rate of Return	5.50%
Gross Rate of Return	7.50%
RRSP Transfer	250,000
Past Service Contribution	100,000
AVC = Additional RRSP Transfer	500,000

Age	IPP Current Service Contribution	IPP IMF Invoice	Total IPP Payment	IPP Fund End of Year
50	24,000	0	24,000	921,410
51	25,800	18,428	44,228	1,017,532
52	27,735	20,351	48,086	1,122,904
53	29,815	22,458	52,273	1,238,375
54	32,051	24,767	56,819	1,364,867
55	34,455	27,297	61,752	1,503,385
56	37,039	30,068	67,107	1,655,023
57	39,817	33,100	72,918	1,820,973
58	42,803	36,419	79,223	2,002,528
59	46,014	40,051	86,064	2,201,098
60	49,465	44,022	93,487	2,418,216
61	53,175	48,364	101,539	2,655,549
62	57,163	53,111	110,274	2,914,910
63	61,450	58,298	119,748	3,198,271
64	66,059	63,965	130,024	3,507,776
65	0	70,156	70,156	3,768,187
Total	**626,841**	**590,855**	**1,217,698**	

Although not locked in under pension legislation, once made, AVCs must remain in the pension plan during the entire period of a person's employment. They cannot be accessed by the employee while still employed. There is one exception to this rule, and it occurs if the pension plan is subsequently amended so that it no longer has the provision allowing AVCs. In that case, the AVCs accumulated in the plan to that date may be rolled over into an RRSP on a once-and-for-all basis.

On termination of a person's employment due to retirement, AVCs are an exception, allowed under the *Income Tax Act*, R.S.C. 1985, c. 1 (5th Supp.), to the rule regarding pension contributions. Although AVCs cannot be withdrawn until the termination of employment, they can be paid on termination as a lump-sum payment should the employee choose to receive it in that fashion, rather than as an annuity for life.

You should note that assets that are held as AVCs are not commingled with the IPP assets at the time of an actuarial valuation. This means that the AVC funds do not impact the surplus/deficit position of the IPP.

The IPP is no longer an isolated product where you only compare the difference of the actuarial funding amounts vs. the RRSP limits to weight the IPP benefits. You should also consider the positive impact of invoicing the IMFs to the IPP sponsor.

CHAPTER 14

UTILIZING EMPLOYEE PROFIT-SHARING PLANS

Overview

This chapter introduces the concept of the employee profit-sharing plans (EPSP). It then describes the long-term opportunity that an EPSP in conjunction with an IPP creates.

Learning Objectives

By the end of this chapter, you should be able to:

- describe what an employee profit-sharing plan is;

- list the benefits that an EPSP provide for both a sponsoring company and for the member of the plan;

- understand how the creation of an EPSP creates funding opportunities for the IPP and what the long-term benefits are.

EPSP: HOW IT WORKS

Established under subsection 144(1) of the *Income Tax Act*, R.S.C. 1985, c. 1 (5th Supp.), the EPSP is a special purpose trust that allows the beneficiaries of the plan to share in the profits of a company. EPSP employer contributions are taxable as income to the employee and tax deductible as a compensation expense to the company. One of the great benefits of EPSPs is that they are treated as IPP eligible earnings for members of pension plans.

EPSPs are non-registered savings plans in which the employer contribution is computed by reference to an incorporated company's profits. The minimum employer contribution is 1% of current year profits or $100 per employee per year. Under an EPSP, investment earnings are taxable, any vesting rules or withdrawal restrictions may be established and no maximum contribution limits or investment restrictions apply. Both employer and employee contributions are permitted.

The flow chart below shows a simplified step-by-step process of how a company sets up an EPSP, and deposits profits into the plan for members.

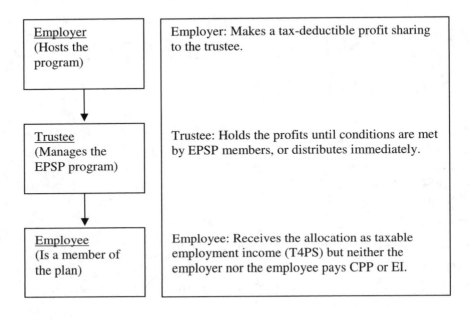

Employer (Hosts the program)	Employer: Makes a tax-deductible profit sharing to the trustee.
Trustee (Manages the EPSP program)	Trustee: Holds the profits until conditions are met by EPSP members, or distributes immediately.
Employee (Is a member of the plan)	Employee: Receives the allocation as taxable employment income (T4PS) but neither the employer nor the employee pays CPP or EI.

EMPLOYEE BENEFITS

- **Maintain RRSP Contribution Room:** Contributions made to the EPSP by the employee and employer will not reduce the employee's RRSP contribution room. Allocated profits qualify as "earned income" for RRSP and IPP purposes and the RRSP carry-forward rules.

- **No Impact On IPP/RPP Contributions:** Members of an EPSP can still accumulate pension credits for their IPPs, allowing their employers to still be able to contribute into their plans on their behalf.

- **Employer Matching:** Many employers will match an employee's contribution to an EPSP as additional compensation.

- **Tax:** Yearly income tax is calculated on an EPSP; however, Canada Pension Plan (CPP) and Employment Insurance (EI) contributions are exempt.

- **"Kiddie Tax":** The "kiddie tax" rules should not apply to income received by minor children from an allocation from an EPSP, if they are *bona fide* employees of the business.

EMPLOYER BENEFITS

- The company accrues a payment to the trust that is fully deductible by the company if it is paid within a certain time period (up to a maximum of 120 days after the sponsoring company's year-end).

- No source deductions (CPP, EI and Income Tax) are required with respect to the amount allocated to the employee.

- An EPSP can be used for income-splitting purposes.

- All amounts paid from an EPSP to an employee are not subject to a reasonableness test, unlike salaries.

- There is no requirement that all employees be included or that those employees be treated equally under the EPSP trust. The decision to share profits and the selection of the employees with whom they are shared are totally discretionary.

How the EPSP works: A trust called the Employee Profit-Sharing Plan for XYZ Company is set up usually using a three-person trust agreement. The EPSP sponsoring company makes the contribution to the trust. All funds in the trust account must be allocated to the participants of the plan at the end of the fiscal year. The company issues a T4PS (profit-sharing) slip.

What you need to know: The table below shows what working Canadians and their employers have been contributing to CPP and EI.

EPSP's — Maximum Combined Employer and Employee Contributions

Year	CPP	EI	Total	Percentage Increase
1966	$158.40	-	$158.40	-
1975	$241.70	$323.44	$564.14	257%
1985	$759.60	$1,348.88	$2,108.48	273%
1995	$1,701.00	$3,051.38	$4,752.38	125%
2000	$2,659.80	$2,245.20	$4,905.00	3%
2002	$3,365.20	$2,059.00	$5,424.20	11%
2004	$3,663.00	$1,853.28	$5,516.28	2%
2005	$3,722.40	$1,825.98	$5,548.38	1%

KEY STRATEGIES OF AN EPSP

The following are examples of how an EPSP trust works and what its benefits in financial planning are.

"Golden Handcuffs" (Employee Loyalty)

An EPSP is an excellent incentive for senior employees. It can drive employee loyalty to an employer by delivering on a payout through continuous years of service. An employer can set up an EPSP with certain stipulations. See the following example:

* Each year, should profit be available, the trustee will receive a payment equal to 15% of an employee's base salary.

* Upon 25 years of service or age 60 the accrued balance plus growth will be released to the EPSP member/employee.

In this situation, the employee is presented with an opportunity so good, so "golden", that the employee becomes literally handcuffed to the employer so as to receive the funds from the EPSP, thus creating "golden handcuffs".

Tax Deferral

EPSPs can also be used as an alternative to salary bonuses to maintain the small business tax rate. EPSP payments must be made within 120 days of the fiscal year-end. If that date happens to fall in the next calendar year, the trustee would have until the end of the calendar year to allocate the payment to beneficiaries. Those beneficiaries would need to remit tax by April 30th of the following year. The end result is the potential for up to 12.5 months of tax deferral. With a traditional approach of paying salary bonuses, source deductions would be due within the same tax year as opposed to the additional 12.5 months of tax deferral gained by the EPSP.

A Practical Application for Investing CPP Contributions Saved in an IPP

Loss or reduction of EI and CPP benefits can be offset by properly investing the savings. In most cases flexibility to invest these contributions should more than make up for the lost benefits. Let's see how!

Imagine that the owner of a Canadian-controlled private corporation (CCPC) establishes an EPSP for the year 2006. In the first year, both this business owner and his spouse are the only beneficiaries of the plan, and each earns more than $41,000 of profit-sharing income (through the EPSP trust).

The business owner, his spouse and his CCPC will not need to make any further CPP contributions. After the EPSP has been established, the savings will include employer/employee CPP contributions equalling $3,722.40 each, or $7,444.80 combined.

If the business owner decides to invest the $7,444.80 CPP savings to fund his Individual Pension Plan into a balanced portfolio that earned 7.5% annually, within ten years the business owner will have accumulated $15,344.

Now let's take this a step further. If our owner invests both the employer and employee CPP contribution into an IPP each year in the same balanced portfolio that compounds annually at 7.5%, assuming his contributions based on savings on CPP contributions will rise with the average industrial wage rate of 2.5% per year for the next 25 years until he turns 69 years old and has to withdraw funds from an IPP, our owner will have contributed $254,305 that would have been ear-marked for CPP contributions into his IPP. The value accumulated within his IPP before it would be needed to be withdrawn as pension at age 69 would be $679,390.

Below is a graph showing how much the savings of not having to make CPP contributions will grow within an IPP over a 25-year period.

IPP Contributions and Growth

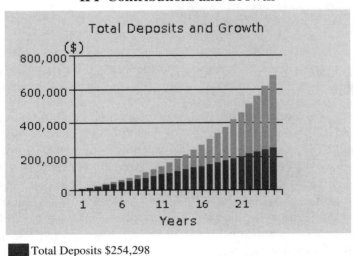

Total Deposits $254,298

Growth $425,074

Income-Splitting Opportunity

This strategy is a practical example of how the EPSP can be effectively used to split income between spouses, generating both tax and CPP savings that can be used to make contributions into an IPP. This example illustrates the benefit of using this money to fund an IPP over a 25-year period.

Business Owner's Gross Income:	$175,000
Income Tax Payable on Income:	$64,400 (36.8% Average Tax Rate)
After Tax Income to Owner:	$110,600

An EPSP is established for the owner and his spouse, who is an employee of the CCPC.

Business Owner's Gross Income:	$100,000
Spouse's Gross Income:	$75,000
Income Tax Payable to Owner:	$30,000 (30% Average Tax Rate)
Income Tax Payable to Spouse:	$19,125 (25.5% Average Tax Rate)
Total Tax Payable:	$49,125
Net Income to Owner:	$70,000
Net Income to Spouse:	$55,875
Total Net Family Income:	$125,875

Note: Difference in net tax payable and net family income with EPSP: $15,275 in 2006 dollars. This tax savings could even be greater if the business owner employed his children, and they were members of the EPSP as well.

LONG-TERM BENEFIT ANALYSIS OF ESTABLISHING AN EPSP

If the business owner and his spouse invested their combined savings of taxes and CPP contributions of $22,719.80 ($15,275 tax savings + $7,444.80 CPP contribution savings), which increased with CPI of 3% to subsidize a joint family IPP for the next 25 years, our owners will have contributed $828,354 into an IPP from these moneys. If these contributions within the IPP portfolio compounded annually at 7.5% for the next 25 years until they retire at age 69, when they will have to start withdrawing theses funds from their IPP, the value accumulated within the family IPP would have grown to $2,173,498.

The graph below illustrates the power for our example of taking the savings from both tax and CPP contributions and investing them into an IPP and letting them grow tax sheltered for 25 years. At the end of this period, because of the implementation of this strategy, the accumulated amount in the IPP will be $2,173,498.

IPP Deposits and Growth

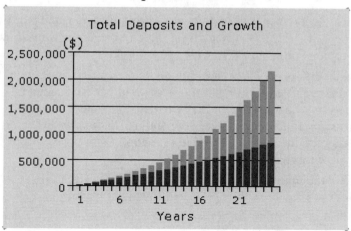

Total Deposits and Growth
($)

Values after 25 yrs

Growth $1,345,144

Total Deposit $828,354

Under certain circumstances, an **EPSP** can be used as an alternative to traditional remuneration strategies to effectively defer tax and facilitate income-splitting.

REQUIREMENTS

There are some guidelines that a company must follow before setting up an EPSP.

- It is essential that the payments from the business to the trust be calculated using the profits of the business. This means that the payments must be a percentage or share or part or all of the profits derived from the business.

- There must be an obligation on the business to make the payments in accordance with a formula in which profits are the principle variable. These payments must be made in any year where the business enjoys profits.

- A trustee is required, and a bank account in the name of the trust must be established.

EMPLOYER NEGATIVES

There are always benefits and negatives to any opportunity in life. The following is a short list of negatives, which you might want to consider before implementing an EPSP trust:

- Like any plan, there are initial costs and maintenance fees to consider. There are legal and accounting fees associated with the analysis and drafting of EPSP trust documents. Average start-up costs for an EPSP trust vary depending on the size of the company. Generally, companies are able to recoup these costs within the first year of this trust being established.

- Like the introduction of the "kiddie tax", CRA always has the ability to cut short the use of legitimate tax strategy.

Remember that an EPSP is a worthwhile consideration when:

- a corporation routinely follows a policy of "bonusing-down" to the small business limit (currently $400,000 federally);

- a corporation is expecting a large one-time increase in income;

- a corporation's current business structure prevents the business owner from effectively income-splitting with members of his or her family;

- a business wants to reward key employees for contributing to the success of the business in a tax and financially effective way.

The creation of an EPSP creates the opportunity for an incorporated business to use money saved that would have been ear-marked for taxes and CPP to be redirected to partially fund an IPP. This is a strategy worth investigating.

CHAPTER 15

RETIREMENT COMPENSATION ARRANGEMENTS

Trevor R. Parry

Overview

This chapter introduces the concept of the retirement compensation arrangement (RCA). It then describes how an RCA can be used in conjunction with an IPP to maximize retirement savings for high-income earners employed by incorporated businesses.

Learning Objectives

By the end of this chapter, you should be able to:

* describe what a retirement compensation arrangement is;

* list the benefits that an RCA provides for both a sponsoring company and for the member of the plan;

* understand how the creation of an RCA will provide additional retirement funding and other opportunity above that of an IPP for top earners within a corporation.

INTRODUCTION

For many companies and government agencies, providing adequate retirement income for their senior and most valued employees presents a problem. Frequently, the pension limits allow for providing only a fraction of required income. It requires innovative planning to address this "pension gap". Historically, annuities were purchased and claimed as deductible expenses by firms, with the future stream of income providing the extra income required to address the shortfall. The RCA rules brought uniformity to the situation, setting out how employers might fund pension gaps going forward. The RCA rules also have been, and are still, used in a punitive fashion as an anti-avoidance mechanism. The general rule is that a firm may wish to establish an RCA, but should avoid having one imposed upon it.

In 1986, the federal government introduced new measures called the retirement compensation arrangement rules. As described in s. 248(1) of the *Income Tax Act*, R.S.C. 1985, c. 1 (5th Supp.), RCA "means a plan or arrangement under which contributions ... are made by an employer or former employer of a taxpayer ... to a custodian in connection with benefits that are to be or may be received or enjoyed by any person on, after or in contemplation of any substantial change in the services rendered by the taxpayer, the retirement of the taxpayer or the loss of an office or employment of the taxpayer ...".

RCA STRUCTURE

The RCA is a trusteed pension structure that allows for higher contribution limits than traditional pension plans. All contributions are tax deductible to the sponsoring corporation and taxed in the hands of the plan member when they are withdrawn. As it is based on a defined contribution structure, there are no inherent required rates of return on the investments held inside the trust, and contributions and withdrawals are at the discretion of the sponsoring company and plan member, respectively. A company may sponsor several different RCAs or a single RCA with multiple members, depending on the situation.

Corporate Employment

One prerequisite for establishing an RCA is having a corporate sponsor in place to settle the RCA trust and to make contributions to the RCA. Partnerships and sole proprietorships are prohibited from establishing RCAs. In addition to a corporate sponsor, the beneficiary of the RCA plan must have a current or prior employment relationship with the sponsoring company or predecessor company. Frequently, a situation develops where an RCA makes good business sense but cannot be put in place because the intended plan member, usually the owner-manager, has not been paid with employment income. Instead, payments of director fees, management fees and dividends replaced traditional earned income. While this may give rise to a short-term tax advantage, it can severely limit tax-planning flexibility. Long-term solutions, including the use of not only RCAs, but RRSPs and IPPs, cannot be implemented.

Trust

RCA trusts vary in how they are drafted. There is no requirement for a corporate trustee to be retained to manage the trust, although in certain situations, the sponsoring company may prefer such a provision. Where the plan member is a U.S. citizen and therefore is required to file with both CRA and the Internal Revenue Service, corporate trustees may be preferred as they are more likely able to deal with this dual filing responsibility. Corporate trustees may also be preferable in situations involving public companies where rigorous shareholder reporting and potential conflict of interest can be avoided.

In most cases, a corporate trustee is not required. A tripartite board of trustees, or, in certain cases, a single individual, will suffice. In the case of the single trustee, the individual should be at arm's length from the company. A lawyer or accountant would traditionally fill this role. The tripartite trust allows for greater flexibility and may suit the owner-manager's situation better than a corporate or single trustee. In this situation, two individuals who are employees of the sponsoring company may act as trustees together with one arm's length individual. The trust itself will vary in the drafting, but it must clearly set out the powers, rights and protections afforded the trustees. This is particularly important in cases where the RCA may be pledged as security pursuant to a leveraging transaction.

Plan Text

The RCA will also include an RCA agreement or plan text. This is a critical document as it outlines the RCA plan. It sets out definitions of parties and the component elements in the RCA. It details plan member eligibility, vesting provisions (if required), nature and timing of contributions, contingencies for change of control of the sponsoring company, benefit descriptions and options, options upon disability of a plan member, options upon death of a member, funding and administration and any and all other issues that the plan sponsor feels the need to dictate. This plan text should also closely resemble a pension document as this is *prima facie* evidence that the structure is in fact an RCA and not a salary deferral arrangement (SDA).

Beneficiaries

Upon the death of the last living plan member, the trust assets are not subject to a deemed disposition as with RRSP/RIF and IPP assets.

Instead, the named beneficiaries will commence a schedule of withdrawals, which will exhaust the assets of the trust within the next 20 years. This can be of significant benefit where the RCA assets are large, and a one-time lump sum withdrawal would result in substantial taxation.

The plan member's spouse will automatically become the primary beneficiary upon the death of that plan member unless otherwise set out in the plan documents. In the event that the spouse has predeceased the plan member, the named beneficiaries, or contingent beneficiaries, will receive the plan assets without probate fees. Where a plan member has minor children, the member should name his or her estate as the contingent beneficiary to avoid the unwanted presence of the Public Trustee, who would otherwise take control of the assets until the individual children reach age of majority.

Actuarial Certificate

Contributions that are made by a sponsoring company to the plan for the benefit of the employee(s) must be reasonable in the eyes of Canada Revenue Agency (CRA). Until recently, there was only conjecture as to what reasonableness would entail; it was not unusual to see some RCA contributions have no reasonable basis.

CRA dealt with this issue in its September 16, 2005 letter:

> As the Act is silent with respect to the determination of whether or not a contribution to an RCA is reasonable, it is always a question of fact and depends on the circumstances surrounding each plan. Contribution amounts that are clearly supported by either an actuarial valuation or the use of some other formula based calculation may be more justifiable; however reasonability must be weighted taking into account all relevant factors.[1]

While CRA says that it will accept formula-based calculations, there is the possibility for misuse and undercutting of the very concept of reasonableness. For instance, inclusion of dividend income, prohibited by the actuarial valuation method, would produce an RCA contribution that does not truly reflect pensionable or earned income.

Concerning the CRA letter, Gordon Lang writes:

> I would assert that the use of a best 3 year earnings formula for the purposes of calculating the earnings base for an RCA, when combined with other reasonable Actuarial Assumptions and Methods is reasonable. In the case of Company Owners, they often have life cycle earnings quite unlike those of regular employees. They will start as Company Founder then as the business increases may take on the titles of Chairman, President & CEO. As they

---

[1] CRA letter: 2005-13240117 (16 September 2005).

wind down their involvement with the business they may ultimately be only a Director of the Company. Their final 5 years earnings as depicted on their Company T4's may well thus relate only to their period of Company service as a Director. Thus, basing their earnings, for the purpose of reasonableness, on the average of the final 5 years earnings is patently unreasonable. Earnings for RCA purposes should be based on actual T4 earnings and not on future earnings which may either be unreasonable or indeed based on fiction.[2]

The actuarial certificate is a document prepared and signed by an accredited actuary setting out the rationale for, and limitations to, any RCA contributions. Earned income, namely T4, T4A and T4PS (profit-sharing) income, may be used to calculate the RCA benefit. The average of the best three years will allow for a comprehensive approach in ascertaining contribution limits. If the plan member has income from a variety of related companies, then each of those companies may contribute to a single RCA, and the actuarial certificate will reflect this. The certificate accounts for how much of the contribution will arise as a result of past service and how much will be able to be contributed each year.

The company may contribute up to the limit set out in the certificate. The contributions are not mandatory, and if the maximum allowable contribution or past service is not used up in a given year, that amount will accumulate for contributions in future years. The chart below sets out a typical contribution ceiling schedule.

RCA inception date:	March 1, 2006	
Age:	49 years old	
Income:	$200,000 (three-year average)	
Retirement date:	65	
Example of current year service and past service amounts		
Maximum Actuarial Unfunded Liabilities (past service)	$1,404,800.00	
Calendar	**Current Service**	
2006	73,800.00	(10 months)
2007	91,900.00	
2008	95,300.00	
2009	98,900.00	

---

[2] May 2005 article available online through Gordon B. Lang & Associates Inc.'s portal <www.gblinc.ca>.

Calendar	Current Service	
2010	102,600.00	
2011	106,400.00	
2012	110,400.00	
2013	114,500.00	
2014	118,800.00	
2015	123,300.00	
2016	127,900.00	
2017	132,700.00	
2018	137,700.00	
2019	142,900.00	
2020	148,300.00	
2021	153,900.00	
2022	159,700.00	

The member's first year contribution is $73,800. When coupled with the past service amount of $1,404,800, his *total first year maximum contribution room is $1,478,600.*

The RCA may also be used in combination with other retirement plans such as the IPP. While participating in an IPP or traditional group pension (RPP) will affect contribution limits to the RCA, the use of a personally funded RRSP will not have the same effect. As the RRSP is a personally funded and held asset, it has no bearing on RCA calculations.

Refundable Tax Account

Once the RCA trust is established and registered with CRA, contributions may be made. To make a valid RCA contribution, the sponsoring company will issue two cheques, each for exactly 50% of the total contribution. One cheque will be made out to the plan custodian, usually an insurance or trust company, bank or investment company. The second cheque, for the remaining 50%, will be forwarded to CRA. This remittance is a payment of refundable tax, and upon registration of the RCA trust, CRA will assign a refundable tax account (RTA) to the RCA for this and any future contributions.

The RCA, unlike an RRSP or IPP, is not a tax-sheltered vehicle *per se*. While final taxation does not occur until the plan member receives a payment of benefit from the RCA, the plan itself is subject to ongoing refundable tax requirements. Fifty per cent of all realized interest, dividends and capital gains, net of fees and losses, is remitted to the RTA annually. For many people, the retarding of asset growth due to refundable tax is something to be avoided and has led to a variety of investment strategies implemented within the RCA.

Filings

Because the RCA is a trust, it has specific reporting requirements that are set out in legislation. The trustees will gather the relevant information regarding investment returns from the plan custodian in order to prepare this annual return. In the case where the RCA invests in a life insurance policy, the insurance company will be deemed to be the plan custodian.

Once the prerequisites have been established, the RCA plan itself can be put in place. The RCA is a trust that is registered with the RCA unit of CRA. Completion and filing of a T733 is required to obtain an RCA account number. It is critical to remember that RCAs must be established and funded before the conclusion of the fiscal year. While CRA will grant a grace period of 14 days following the fiscal year end to receive the refundable tax remittance, those individuals establishing these plans, and their advisors, should be conscious of deadlines. The penalties for late remittance are onerous; 10% of the refundable tax is assessed for first-time tardiness, and this increases with each subsequent transgression.

In addition to the initial application for an RCA account number (Form 733), the trustees are also required to file a series of documents by March 31st of each year. Those documents include a Part X1.3 Tax Return, a T737-RCA Return for reporting employer contributions, a T4A-RCA Summary and a T4A-RCA Form for refunds of contributions to the employer and payments to beneficiaries. If payments are to be made to non-resident beneficiaries, an NR4 Summary and an NR4 Form for payments must be filed as well. The annual RCA Guide prepared by CRA is an excellent and user-friendly resource for all those individuals responsible for the administration and reporting of RCAs.

RCA Flow Structure

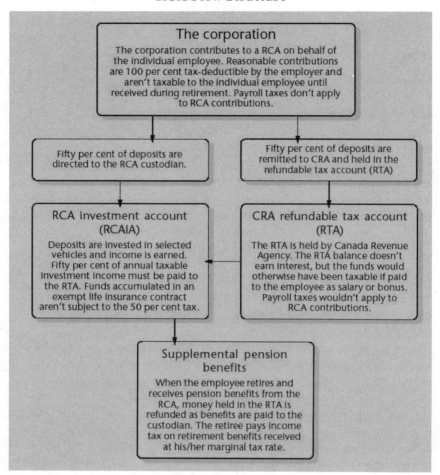

Flow chart above provided by Professionalreferrals.ca Inc.

RCA APPLICATIONS

To understand why an RCA is used, and to identify scenarios where its introduction might be of aid, we must first determine the benefits or effects of the RCA. Generally, the RCA is a retirement planning tool that allows the plan member to defer income to a time and place of his or her choosing.

Advantages

By understanding the key benefits of the RCA — postponement of significant tax payments, flexibility of contributions and withdrawals, creditor proofing and estate planning — we can determine the scenarios where the RCA may be a timely and beneficial strategy.

RCAs offer a great deal of flexibility both in contributions and withdrawals. Once the limits are set, companies can fund any amount not exceeding those limits. The creation of an RCA does not automatically confer a liability on the employer. Also, remaining funding room can be carried forward, allowing almost complete company discretion in when and how much a company will contribute to the RCA. Likewise, once the plan member has undergone a material change in employment, he or she has complete flexibility in when he withdraws the funds. There is no set schedule and no age at which he or she must begin drawing.

The principal advantage of this flexibility is tax deferment. Contributions made into an RCA are not taxable until they are withdrawn from the plan. This allows the plan participant to take money that would normally be taxed at a high rate and instead have it placed in an RCA, intending to withdraw it in years when he or she is in a lower tax bracket. Additionally, some foreign tax jurisdictions may allow for the funds to be withdrawn at significantly lower rates than if the participant remained a Canadian resident.

Being that it is a trust, the RCA is protected from creditors of both the sponsoring company and the participant, unless otherwise bound by an agreement pledging the RCA assets as security. This may be of significant interest to those companies and professional corporations that find themselves in markets in which the risk of litigation is a practical concern.

The RCA documents may be prepared to remove any company roll after initial contribution, or a letter of understanding may be prepared by all relevant parties setting out that the RCA is to be funded with a single contribution, and the sponsoring company will have no legal tie or future responsibility to the RCA or plan member after funding.

Where a business has multiple family generations employed, a single RCA can be created for the whole family unit, allowing contributions that were driven by the parents' income to be passed down to the children, taxed only on withdrawal by the children, not on the death of the parents. Even with only a single participant in the plan, on death the beneficiary has a full 20 years to collapse the RCA, spreading out the tax burden.

Drawbacks

There is no firm case law or legislative direction that subjects RCA assets to inclusion in net family property (NFP) calculations in divorce proceedings. While there is reason to argue that these assets might be exempt from such proceedings, it is more probable that the RCA will be included and therefore not survive divorce. The RCA is likely to be seen as a pension plan, and a review of the key documents would in most cases indicate intention to create something very much akin to a pension plan. All of this forces the conclusion that the RCA is more likely to be incorporated into NFP calculations.

An employer must avoid creating a salary deferral arrangement when establishing an RCA. If an employee is otherwise entitled to an amount of remuneration pursuant to his or her employment contract, and that remuneration becomes an RCA contribution, CRA is likely to find an SDA and levy tax, interest and penalties. If, however, an employment contract clearly stipulates that the amount and nature of remuneration are to be determined solely at the discretion of the employer, then it is likely that no SDA will be found to exist. Finding an SDA in the situation where an owner-manager contributes to an RCA is highly unlikely as these individuals' overall compensation varies each year with the profitability of the firm.

If an employee were to leave the company, and the vesting provisions had not been satisfied, that employee may have a cause of action where it can be proven that the employee was otherwise entitled to the plan contributions as a performance bonus pursuant to the employment agreements. While not insurmountable, this presents a challenge to counsel in drafting such agreements to allow for the RCA to be established and funded, without the threat of future litigation.

Employee Contributions

In certain circumstances, an employee may be required to contribute to his or her RCA. This was addressed by CRA in the aforementioned letter:

> The Act does not specifically dictate what level of benefits may be provided under an RCA. However, an employee may only deduct amounts paid in the year as contributions under an RCA to the extent that the conditions in paragraph 8(1) (m.2) was intended to be a relieving position which would in part permit, within limits, the deduction of employee contributions where they are required under the terms of an unregistered pension plan that also meets the RCA definition. Consequently, before any amount will be deductible under paragraph 8(1) (m.2), the plan or arrangement has to be a pension

plan. Where it is established that the plan or arrangement constitutes a pension plan, an employee contribution will be deductible under paragraph 8(1)(m.2) of the Act where all of the following conditions are satisfied:

(a)   the amount is paid to a custodian of the arrangement who is resident in Canada;

(b)   the taxpayer was required, by the employer's conditions of employment, to contribute the amount; and

(c)   the amount contributed to the RCA in the year does not exceed the amounts contributed to the RCA in the year by any other.[3]

Where the above requirement has been satisfied, the employee contribution can be accepted by the custodian and be deducted by the employee. This situation is rarely encountered, but may exist where a company wishes to put an RCA in place but missed the filing deadline. As a result, contributions are made by the employees and matched by the sponsoring company, with the resulting deduction facilitating the intended tax result.

RCA INVESTMENTS

There are effectively no rules as to what an RCA can invest in. CRA has recently opined that direct or indirect investment of the assets of the RCA trust in the sponsoring company is something that should be avoided as it may result in a questioning of the intent behind creating the RCA in the first place. If we therefore assume that RCAs will invest in arm's length investments, there is a wide array of choices open to the RCA trustees. In certain cases, the RCA trustees will direct the investments of the trust, and in other instances the company may appoint an investment manager to direct these affairs.

While an RCA may invest in any securities, it might be advantageous to look at investments that have certain tax-efficient characteristics. Tax-sheltered or tax-efficient investments that minimize the annual remittances to the refundable tax account are, *ceteris paribus*, preferable to other types of investments. There are a whole host of investment options that will wholly or partially achieve this goal, including life insurance and certain tax-efficient types of pooled investments.

Insurance

For many people, the use of permanent life insurance contracts, either whole life or universal life, inside the RCA is the preferred investment

---

[3]   Document 2005 — 13240117. Page 3. Canada Revenue Agency.

option. Offering a wide choice of underlying investments, the cash value (CV) of the contract will grow tax-sheltered, eliminating the need to remit annually to the RTA.

When the plan member commences withdrawals from the RCA, he or she may do so by either "leveraging" the insurance policy or taking cash withdrawals from the policy. The former strategy would see the policy pledged as collateral to a financial institution which, in return, would forward a loan or loans to the plan member. The death of the plan member results in the death benefit being paid to the RCA trust, which in turn repays the lending institution. The latter strategy does not require a lending institution but gives rise to ongoing refundable tax remittances. These withdrawals are deemed taxable dispositions requiring 50% of that disposition to be remitted.[4]

One drawback of the "insured RCA" approach is that on the death of the insured, the normally tax-free death benefit is received by the RCA trust and is paid out to the named beneficiary(s) as taxable RCA income. This is unfortunate as these death benefits are usually a considerable amount. The sponsoring company should give consideration to a "split dollar" insured RCA strategy. In that instance, the RCA and the company would share the ownership of the insurance contract, with the CV being owned by the RCA trust and the death benefit being owned by the sponsoring company. With the growth of the CV sheltered, the value of the RCA asset is maximized due to the lack of annual remittance. Upon retirement, that CV may be drawn down or leveraged to provide for the income needs of the plan member. Upon the death of the plan member, the death benefit will be paid to the corporation, creating a credit to the capital dividend account. This in turn will be paid out to the shareholders tax-free.

The split dollar strategy, while initially more expensive since it requires a specially tailored contract and actuarial report on the validity of the split, allows for more comprehensive financial planning.

The buy-sell provisions, common in most shareholder agreements, and frequently unfunded by the company, may now be funded, making corporate succession planning a reality. The company also bears the cost of insurance as a non-deductible expense above and beyond the RCA contribution (which of course remains deductible).

While the insured RCA route may be preferable in many cases, it is not unusual to see a combination of insurance- and investment-based

---

[4] J.T. Cuperfain and F. Marino, *Canadian Taxation of Life Insurance*, 2nd ed. (Toronto: Thomson Carswell, 2002), at p. 203.

product solutions. Often lack of insurability due to medical issues, or lack of time needed for accumulation in the CV, mitigate against the use of insurance in an RCA. It is also possible that as a result of the underwriting process, the contribution to the RCA cannot all be sheltered in an insurance contract, and provision should be made to find a suitable tax-efficient investment vehicle.

Tax-Efficient Investments

Certain types of mutual funds, known as corporate class funds, may operate tax-sheltered, providing a significant benefit inside an RCA. Exchange-traded funds and certain hedge funds have been used to satisfy a need for tax efficiency. The trustees, investment manager and investment advisor will have to thoroughly examine the tax efficiency and risk of each proposed investment.

LEVERAGED RCAS

The ability to use the RCA for corporate financing is an opportunity in financial planning that is attractive for many candidates, both lenders and borrowers. For that reason most of Canada's chartered banks have established lending programs to allow for the front end leveraged RCA. Banks and other lenders find the secured nature of the transaction attractive, and, as the RTA is a receivable of the trust, banks will often lend up to 90% of the total value of the RCA.

In essence, the ability to leverage an RCA lives in the laws of trusts. It is a standard provision of most trusts that the trustees may pledge the assets of that trust as collateral or security to facilitate lending. While the trust indenture will have some substantial modifications and characteristics germane to RCAs, the provision for the trustees to pledge the RCA assets will be found in most RCA trust indentures. That said, the RCA is a retirement plan and must always maintain its *bona fide* status as such. There is generally believed to be a stipulation that the plan members must have unimpeded access to the trust assets, as benefit payments, upon the stated retirement date of the individual.

This rule has been translated into a practice enforced by lenders that the loans which are made, and secured by the RCA, must be repaid in full by the retirement date of the plan member. To do otherwise would create an "evergreen" scenario in which the loans are not repaid during the lifetime of the plan member. A loan on trust assets of a retirement plan that is not repaid until the condition that follows retirement, that is death, is at its core not a retirement plan and consequently such a plan is not an RCA, and will, and should, attract the scrutiny of CRA.

Proceeding carefully and with the right team of professionals advising all parties is the only way to undertake leveraged RCA transactions. The sponsoring company will retain legal counsel to advise it on the terms of the loan. The bank or client will be required to obtain a tax opinion from an approved accounting or law firm, setting out to the lender that the RCA is an RCA and not a salary deferral arrangement or other non-RCA structure, and, as such, the bank can realize on its security interest in the event of default or in enforcing the terms of the lending agreements.

Each lender will have a somewhat different approach to the transaction. Some will insist on acting as trustee, while others will insist on a separate corporation (investment corporation) to be created to service the loan between RCA trust and the sponsoring company.

The lender will insist on low risk investments in the RCA trust. Often, the assignment of a death benefit of a life insurance policy will be part of the transaction. Some lenders will insist on a personal guarantee provided by the principals of the sponsoring company. Each lender will have different requirements, and costs will reflect this.

In addition to the due diligence that the lender will perform on the prospective borrower, the purpose of the loan must be considered. A direct payment of the loan proceeds or diversion of those proceeds to an individual shareholder or shareholders will likely not meet with approval.

Care should be given not to lend the invested portion of the RCA back, directly or indirectly, to the sponsoring company. While not strictly prohibited, CRA has opined that this type of transaction might question the intent of the RCA.

WITHDRAWING FROM RCAs

Withdrawals from the RCA may commence upon a substantial change in the nature of employment of a plan member. The plan member will request payment from the trustees who, provided that they are satisfied the member may make such a withdrawal, will pay out the requested amount. The trustees will make all necessary withholdings and remit to the proper authorities. The individual will then claim this income on the annual T1 General return.

Before any distribution is made, the trustees will need to inform CRA of the intention to commence withdrawals. This is done by obtaining a Remittance Number for Tax Withheld from a Retirement Compensation Arrangement. The trustees will complete a T735 form to initiate this process. The particular regime for withdrawals is set out in a very detailed fashion in *Retirement Compensation Arrangements Guide* available from CRA.

For every dollar withdrawn from the RCA trust, the RTA will refund 50 cents to the investment account.

If the plan member is not a Canadian resident, the trustees will be responsible for remitting the required withholding tax to CRA.

APPLIED RCAs

In practice, the RCA is an effective solution in many different cases. As CRA is also now looking toward intent in assessing RCAs, retirement must always be the primary planning goal in RCA practice.

There are two primary focuses of RCAs: employee compensation and owner-manager solutions. Employee compensation includes executive compensation planning, severance, non-resident issues and employee retention. Owner-manager solutions include profit management, leverage strategies, business exit strategies and non-residency planning.

Employee Use

Executive Compensation

Supplemental Executive Retirement Plans (SERPs) have existed in Canadian business for years. They are promises, usually put in place through a resolution of the board of directors, that establish a retirement plan for a key employee that goes beyond the pension limitations set out by CRA. Often, the retirement package offered to a key executive is a make-or-break element of the employment relationship. For many large Canadian companies, these SERPs appear as unfunded liabilities; they are paid out of cash flow as needed.

This unfunded, non-segregated structure creates significant problems for both the employer and employee. A change in control or bankruptcy of the sponsoring company could result in the SERP promise being unenforceable, leaving the employee in a rather precarious situation. The company may also not like to have large unfunded liabilities on its balance sheets. These concerns make funding the SERP critical. Some firms have used letters of credit to fund SERPs, but this must be seen as a stop-gap measure.

Corporations are beginning to address this funding challenge by embracing the RCA. The RCA may be established for either a single employee or an entire class of employees. The employees' retirement needs are being addressed through a creditor-proof vehicle. The employer has cleaned up its balance sheet. Employee loyalty is enhanced.

In this situation, the RCA acts very much like a large RRSP where assets can grow and pay out enhanced but not specific income upon retirement of the plan member.

Care must be taken to assure that a SERP does not constitute a salary deferral arrangement.

Severance

One of the unfortunate facts for today's employee is that lifetime employment with one company is an exception to the rule. Severance is therefore something that companies should incorporate in their planning. The RCA is of particular use in this area.

A large severance package in one year will give rise to significant taxation. If the departing employee can mitigate the tax liability by dividing the large lump sum into smaller amounts occurring over several tax years, the result is usually a significant reduction in overall tax paid. The RCA is the vehicle that will accomplish this.

The RCA is funded as the plan member is terminated. Because termination constitutes a substantial and material change in the nature of employment, the former employee is legally entitled to commence withdrawals at leisure.

If an individual finds employment soon after his or her termination from the previous firm, he or she may not need to access the RCA for many years. The RCA can then provide a new source of retirement income for the future. If the plan member needs income, the member may withdraw it in amounts of his or her choosing. Using Ontario tax rates, a $400,000 severance payment (excluding other income) would result in taxation of $168,055, while redirecting that lump sum payment into four $100,000 RCA payments, each occurring in a separate year, would result in tax of $29,374 annually, or $117,496 in total. That is a considerable savings in tax.[5]

Non-resident

International firms with subsidiary operations in Canada may find the RCA quite useful because it provides a means of equalizing benefits that

---

[5]   Ernst & Young 2006 Personal Tax Calculator, online: <http://www.ey.com/GLOBAL/content.nsf/Canada/Tax_-_Calculators_-_2006_Personal_Tax>.

executives in other countries are able to receive. For instance, both the United States and United Kingdom have far more expansive pension limits. The RCA allows the Canadian executive to receive a pension comparable to his or her foreign colleagues.

Retention

The use of vesting is critical in understanding the efficacy of a group RCA. In traditional pension plans, the plan member is said to be vested (entitled to the beneficial ownership of his or her pension asset) after two years of membership in the plan.

The RCA has no such rules concerning vesting. The plan sponsor may include in the RCA agreement/plan text a deferred vesting provision. While we encourage firms to avoid being draconian with regards to vesting, the use of this provision will go a long way to retaining a key employee. Traditionally, the plan member would see the benefit vest after five or ten years of service. There would likely be an acceleration clause that would result in immediate vesting upon change of control of the sponsoring company.

As the majority of the employee group that would be party to this type of RCA will not be fully vested for many years, the employer should give consideration to creating a single group RCA. The plan custodian, or retained actuary, can demonstrably assist the trustees in preparing the annual filing requirements, such as accounting for each plan member's share of the RTA.

Owner Use

Profit Management

Where a company's overall tax strategy is to limit profit to $300,000 (soon to be $400,000) to take advantage of the small business tax rates for qualified business corporations, the usual means of achieving this is to pay bonuses to the shareholders. The company is then able to pay a low rate of tax. This strategy, while advantageous to the corporation, gives rise to considerable tax payments for the individual owner-manager. The company, if operating in provinces that impose payroll or employer health taxes, will also have to pay these as a result of the "bonus down" strategy.

In many cases, the creation of an RCA may be a preferable strategy. RCA contributions would likely be equal to what otherwise would have been paid out as a shareholder bonus. The company receives tax relief for the contribution, and escapes having to pay the provincial tax, finding itself in the same or preferable situation as having paid out bonuses.

The individual may find this strategy preferable. Typically, the person receiving the bonus will already be in the top tax bracket; the bonus is thus taxed at the top rate. If tax rates at withdrawal are lower than when the initial contribution was made to the RCA, then the taxpayer has reduced his or her overall taxation.

Leveraging

The most common uses for a leveraged RCA are:

- providing additional working capital to the sponsoring company;
- expanding of business operations;
- acquiring competitors;
- buying out other shareholders; and
- flushing the shareholder loan account.

The primary determination for leveraging the RCA is: Will the strong internal rate of growth outweigh the cost of borrowing? While loans are usually quite favourable in terms of interest, the associated legal, actuarial, banking and accounting costs must be considered.

Businesses that enjoy strong cyclical growth, such as builders and real estate developers, are just two categories of businesses that have utilized this strategy. The strategy is now being used to facilitate orderly transfer of ownership amongst shareholders, or between generations in family business scenarios.

Exit Strategy

It is an unfortunate fact that entrepreneurs, while they may do some planning for their own retirement, do little planning for the retirement of their business. Too often, owners assume that their real retirement income will come from the sale of their business. They plan on the $500,000 life capital gains exemption for sale of shares of a qualified small business corporation. The unfortunate fact is that the sale that the owner intends to undertake is rarely the sale that the owner ends up getting.

The vast majority of Canadian business owners do not sell the shares of the corporation, but rather enter into asset sale transactions. Typically, the purchaser does not in most cases wish to purchase the liabilities of the business that would attach in an equity sale. Most franchises require a franchisee to sell the franchise back to the parent company through an asset sale.

The effect of this is profound. Entrepreneurs who expect to pay very little tax on the sale of their company because of preferential tax treatment on capital gains will find that they face a rather daunting tax bill in the year of sale. This is because selling assets generates income to the company. When the final accounting is completed on the sale, an entrepreneur might find a tax debt equivalent to almost half of the value of the business.

The use of a tax postponement strategy, made possible by instituting an RCA, may be the critical and timely piece of financial planning that the business owner needs. The strategy is straightforward. Once the contribution limits have been established, the sponsoring company will fund the RCA. In many cases, the long period of employment that the owner-manager(s) has accumulated allows for considerable contribution room. The contribution will often offset all of the tax liability associated with the sale of assets.

The result is secure income, enjoyment of retirement and substantial reduction of tax. Of course, the efficacy of the RCA strategy is reduced with substantial income from other sources such as rents, royalties or associated fees from other business interests. However, for the vast majority of Canadian business owners, the primary retirement income will be from the RCA and other registered plans.

A company that sells its assets, creating a taxable income of $3,000,000, would normally attract considerable tax, even with two owners to split the bill. In Ontario, they would each owe $666,801 in taxes, and the company would have $50,700 of Employer Health tax to pay. Even in Alberta, which enjoys much more reasonable levels of tax, the shareholders would owe $573,247 each on their 50% ownership of the company.

The advantages of tax postponement as allowed through the use of the RCA are clear. It is unlikely that the business owner will need to take a single payment of $1,500,000. He or she is more likely to need income of $150,000 per year. That would mean that the tax on that income (excluding other income) would be $52,030 in Ontario and $46,747 in Alberta. Projecting forward, that would result in tax savings of about $150,000 per person over a ten-year period.

An RCA may have a roll in an anticipated share sale. In order to safeguard the ability to claim the lifetime capital gains exemption, the RCA could be put in place in earlier years to create an ongoing corporate purification strategy. Passive asset problems, which may jeopardize the exemption, can be avoided by managing the creation of retained earnings through RCA contributions.

As the vast majority of Canadian entrepreneurs will attempt some form of change of control of their business (most through asset sale) in the next 15 years, it is essential that they learn about the benefits of tax postponement through the use of a properly established RCA.

Non-resident

An RCA participant who changes his or her legal residency may be able to withdraw his or her RCA pension assets at considerably lower tax rates (15% to 25%) than he or she could by remaining in Canada. Care should be taken to consult with an international tax expert to make sure that the participant meets the residency requirements and to determine the actual tax treatment.

CONCLUSION

The RCA is a vehicle that has enjoyed expanded use in recent years. For employers wishing to fashion superior compensation, retirement and retention strategies, the RCA can be a straightforward approach to achieve these key goals and to remove unfunded liabilities from the balance sheet. For the business owner looking to defer or reduce tax, find alternative financing strategies and reduce tax upon the sale of his or her enterprise, the RCA is a vehicle that he or she must consider.

With taxation burdens staring employers and entrepreneurs in the face, the time to consider the RCA, in the light of its flexibility and positive consequences, is now.

CHAPTER 16

STRATEGIES OF BALANCING EMPLOYEE HEALTH CARE COSTS WITH AN OWNER'S RETIREMENT GOALS

Andrew Duckman
Peter J. Merrick
Trevor R. Parry
Stan Risen

Overview

This chapter will explore in depth some of the key issues currently challenging the traditional insurance model and will show how an alternative insurance solution known as an ASO (administrative services only) model offers an attractive cost-effective option that can impact the owner's retirement strategy in a positive way by finding money to fund the owner's IPP solution. It concludes in providing tax-effective methods to turn health care costs that are not covered by traditional medical and dental plans into legitimate deductions for employers and non-taxable benefits for employees.

Learning Objectives

By the end of this chapter, you should be able to:

*   understand the new developments in health care;
*   develop a basic understanding of the administrative services only (ASO) model to manage rising health care costs for employees;
*   understand how adopting the ASO model for health care can help fund a business owner's IPP;
*   understand the benefit of creating health spending accounts for both executives and business owners.

FINDING THE MONEY

One of the reasons the IPP solution remains relatively underutilized by owners of small to medium-sized companies in Canada today is due to a lack of available corporate funds to make the large initial and ongoing investments that are required into the IPP to ensure maximum results.

One fruitful area to look for potential funds is at the business' group employee insurance. Most owners of small and medium-sized businesses offer their employees group benefit plans from traditional insurance carriers. Perhaps the greatest difficulty with this model is the constant rise in annual premiums, often as high as 15% per annum. In many cases, a simple re-evaluation and subsequent remodelling of the group benefit insurance model can deliver significant cost reductions and contain the year-over-year escalation. By adopting an alternative insurance solution, businesses owners will not only realize these cost savings but can also use these new found savings to fund their IPP.

In the face of Canada's public health care crisis, providing employees with adequate and competitive health and dental coverage has never been more important. In 2005, more than $142 billion was spent for health care in Canada with 70% of the costs paid for by the federal and provincial governments' publicly funded system. Corporate Canada paid for most of the remaining 30% of non-essential medical and dental expenses, according to the Canadian Institute for Health Information and Statistics Canada.

While employer medical and dental plans were originally designed to be supplementary to the publicly funded government plan, as a result of the federal and provincial cutbacks in health care services, employers and private insurers across this country have had to alter and redesign their medical and dental plans to keep up with emerging trends of higher claims and new cost realities. In an age where publicly covered services continue to be reduced, we are likely to see Corporate Canada's share continue to increase in the coming years.

In the midst of these economic pressures on the current health care system, employees are demanding an enriched company medical and dental benefit plan. While the traditional corporate employee medical and dental benefit plan in Canada provides coverage for semi-private hospital rooms, prescription drugs, dental, chiropractors, physiotherapists, vision care, extended health coverage and travel medical insurance, employees are asking for more options then ever before. Opinions on what to add are largely influenced by age and experience — items like teeth-whitening can compete with orthotics. Older employees want expanded drug coverage, while younger workers are concerned about their deductibles. The end result is employees want choice and employers want/need to contain their costs.

The vast majority of Canadian small and mid-sized businesses offer medical and dental benefits to their workforces by utilizing insurance carriers. With the consolidation frenzy of the last decade, the number of insurance carriers has dwindled in an effort to make the Canadian players more globally competitive. This new, streamlined landscape has been good for the carriers, but not for the small and medium-sized Canadian businesses, which have been underserved by the carriers, because the carriers are focused on delivering shareholder value with big premium clients that pay $500,000 or more in annual premiums.

The increasing pressures on the current health care system, the consolidation of the insurance industry and the growing employee demand for more flexible and expanded coverage is having the greatest impact on the small and medium-sized Canadian business. With health and dental care coverage escalating by approximately 15% for health and 7% for dental, small- and medium-sized employers are facing uncontrollable and unpredictable costs to their businesses to provide these benefits. Employers have tried to curtail these costs by introducing annual limits, co-insurance, deductibles and exclusions to their medical and dental plans.

Upon closer review of the average group medical and dental policy for small to mid-sized businesses, usually only 60% to 75% of the overall premium dollars are ear-marked for payment for eligible claims. The remaining portions of these premiums are used to pay administration cost, create reserves, pay commissions and earn insurance carriers profits for shareholders.

As an alternative to the traditional medical and dental insurance solution, some employers are choosing to move towards the administrative services only (ASO) model offered by traditional insurance companies and third party administrators. There are generally three components to this model:

(a) *Self-Insurance* — The employer self-insures, assuming the cost of all claims.

(b) *Stop Loss Insurance* — To reduce the risk of a large employee claim, stop loss insurance provided by a traditional carrier or specialty provider is combined with the self-insurance to pay out claims beyond a certain level. The premium for this reduced level of insurance is reasonably affordable.

(c)   *Third Party Administrator* (TPA) — In order for Canada Revenue Agency (CRA) to allow the cost for medical and dental plans to be tax deductible for the employer and the benefits to be non-taxable in the hands of employees, the administration of these plans operated through the ASO model must be handled by a third party.

By avoiding a great deal of the administrative costs and reserves incurred by traditional insurance companies, this model allows the employer to pay more claims with every dollar spent, and offers greater flexibility when designing a plan. Under the ASO model, the company assumes the cost of predictable claims, and purchases stop-loss insurance for the catastrophic risk for unpredictable large claims.

But what if an employee has a large drug claim or hospital claim? Can the plan sponsor afford the risk of self-insurance?
To reduce the likelihood of incurring a significant claim from an employee, insurance is still a wise purchase. Statistically, most employees spend less than $1,000 on eligible health claims. Therefore, the premium for insurance over this amount is reasonably affordable. In this case, insurance is truly insurance. The company is assuming the cost of predictable claims, and purchases insurance for the catastrophic risk of unpredictable large claims. This type of insurance is referred to as stop-loss insurance.

For companies with less than 150 employees, the key factor is selecting the appropriate stop-loss level. As the deductible or stop-loss level increases the corresponding premium is reduced. However, the level of risk increases should the company incur a major claim. Regardless of the cost of the stop-loss insurance, the company will only tolerate a certain level of risk. The key is understanding claims activity and choosing a level of stop-loss insurance at which the risk tolerance and savings are in harmony.

To illustrate the savings from the ASO model with stop-loss insurance, we will use a ten-employee company. The total health claims for the previous 12 months were $9,000, and the total dental claims were $7,000.

	Traditional Insurance
Health premiums	$13,000
Dental premiums	$11,000
Total cost	$24,000

	ASO with stop-loss ($1,000 level)
Health claims	$3,800*
Dental claims	$7,000**
Stop-loss premium	$6,000
Administrative cost	$1,680
Total cost	$18,480
Saving	$5,520 (23%)

*   As a rule of thumb, 80% of all claims come from 20% of all employees — in this scenario, two employees incurred $3,600 worth of health claims each, costing the stop-loss carrier $2,600 per employee based on a $1,000 stop-loss deductible. Deduct that cost from the initial $9,000 and $3,800 is borne by the company.

**   The dental claims are fully self-insured by the company and will cost the company the full $7,000. There is no stop-loss for dental. Unlike health, which could have a catastrophic event, dental has built-in limits of coverage and therefore there is no need for dental stop-loss insurance.

In the example, the company would save $5,520 or 23% by converting to a self-insurance model with a stop-loss policy. In the worst-case scenario, where all employees have high health claims one year, the company's exposure is still capped at $1,000 stop-loss level per employee, and, therefore, the health claims would increase from $3,800 to $10,000 — an increase of $6,200. There would also be an additional administration cost of $620. If this was the case, the total cost for that year would be $25,300. However, while the likelihood of such an event occurring is extremely minimal, the impact on the following year with ASO would still be less than with traditional insurance that reimburses from the first dollar.

ASO AND INSURED PLANS IN ACTION ENABLING A BUSINESS OWNER TO FUND HIS IPP

Imagine a 55-year-old man who owns a small transportation company in Ontario with approximately 90 employees, who has drawn a T4 income since 1991 of $100,000 annually and who has struggled with the rising costs of his company's group benefit premiums, which have been increasing at an annual rate of 10% per year over the last three years. In a competitive industry with only 5% profit margins, the company had to take immediate action. The company outlined that it wanted to achieve three objectives when reviewing its group insurance plan with its employee benefit specialist:

(1) Provide an enhanced medical and dental plan that would be attractive to new and existing personnel.

(2) Maintain and, if possible, reduce expenditures on its balance sheet.

(3) Fund an IPP for the business owner's retirement.

After a thorough consultation, the corporate benefits program was re-engineered to meet the company's main objectives. This was accomplished by modifying the existing fully insured group plan to an ASO model with stop-loss insurance. After the new solution was implemented, annual premiums went from $403,562 to $239,706, a 40% savings in year one alone. In year two, the premiums for the ASO and stop-loss insurance increased by only 5.5%, down from the 10% premium increases seen under the traditional group insured plan.

Based on the above assumptions, this company will realize an accumulative savings by transitioning from the traditional group insured plan to the new ASO and stop-loss insurance plan totalling $3,345,439 over the next ten years (see the table, below). Had the employer paid for the entire plan, these savings would have been equivalent to the company generating $67 million of gross revenue during the same ten-year period.

Projected Ten-Year Savings

Year	Traditional Insured Annual Premium Based on an Annual 10% Renewal Increase	Cumulative Premiums Paid	Annual Premiums for ASO and Insured Model Based on an Annual 5.5% Renewal increase	Cumulative Premium Paid for ASO plus insured Model	Cumulative Savings for Transitioning to the ASO and Insured Model	Gross Revenue Equivalent to Cumulative Savings
1	$403,562	$403,562	$239,706	$239,706	$163,856	$3,280,397
2	$443,918	$847,480	$252,890	$492,596	$354,884	$7,104,777
3	$488,310	$1,335,790	$266,799	$759,395	$576,395	$11,539,427
4	$537,141	$1,872,931	$281,473	$1,040,867	$832,064	$16,657,921
5	$590,855	$2,463,786	$296,954	$1,337,821	$1,125,965	$22,541,819
6	$649,941	$3,113,727	$313,286	$1,651,107	$1,462,620	$29,281,652
7	$714,935	$3,828,662	$330,517	$1,981,624	$1,847,038	$36,977,700
8	$786,428	$4,615,090	$348,695	$2,330,319	$2,284,771	$45,741,115
9	$865,071	$5,480,161	$367,874	$2,698,193	$2,781,968	$55,694,999
10	$951,578	$6,431,739	$388,107	$3,086,300	$3,345,439	$66,975,688

COST-SAVINGS OF THE ASO MODEL USED TO FUND AN IPP

In the example provided above, the business owner saved his company $163,856 in the first year by having his company adapt the ASO model, which goes directly to the company's bottom line. The savings created could be easily redirected to fund the business owner's IPP, helping him meet his last objective of funding his retirement in a cost-effective way.

This business owner, at 55 years of age, with a T4 income of $100,000 from his company since 1991 has now found existing money within his company to make the $161,851 contribution to fund the IPP. The $161,851 IPP contribution will be a full deduction for the business and a non-taxable benefit for the business owner in the first year of the IPP. All future contributions into the IPP will also come from the savings from switching to the ASO model.

HEALTH AND WELFARE TRUSTS

Adopting the ASO model allows employers the additional benefit of providing either health and welfare trusts (HWT) or enhanced benefits for key executives within an organization. An ASO can be structured to provide varying reimbursement limits to different classification of employees (*e.g.*, executive, part-time staff, *etc*.). Each employee classification can be assigned an annual reimbursement limit, with different classes of employees having differing reimbursement limits.

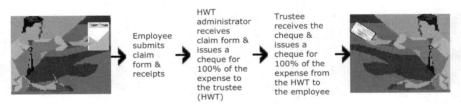

Illustration was provided with the permission of Gordon B. Lang & Associates Inc.

In this competitive employment environment, employers looking to attract and keep key people are finding that offering enhanced executive medical and dental plans gives these employers an edge over their competitors aiming to achieve the same results. Enhanced executive medical coverage using the ASO model for key people within an organization in addition to traditional health care coverage can include the rest of an individual's costs, such as the following:

- insurance premiums paid by the executive/employee or the individual's spouse for private health and dental plans;

- cosmetic dental and medical treatment;

- over-the-counter drugs, provided they are prescribed by a physician;

- drugs for conditions sometimes excluded under conventional plans;

- laser eye surgery;

- professional services of a dietician, acupuncturist, psychologist or nutritionist;

- dental care (preventive/restorative/orthodontic);

- medical equipment and devices;

- allowing of critical illness (CI) and long-term care (LTC) insurance premiums to be deductible to the company;

- facilities and services — special school, alcohol/drug addiction counselling, nursing home care, institution for mental or physical handicap, licensed private hospital, semi-private or private charges in a hospital, care of a person who has been certified as mentally incompetent, care of a blind person, full-time attendants in a nursing home, and fertility clinics;

- specialized private schools, camps and other educational institutions — an owner of an incorporated business (and/or his or her dependants) who has been diagnosed as having a learning disability has the ability to make business tax deductions for expenses that are related to the learning disability through the use of the health and welfare trust solution.

The cost of specialized private schools, camps and other educational institutions can be put through a health and welfare trust in accordance with the rules set down in subsection 118.2(2) of the *Income Tax Act*, R.S.C. 1985, c. 1 (5th Supp.), provided that the following three criteria have been met:

Criteria One: A qualified person has certified that the individual has a learning disability.

Criteria Two: A qualified person certifies that the individual with the learning disability requires the equipment, facilities and personnel specialties provided by a named private school, camp or other educational institution.

Criteria Three: The specialized private school, camp or other educational institution has the required equipment, facilities and personnel to assist the individual with his or her learning disability needs.

"The Numbers Speak for Themselves ..."

Imagine that you have a client who has an incorporated business in Ontario, earns a T4 income of $200,000, and has a marginal tax rate of 46.4%. This client has a son who has been diagnosed with a learning disability by a certified child psychologist (Criteria One met).

The psychologist recommends in writing that the best educational facility in Canada to meet this boy's learning and developmental needs as a person with a learning disability is Robert Land Academy (RLA), a boarding school in Wellandport, Ontario. RLA has been widely recognized by qualified persons during the past 28 years in meeting the special needs of boys with learning disabilities (Criteria Two met).

RLA currently has in place the facilities and personnel to meet the educational needs of boys who have been diagnosed with learning disabilities (Criteria Three met).

The school fee for attending RLA for the entire 2006-2007 academic year is $35,500.

Now let us compare this client's two options and find out what the final financial outcomes for each are. In Option 1, the client plans to pay for the entire school fee with his after-tax dollars. In Option 2, the client has set up a health and welfare trust with his company and plans to pay for the entire school fee through the trust.

In Option 1, the client will have to earn approximately $66,231 of personal income before taxes to pay with after-tax dollars the school fees of $35,500. The school fees will have to be paid before the client can be eligible to apply for a personal medical expense tax credit (METC).

In Option 2, the client's company, through the health and welfare trust solution, will pay $39,000 ($35,500 school fees plus $3,500 administration fee of 10%) into the trust. The total savings this client and his company receive for opting for Option 2 and setting up the health and welfare trust and then claiming the RLA school fees through the trust is $27,231 over staying with Option 1. This savings equals approximately 75% of RLA's entire school fees.

Critical Illness and Long-Term Care Through a Health and Welfare Trust

For many businesses, the use of a health and welfare trust can be instrumental in providing health benefits and planning for contingencies. The use of an HWT to make the pure insurance portions of CI premiums and long-term care premiums deductible allows a company to provide these benefits on a more cost- and tax-effective basis.

CRA has issued various rulings concerning CI and LTC policies purchased by a health and welfare trust over the last few years.

1. CRA Interpretation Bulletin IT-85R2, July 31, 1986, set out key requirements needed to constitute an HWT and requires that benefits would be restricted to one or more of the following: group sickness and accident insurance plans and private health service plans.

2. CRA Technical Interpretation TI-2003-0026385, December 10, 2003, held that CI policies, which provide only CI coverage, would constitute an accident and sickness plan.

3. A CI insurance policy held by a health and welfare trust is not considered a "life insurance policy" and, therefore, is not a taxable benefit to an employee. A return of premium benefit payable on death, or at the expiry of the term of the coverage or after a certain claim-free coverage period, may result in the disallowance of tax deductions of all contributions to the HWT.

4. Under CRA Interpretation Letter 2002-0160155 dated April 3, 2003, and subsequent CRA letters, a group CI policy may be purchased by the plan, and where such a policy contained no provision for life insurance coverage or for a refund of all, or a portion, of the premiums paid on termination of the policy or on death of the insured employee, it was viewed as a legitimate investment by the plan resulting in no taxable benefits to the employees.

5. A similar situation applies with an LTC policy, where such a policy would be a legitimate investment by the plan, providing it did not contain any return of premium benefits providing a premium refund similar to that for CI policies.

There are two types of CI and LTC policies — individual and group plans. These are generally issued by distinct departments of life insurance companies. Either type of policy may be purchased through a health and welfare trust.

Individual Policy and Split-Dollar Agreements

Individual policies generally provide additional benefits or riders in the form of return of premium benefits. Although the company may find such riders highly attractive, should the premium for such riders be paid through the HWT, it invalidates the HWT, *i.e.*, it disqualifies the eligibility of all contributions made to the HWT. The approach is to prepare a "split-dollar" or "shared ownership" agreement. The cost of pure insurance is funded through the HWT, and the company will pay the premiums for all of the various return of premium benefits and riders. Care must also be taken to ensure that shareholder employees are eligible for such benefits as a result of their employment with the company as opposed to their company ownership and that a policy would be issued on each life.

Flow Chart of an HWT with Critical Illness Insurance or Long-Term Care

(Individual Policy Situation)

1. Health and welfare trust is established
2. Sponsoring company purchases CI insurance or LTC insurance

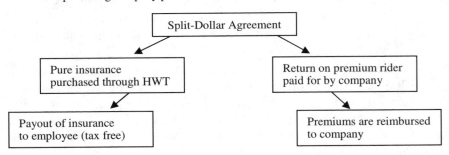

Group Policy

Group CI policies tend to be simpler than individual policies and can usually be issued without any return of premium benefits or riders.

Requirements

Whether individual or group policies are used to fund critical illness insurance through a health and welfare trust, the company should ensure the following:

1.   The HWT has been properly set up and that no taxable employment benefits or shareholder benefits have been created.

2.   The critical illness and/or long-term care benefits constitute a "group sickness and accident plan" by purchasing either a group plan or series of individual plans which will be deemed part of the company plan.

3.   No form of return of premium benefits or riders are funded through the HWT. If the company wishes to purchase these riders, they should have their employee benefit consultant prepare a split-dollar/shared ownership agreement. If the company does not require these riders the insurance company should be instructed to issue the policy as pure insurance without any such benefits riders, in particular, any embedded return of premium benefits on death.

FINAL ANALYSIS

Regardless of whether employers continue with traditional group insurance plans or adopt the ASO model, employers need to review their plan designs and understand where employee spending is occurring. It is strongly recommended that the employer include stop-loss insurance coverage with a reputable provider, along with a group pooled out of province, out-of-country travel insurance program. Under the ASO model, the cost of benefits is directly claim-driven versus premium-driven under the old traditional insurance carrier plan model.

Third party administrators and insurers will report all claims made by the employee by category (drug, dental, paramedical, hospital, vision) to the employer. In accordance with the *Personal Information Protection and Electronic Documents Act*, S.C. 2000, c. 5 (PIPEDA), the employees' names are not disclosed due to federal privacy laws. With this information, employers together with their administrators are equipped to act to control skyrocketing medical and dental costs. If an employee or employee's family has large drug claims, a drug cost management program can be initiated.

While it is strongly recommended, if the employer chooses not to include stop-loss insurance coverage in its ASO program, there are additional provincially funded drug programs that employees can access that have high drug utilization. This falls outside of the scope of employer-provided coverage but represents an additional option that individuals can access when drugs are not covered by their employer. In the case of Trillium, Ontario's provincial drug program, residents must pay an out-of-pocket deductible based on their family net income and the number of their dependent children. The provincial drug formula is reviewed regularly, and not all drugs are covered by these provincially funded drug plans.

A FINANCIAL WORD

Health and welfare trusts require specialties in employment compensation, adjudication of eligible claims and benefit plan construction. Therefore, if you are evaluating the suitability of an HWT for your clients or for yourself, it is well worth the time and money to hire the right professionals to assist in the design, implementation, maintenance and adjudication of claims within the HWT solution.

There are clearly several unique benefits in foregoing the traditional insurance model and, instead, adopting an ASO model. In addition to increased flexibility and greater control over the plan, the alternative model offers a considerable cost savings. By playing a more active role and taking on the increased risk associated with the ASO model, the business owner is able to reduce administration fees, eliminate reserves and cut out unnecessary benefits.

For the individual business owner looking for the most effective way to save for retirement, this alternative model also has the added "benefit" of providing the means to fund an individual IPP along with a whole host of other cost and tax-saving benefits.

CHAPTER 17

DISABILITY AND INDIVIDUAL PENSION PLANS

Ian Quigley

Overview

This chapter looks at the issues that impact the Individual Pension Plan when a plan member becomes disabled. It explores strategies that allow both an IPP sponsor and IPP member during a member's disability to maximize the IPP and other retirement benefits while minimizing costs to the employer through the use of salary continuation plans.

Learning Objectives

By the end of this chapter, you should be able to:

* understand the risks of an IPP member becoming disabled during his/her working career;

* list the options for both an IPP sponsor and IPP member to fund the IPP in the event of the member becoming disabled, depending on whether the IPP member is either a connected or a non-connected member; and

* understand how the implementation of a salary continuation plan can be an effective strategy that complements the IPP solution.

A REAL RISK REQUIRING REAL ATTENTION

Individual Pension Plans are back in vogue as a retirement planning tool in the small business environment. The target seems to be senior executives and owner-managers looking to generate a tax-sheltered pool of retirement savings in excess of what RSP programs will allow. While retirement remains a stiff challenge for many, other risks inherent in the financial planning process should also be reviewed, including the risk of disability.

Disability risk is called "morbidity" risk. Morbidity risk is real and a serious threat to the net worth of many Canadians including those contemplating Individual Pension Plans. While death only causes 3% of mortgage foreclosures in Canada, disability is reported to cause 48%. This comes as an alarming statistic to many advisors and planners. Various options exist to offset the financial risk of being disabled, including a number of approaches from a tax perspective. Here lies a strong area for solid financial planning and advice giving.

In 2001, a research organization (LIMRA) did a survey called "Tracking the Opinions of the Public in Canada". This survey measured the public's attitude toward insurance and other financial products in Canada. Some of the interesting facts to note from this survey were that only 39% of households reported to be using an insurance agent or broker, and of those households, only 47% had discussed disability insurance. This is somewhat surprising in light of the risk of disability and the need for attention in planning against this risk. The survey went on to illustrate that while few had addressed the issue, many Canadians are concerned about their ability to replace their income in the event of a disability. As a matter of fact, it ranked third on the list of concerns, with 70% of Canadians commenting that they share this concern.

Looking at a Statistics Canada "Health and Activity Limitations" survey from 1991, we see that the disability rate in Canada is 17.7%, meaning one in five Canadians are struggling with a disability issue. A 1985 Statistics Canada Commissioners Disability Report further illus- trates the risk of a disability occurrence with the chance of a disability lasting 90 days or more exceeding 30% for males and females all the way up to age 50.

Statistics such as these may lead a person to question the threat a disability would have on the planning available within an Individual Pension Plan. Certainly, the effect of a disability needs to be addressed by all planners reviewing such pension plans for their clients.

DISABILITY CREDITS

The effect of a disability event on an Individual Pension Plan depends on whether the plan has been registered for a connected person. Many IPPs are arranged for senior staff including owner-managers. As a result, many IPPs are considered what are termed "connected person" plans and, therefore, subject to connected person plan rules.[1] A connected person is one who:

- owns, directly or indirectly, at least 10% of the issued shares of any class of the capital stock of the employer, or of any other corporation that is related to the employer;
- does not deal at arm's length with the employer; or
- is a specified shareholder of the employer under paragraph (*d*) of the definition of "specified shareholder" in subsection 248(1) of the *Income Tax Act*, R.S.C. 1985, c. 1 (5th Supp.) (ITA).

In a connected persons plan, disability periods are exempt from creditable service. This means that even if the employee receives taxable employment income during a period of total disability, the pension plan would not be able to generate pensionable service.

This fact will then lead a planner to recommend a potentially different set of options to a disabled connected person versus a disabled non-connected person.

DISABLED CONNECTED PERSONS

A disabled connected person is the most likely candidate requiring such advice, as most Individual Pension Plans are set up for this market. You may note that the plan text required of these pension plans defines disability as "total and continuous disability". As a result, if you give advice to a disabled connected plan member, you may want to establish the details and conditions of the disability. For example, a person may qualify for disability benefits under an insurance contract but not be severely enough disabled to lose pensionable credits from the pension plan. If this is the case, more options present themselves as discussed for non-connected persons later in this chapter.

In the event of a total disability, most connected plan members will probably look at terminating their Individual Pension Plan. At plan termination comes the potential to negotiate a terminal contribution from the plan sponsor that may pair well with the disability planning outlined in the unanimous shareholders' agreement (USA).

[1] Subsection 8500(3) of the *Income Tax Regulations*, C.R.C., c. 945.

Terminal Funding: A Retirement Enhancement

Retirement enhancements become available to plan members when the plan is terminating,[2] and result in a negotiation between the plan member and the plan sponsor (often the same party with a connected person plan). Some people view this as offering a "retirement package", and it is paid into the pension trust by the sponsoring company on a tax-deductible basis. Plan members can secure packages as follows:

- an early unreduced retirement prior to age 65;

- improving the pension payout to full indexation from (CPI) − 1%; or

- "bridging" the equivalent CPP payout until age 65 paid from the pension plan.

A retirement with plan enhancements will cause the obligations of the plan to increase. This will increase the funding requirements of the plan and, therefore, the tax-deductible contributions of the plan sponsor. This funding comes from the company (tax-deductible contribution) and goes into the tax-sheltered pension trust on behalf of the member(s).

Estimates made on terminal deposits[3] are dependent on the age of the plan member and how long the plan member was in the pension plan (including backdating from past service benefits).

Below is a chart that illustrates how much money can be terminally funded at specific ages for plan members who earn the maximum pensionable income.

Age entering the plan:	Age of Retirement: 60	62	64
45	$ 500,000	$ 400,000	$ 300,000
50	$ 300,000	$ 250,000	$ 200,000
55	$ 180,000	$ 170,000	$ 120,000
60	$ 125,000	$ 90,000	$ 70,000

Note that if the trust is dispersed, there are *Income Tax Act* prescribed maximums that can be transferred into a LIRA or LIF/LRRIF account.

---

[2] Unless they are a federal member of Parliament, their terminal funding has been prenegotiated.

[3] Ian Quigley, *Tax and Compensation Strategies* (Toronto: Thomson Carswell, 2005).

Terminal Funding: Disability Buy-Out Programs and Disability Lump Sum Insurance

Coincident to the terminal funding opportunity may rest a disability buy-out clause in the USA. Some USAs will offer to repurchase shares of a disabled person after a set period of disability.[4] Some, or all, of this can be insured on a lump-sum basis with an insurance company. Basically, the insurance company pays the policy amount to the company tax-free, and the company then has funding available for the share repurchase. A challenge is that the share repurchase[5] will often lead to taxable gains to the disabled person and then be invested in a taxable environment going forward.

If the share repurchase, outlined in the USA, were to be worded in a flexible manner, it might be able to coincide with the terminal funding available in the pension plan. The issue here is that the USA contractually binds the company to the disabled member, when the terminal funding in the pension plan cannot be predetermined. Nonetheless, the two events can work well together.

For example, a partner becomes disabled. One year later, the insurance proceeds are received by the sponsor company tax-free. The sponsor company then decides to pay out the pension plan on a tax-deductible basis. The disabled member of the pension plan now has a boosted IPP with tax-sheltered investing. Hopefully, the tax boost will better prepare the member to deal with the financial consequences of being disabled.

DISABLED NON-CONNECTED PERSONS

Non-connected persons can continue to receive pensionable service on employment income received even if they are disabled. This may sound contradictory to many people, as how would a disabled employee receive taxable employment income while being disabled? The answer depends on the structure of the disability insurance.

One traditional approach to obtaining disability insurance is through an employer sponsored plan. Here the employer simply sponsors the plan and the plan is considered by Canada Revenue Agency (CRA) as an "employee-pay-all plan". Employee-pay-all plans are programs where the employee pays out of his or her after-tax income the cost for the disability insurance. The employer simply acts as a facilitator of the

---

[4] Often 12 months.
[5] Either corporate or personal repurchase.

disability coverage. As the premiums are paid with after-tax dollars, and the contracts are in essence owned outside of the corporation, the potential payout is paid as tax-free dollars to the disabled employee.

The other traditional approach of obtaining disability insurance on an individual basis is through an individual disability contract. Here as well, the premiums are paid with after-tax dollars, and the contract is in essence held individually or outside of the corporation. The contract as it is paid with after-tax dollars will have a payout that is characterized with tax-free dollars.

WAGE LOSS REPLACEMENT PLANS

A "wage loss replacement plan" or "salary continuation plan" (SCP) is a formal arrangement between the employer and its employees. Here, the arrangement offers provisions for indemnification of lost income in the event of sickness, maternity or accident. Simply put, lost wages are covered.

Most income and benefits earned by an employee are taxable in the year earned. This includes the value of board, lodging and other benefits with only a few limited exclusions. One of these exclusions is the cost of a "group sickness or accident insurance plan". An employer may therefore outsource the risk of covering wages in the event of a disability by purchasing a disability insurance contract. The cost(s) of this contract is borne by the employer on a non-taxable basis to the employee.[6]

In the event of a disability, the benefits received by the employee will be taxable due to a loss of income and pursuant to a sickness or accident insurance plan, disability insurance plan or income maintenance plan.[7]

Items to note[8] with regards to a wage loss replacement plan include the following:

- Benefits are paid on a periodic basis.

- The arrangement may be formal or informal.

- If a contract of insurance is used, it is part of the plan but not the plan in itself.

- CRA will assume the program is a wage loss replacement plan unless the contrary can be established.

---

[6] Subparagraph 6(1)(*a*)(i) (ITA).
[7] Subparagraph 6(1)(*f*)(ii) (ITA).
[8] IT – 428 "Wage Loss Replacement Plans".

- The plan must be an "insurance plan" but does not require an insurance company.

In a Technical Interpretation letter written in 1997,[9] a proposed wage loss replacement plan was reviewed where an individual was both an employee and a shareholder. CRA stated it was a question of fact whether a benefit had been conferred on the individual in the capacity of a shareholder or in the capacity of an employee. Where a benefit is granted to an individual, the benefit will be presumed to have been conferred upon him or her by reason of being a shareholder, unless the benefit is available to all employees of that corporation or the benefit is comparable in nature and quantum to the benefits generally offered to employees who perform similar services for and have similar responsibilities to other employers of a similar size.

This is an important comment because it removes the issue of shareholder versus employee and reminds us that programs such as a wage loss replacement plan are specifically designed for employees. The issue of shareholder status is not one of concern unless a bias has been taken to offer benefits specifically to those with shareholdings. This TI letter moves on to discuss a situation of multiple wage loss replacement plans and comments that it is possible for an employer to offer multiple wage loss replacement plans to employees under different terms and conditions. The TI letter concludes with comments in regards to individually purchased disability contracts being grouped together and used as part of a wage loss replacement plan, and favourably comments that this is a reasonable strategy to be undertaken.

Each province carries its own Insurance Act, which may affect the ability of an employer to offer a wage loss replacement plan. Specifically, the Province of Alberta has made it illegal to self-fund a wage loss replacement plan, but an insured arrangement through an insurance provider is considered onside. This is a trend that we should see in Canadian provinces as a response to events like the Eaton's bankruptcy, where employees lost disability benefits due to the bankruptcy of their employer.

Tax Savings Used to Purchase More Insurance

A properly structured wage loss replacement program would take the tax savings from the deductible premium and apply it towards a larger insurance policy. With the larger taxable insurance policy, you then have

---

[9] TI9640485.

to look at the post-disability tax rate to determine where the higher net payout would be achieved.

Assuming tax rates do not change, the wage loss replacement program should offer an employee the same net income as the employee-pay-all approach. It has to be this way, as insurance companies cannot offer preferential underwriting to one method versus the other, or arbitrage would enter the system.

For example, an employee wanting to purchase a $48,000 disability policy outside the corporation will have a policy cost of $200/month ($2,400/year). The policy pays $48,000/year tax-free in the event of disability. To pay the $2,400/year policy cost, the employee will have to draw $4,000/year of salary at a 40% tax rate. The premiums are paid with after-tax dollars and the payout is tax-free.

The same employee could be offered participation in a wage loss replacement plan. Here, the disability premiums would be a non-taxable benefit, but any payout would be taxable. The underwriter of such a policy would need to ensure that based on circumstances today, the policyholder could not arbitrage against them by preferring one strategy over the other. As a result, the employer for the employee should be able to purchase a larger taxable policy. At a tax rate of 40%, the employee would have to have obtained a $6,667/month benefit so that after 40% tax ($2,667), the same net income is achieved. There is no extra risk for the insurance company as the same net income is found in both approaches. Using similar logic, the cost of the policy should also be the same. The $2,400/year after-tax cost would now become a $4,000 pre-tax cost.

Here is the point of indifference:

Personal Policy

- Premium cost $4,000 in taxable salary, leaving $2,400 after-tax.
- Policy offering $4,000/mth in tax-free disability benefits.

Wage Loss Replacement Program (Taxable Policy)

- Premium cost $4,000 as a direct business expense.
- Policy offering $6,667/month in taxable disability benefits. After 40% tax, this would leave the executive $4,000 of net income.

In reality, most taxpayers will find that their tax rate decreases during a disability period. A salary continuation program can be arranged for those starting at a high tax rate (executives) as simply an arbitrage on underwriting assumptions. If the underwriter assumes that there is to be no tax rate change pre- and post-disability for the insured, but the executive/the insured feels that there could be a spread achieved in the system, this is a worthwhile strategy to investigate.

More Than a Simple Tax Arbitrage

Although there is clearly a tax arbitrage available for those starting at a high tax rate, there is more opportunity for planning in a salary continuation program than a tax arbitrage. An SCP offers an employee a non-taxable employee benefit that the employee could not achieve independent from the company. The company would in essence own the disability policy and could use it as a negotiating tool for executive compensation purposes. In addition, some corporate taxpayers simply find it easier to cut a corporate cheque for things such as insurance coverage, rather than a personal cheque.

It is possible that the disabled employee would qualify for a disability tax credit, thereby reducing his or her post-disability tax rate.

Should the disabled employee require medical needs not offered by the health care system, he or she could use the medical expense tax credit again, reducing his or her disability tax rate.

As the disability income is paid in a taxable format, it is possible for the employee to do other tax planning in the disability period, working to achieve a disability rate lower than assumed by the program. Enter the Individual Pension Plan.

Wage Loss Plans and an IPP

Because the income from an SCP program is considered employment income, it would create pensionable contribution opportunities for non-connected plan members. Income is paid to the employee from the insurance contract, but is considered taxable employment income. The sponsor company could continue making IPP deposits on behalf of the employee allowing the employee to maintain retirement savings plans while dealing with the disability disruption.

A second perspective is to leave the pension plan. A connected member who would not continue to gain pensionable credits from the IPP could return to an RSP program. Deposits made into the RSP account would reduce taxable income and boost the results of the wage loss program. This could offset the lost tax benefits from the pension plan for connected persons due to a disability event.

CHAPTER 18

PLANNING FOR CHILDREN WITH DISABILITIES, AND ESTATE PLANNING

Kenneth C. Pope

Overview

This chapter explores the strategies that either parents or guardians can use when planning their estates to provide the maximum benefit for their adult disabled child using the IPP and Henson Trust solutions.

Learning Objectives

By the end of this chapter, you should be able to:

*   understand the issues surrounding estate planning for parents and legal guardians of adult disabled children using pension plans and Henson Trusts.

Pension plans are a valuable part of estate planning. They result from hard work, prudent investments and frugal expenditures while we are actively engaged in our work or vocation. They are intended to provide financially for us and our loved ones in the later periods of our lives.

Pensions typically have a survivor pension, as we plan to provide for our spouses and children when we are gone. This is a natural evolution of our lifelong efforts to care for our families.

We realize that a spousal pension may well result in the loss and clawback of other benefits, such as federal and provincial income supplements (GAINS) and old age security benefits (OAS). The efforts we make to split income and reduce the usurious rates of taxation in Canada are generally defeated when one spouse dies and passes on pensions, investments earning income and other family assets to the surviving spouse.

A family with a child or children with disabilities, in which both parents have committed themselves to caring for all their children as their needs require, would benefit from specialized advice when planning for retirement with private corporate Individual Pension Plans (IPP) as well as public sector pensions across Canada.

Children with disabilities, when they reach the age of 18 years and become adults, usually qualify for provincial disability benefits that include both financial and other life support benefits. The benefits vary from province to province, decreasing as you move from west to east.

The optimal estate planning arrangement to provide for them after the parents have passed on is a "Henson" trust. Named after a landmark case in Ontario which resulted in settled common law for almost all provinces in 1989, assets left by way of a will or other designation to the trust do not disqualify the child from these benefits as assets in excess of the asset test (assets in excess of $5,000 in Ontario for example),

Inheritances from a parent (or grandparent) left to a Henson trust, intended to provide for the child just as the parents did while alive, are exempt from the asset test. In conjunction with the very modest financial benefits provided by the provinces (maximum $959 per month in Ontario), the Henson trust can help to provide for the supplementary needs of the child.

It is entirely feasible for an IPP to designate a survivor pension for a spouse, obviously, and from there, a pension for an "adult dependent survivor", such as a child with disabilities, is a small step.

The difficulty is that pension income will be offset dollar for dollar from provincial disability benefits! A 100% offset is not a good use of well-earned pension income. This is not why parents work hard all their lives, to remove and replace the provincial share of support for their children. The legislative intent of provincial disability benefits is to continue a sharing of support from the province, the community, the family and the person with disabilities.

The better plan is to have the pension income paid to a testamentary Henson trust, created by the will of the parent, rather than paid to the child. It is also feasible to have the pension paid to the trust upon the death of the pensioner rather than on the death of the spouse if this is preferable for tax efficiency, depending on the tax bracket of the surviving spouse. There is no sense giving income to a surviving spouse to be taxed at high marginal rates, thereafter used to provide for the child, when it may be taxed at reduced rates at the start.

Another alternative, which will be appropriate when considering the future plan of care for a child with disabilities, is to commute the pension into a lump sum and have this directed to the trust. This could then be used to purchase shelter for the child, or to be reinvested according to "prudent trustee investment guidelines". In Ontario and other provinces, such guidelines have replaced the approved list of investments defined by statute (which lawyers had always worked around anyway). For example, it may be appropriate to invest in dividend-earning stocks rather than interest-earning assets, to make use of the dividend tax credit and further reduce taxation.

The "preferred beneficiary election" available to trustees of trusts when the beneficiary qualifies for the disability tax credit due to his or her being "markedly restricted in the activities of daily living" provides an alternative to attributing income to the low income child by following the "paid or payable" rule.

Income can be deemed to be income to the child without actually giving it to the child, in turn spending it as after-tax capital in ways that benefit the child without affecting provincial disability benefits.

In addition to IPP beneficiaries, there are going to be hundreds of thousands of unwitting "adult dependent survivor" pensions coming into play as the "baby boom" generation retires. Relatively few of these employees even know that such pensions for their children exist. These pensions often become known to the family only after the pensioner has passed on and the family seeks estate settlement assistance from knowledgeable accountants, financial planners and lawyers.

A client of mine who is a retired teacher, Lola, called recently to ask if there have been any developments that would affect her situation. I was obliged to advise her that although we are working on changes, her son's benefits would still be affected by her teacher's pension, which has an adult dependent survivor provision.

The same is true of the OMERS pension, another provincial legislative pension, which provides a pension for adult children with disabilities. The general rule for Canadian pensions is that the disability must be a result of early onset or young adult disabilities.

The disabilities may be any combination of physical, mental health and cognitive developmental disabilities. Establishing the facts of the disability and pension applicability takes place after the parent(s) death, but documentation can be put in place beforehand.

The cause of disabilities may include injuries at birth, which is still unusually common as a result of the hurried time schedules for doctors and nurses, quick admittance and dismissal and policies during childbirth that result in induced or forceps deliveries to meet a shift change or free bed requirements.

We have reduced infant death and maternal death rates phenomenally in the western world, but the number of premature births, multiple births and forced births resulting in disabilities is not well documented.

Across Canada, the huge number of families who have children with disabilities is astounding, and constitutes a segment of the population that is both large and identifiable — if professionals are aware enough to realize that not asking the simple questions necessary is akin to professional negligence.

For example, December 2004 statistics provided by the Ministry of Community and Social Services of Ontario indicate that there were 206,884 cases of people receiving Ontario Disability Support Payments (ODSP). These cases involve one or more individuals between the ages of 18 and 65, with a total number of beneficiaries in the family unit being 286,465.

These numbers reflect only approximately two-thirds of the actual total number, since it excludes those over or under these ages with disabilities. (People under the age of 18 and over the age of 65 do not receive ODSP.)

The parents, siblings, grandparents, aunts, uncles, cousins and more distant relations typically share a common and unending concern for the family members with disabilities. This perpetual support and advocacy for the child may vary across families and require differing amounts of financial and other assistance, but it is usually a lifelong, intergenerational concern.

As one client mother said to me, "All I want is to live 60 seconds longer than my daughter". This statement simply enunciates this core estate planning concern for these families. Due to significant advances in medical science, parents no longer outlive their children with disabilities, and these children for the first time will become senior citizens themselves in record numbers, as the baby boom ages.

The issue of developmentally disabled adults requiring long-term care like any aging senior citizen, often with markedly higher mental deterioration and dementia setting in at early ages, as recent studies are indicating, is starting to receive the active attention of developmental services and long-term care providers.

If on average we presume that each of these adult children with disabilities has two surviving parents, has just one sibling who is likely to be the trustee of the Henson trust when the parents do pass on and has just one surviving grandparent, we conservatively calculate there are 827,536 intimately concerned citizens needing specialized estate planning advice. If we total these family members along with the 286,465

ODSP beneficiaries, we have 1,114,001 close family members in Ontario alone.

From an accounting standpoint, if these families are properly advised, they will create testamentary and *inter vivos* Henson trusts to provide for their children. These trusts will be created both while the parents are alive, and upon each of their deaths. This will generate trust accounting and tax filing work equivalent to at least 206,884 new client files in Ontario alone.

Due to the common use of the "preferred beneficiary election" for the trusts, depending upon circumstances, the tax returns for the beneficiary will also require attention.

From a financial planning perspective, these families have a critical "know your client" issue. Their financial planning, insurance and investment needs are often weighted by concerns about the child with disabilities. Insurance products often play a key role in their planning to fund Henson trusts.

From a marketing perspective, the 2001 Canadian census gives an Ontario population of 11,410,046 souls, almost one in ten of whom are directly affected by disability issues. This is a very identifiable niche market that is unknown to many professional advisors.

These numbers reflect reality all across Canada. The percentages will vary from city to city, but I find they increase from this benchmark, not decrease. In formerly industrial towns from which industry has fled, the numbers move towards one in five, not one in ten. My hypothesis is that when jobs leave, the only people who can remain are pensioners and the services and retailers who serve them.

Pensions are a major source of later life income for both wealthy families and lower income families. Both will also often have a Registered Retirement Savings Plan (RRSP/RRIF). For higher income earners, this is a component of their overall investment and retirement strategy, designed to allow asset growth without annual taxation of the income earned. Unfortunately, upon retirement this RRIF income is subsequently taxed at high rates in the hands of the contributor or the spouse. (To digress briefly, I think that some of my most interesting work is for clients who live in other countries and tax havens. Did you know that it is not sufficient to simply reside on the Isle of Man and die there? You must provide for interment there as well to preserve your tax status.)

For lower income families, RRSPs are often a cruel trick played on them by well meaning financial advisors and institutions. When retired, drawing on the RRSP may often result in substantial clawbacks of GAINS and OAS income. Every dollar of other income starts to come into the clawback equation for both GAINS (at 50% of each GAINS dollar) and a graduated clawback of OAS at higher levels of income. Financial advisors in particular should consider these factors from the client's perspective when also considering their commissions and fees.

What both tax bracket families would like to do is shelter this RRSP asset and have it available at lower rates of taxation or clawback for the benefit of their children with disabilities when they have passed on.

To do so would require that it be "rolled over" to the child or to his or her Henson trust to protect provincial disability benefits. It is common knowledge that such a rollover can be made to a dependent child under age 18, subject to annuitizing the fund and paying it out in equal shares in the years remaining until age 18. For a child over age 18, the rules are less well known.

This adult dependent rollover is now feasible. As a result of federal regulatory changes in 2003 after the budget in February of that year, the financial dependency test (income of the child in the year prior to death of the parent being less than the personal tax exemption level) which a child with disabilities must meet to allow this rollover has been adjusted upward, and, in the majority of cases, the test can be met.

Until raised by amendments to the applicable regulations to the *Income Tax Act*, R.S.C. 1985, c. 1 (5th Supp.), the test was the amount of the personal exemption, which is $8,648 in 2006. If the adult child had income greater than this amount, which virtually all adult children with disabilities do, resulting from provincial disability benefits, they were disqualified from a tax-deferred rollover of registered retirement assets.

This test amount was raised to $13,814 in 2003 and indexed, making it greater than disability benefits in all of the provinces; thus, the rollover is achievable subject to other factors which may make such a designation complicated or self-defeating.

Foremost is the fact that the rollover of an RRSP in excess of certain limits directly to a child receiving ODSP will disqualify him or her from benefits, and the receipt of funds from the RRSP will again affect benefits. This is the case in all provinces. Specialized advice is needed to decide on the parent's best course of action.

If a parent designates an RRSP to a child with disabilities, which is very common when a spouse is out of the picture due to death or divorce, there are factors which a professional advisor must consider and discuss with the parent. A financial advisor who places the annual contributions might well know of this designation, while an accountant or lawyer often would not unless he or she was aware that the parent must ask.

Accountants doing the tax returns for clients who do not ask are particularly at risk. They will know there has been an annual contribution, but may think their job is done when preparing the tax return for filing. Knowing but not advising about the implications of beneficiary designation will come back to haunt them in the very near future. The fees they may have earned preparing the tax return will not warrant claims made for negligent advice. This sort of claim is already coming back to bite the tail of lawyers who did not prepare Henson trusts for clients when they "knew or should have known" there was a child with disabilities. Most of my estate practice involves sorting out "no trust" estates or advising executors when flawed trusts have been drafted.

One result will be that my own errors and omissions insurance premiums will be going up. The courts will hold lawyers and other professionals to the test of perfection and find against them without relent or qualification.

Another result will be the liability of the partners of retired accountants, advisors and professionals who find themselves liable as partners of retired professionals. In the majority of cases, I have been able to find a "fix" to this problem, by mitigating the damages and putting the estate and beneficiary on side with the provincial authorities. We are now starting to see situations where my best efforts are not enough, and disability benefits and other life supports are being cut off. This is tragic and unnecessary for all concerned.

I have a client situation in which we were able to have a sympathetic judge in a small town actually amend by court order the terms of a will with no Henson trust, thus creating one! This is cutting edge, but it won't be available across the board.

Much to the advantage of the partners of the senior retired solicitor who drafted the will, their liability has ended, and a quantified settlement will be reached with LawPro, the lawyers' indemnity company.

This brings us to the question of designating the RRSP to a Henson trust. This is not presently workable except for IPP owners. Proposed amendments to the *Income Tax Act* which would allow this for average citizens have not been brought into effect.

An IPP owner, however, is free to have the RRSP transferred over to the IPP by way of an additional voluntary contribution as discussed in Chapter 13 of this text, and the benefits then directed to a Henson trust. This is the ideal solution to the problem.

CHAPTER 19

APPLICATIONS OF UNIVERSAL LIFE INSURANCE WITH IPPs

Gordon Berger
Bob Kirk

Overview

In this chapter you will learn how to complement the IPP with the universal life insurance solution.

Learning Objectives

By the end of this chapter, you should be able to:

- understand the value of utilizing universal life insurance to create and maximize wealth;
- understand the value of leveraging the cash value within a universal life insurance policy to fund IPP contributions.

WHY UTILIZE UNIVERSAL LIFE INSURANCE?

It is quite clear that the most elusive strategies from a financial planning perspective are those that provide integrated solutions to real problems. To create a vehicle that will provide the user with "the missing link", the piece that draws everything together into a package that provides the client with a unique financial solution for now and tomorrow is the real goal or nirvana of wealth creation.

A lot has been said about using leveraged life insurance programs, but there are different ways in which they can be utilized. Select clients can take advantage of the universal life concept through the use of this seamless strategy that provides value with the following benefits:

- allows deposits to be deductible over time;
- has low captive capital;

- grows deposits tax-sheltered;
- transfers the growth to the next generation tax-free;
- allows for the use of the growth tax-free.

There are only four "real" tax shelters in Canada today:

- principal residence (home);
- Individual Pension Plans;
- RRSPs;
- life insurance.

Sometimes it is not possible to use your home, although recently, lines of credit and concepts such as the reverse mortgage have become all the rage. RRSPs are entirely too constrictive in that they have limited deposits, must be unwound at age 69 and are taxable when used, often at the highest marginal tax rate. That leaves life insurance ...

Section 148 of the *Income Tax Act*, R.S.C. 1985, c. 1 (5th Supp.) (ITA), allows for properly structured life insurance plans to "grow deposits sheltered of tax" and "transfer the growth to the next generation tax free". This is why life insurance policies can provide the essential value that makes them a viable chassis for the universal life solution.

However, generally speaking, deposits to life insurance are not deductible. This process allows for the creation of tax deductions using the above section 148 of the ITA.

THE SCENARIO

The scenario below illustrates how a life insurance policy provides the greatest flexibility for a business owner to maximize his or her wealth.

- *Business owner is a 55-year-old businessman.*
- *Business was incorporated in 1985.*
- *Company can sponsor and fund for our business owner an IPP for past service back to 1991 and current service for $161,851 in 2006.*
- *Qualifying transfer is needed to fund for past service is $242,600.*
- *The second year (2007) after the IPP has been created, the contribution made into the IPP by the company will be $27,934. These corporate deposits into the IPP for the years that follow will increase at 7.5% per year.*
- *The business owner did a reorganization in 1999 and opened a holding company (HoldCo).*

- *He has flowed over $2 million from his operation company (OpCo) to his HoldCo, where it sits in retained earning.*
- *The business owner has $1.5 million sitting in his RRSP.*

THE PROCESS

The client has already moved money from OpCo to HoldCo and, therefore, has already placed cash into retained earnings of HoldCo.

HoldCo could make a large deposit to the insurance contract — let's say $1 million — and then could subsequently borrow by way of a policy loan back to HoldCo. In actual terms, approximately $700,000 could be borrowed back to HoldCo; the additional $300,000 will pay cost of insurance and grow tax-sheltered within the insurance policy and provide funds for future policy loans as they become available. HoldCo now needs to invest the $700,000 to provide for the possibility of interest deductibility on the policy loan.

When the funds are withdrawn from the insurance company, the client must invest that money. The investment must be an investment that would allow for the deduction of interest expenses. Why?

Because the withdrawal from the insurance contract is by way of a loan.

Perhaps HoldCo loans a portion of the funds to OpCo at an interest rate slightly higher than that being charged by the insurance carrier — this creates a reasonable expectation of profit scenario. HoldCo could also take out a general security agreement or other security to ensure that it is "first in line" in the event of insolvency of OpCo.

Each year the insurance carrier will ask for interest on the policy loan, and each year HoldCo will ask OpCo for interest on its loan. The net result is that the deduction in HoldCo offsets the income from OpCo to HoldCo, and there is no tax on this transaction other than a small amount on the income difference between the loan interest paid to the policyholder from OpCo and the loan interest paid by the policyholder to the insurance carrier. In essence, HoldCo has a deduction it did not have before.

Now to the funds, which are now in OpCo. A portion of the funds can be used to deposit into the Individual Pension Plan to satisfy the past service requirement, and funds would be moved from the RRSP into the IPP as well. This is completed in satisfaction of the opportunity to deposit 15 years of past service to the Individual Pension Plan. In order to make these deposits, our client would have to have enough funds in his RRSP to allow for a transfer from the RRSP into the Individual

Pension Plan as well. In our example above, this would mean that a deposit of $161,851 would be made into the Individual Pension Plan, and $242,600 would be transferred into the Individual Pension Plan from the RRSP. The main benefit of this is that the deposit from OpCo to the IPP will be deductible, thereby building a retirement plan with deductible funds. It is of special note that funds can be borrowed to contribute into an Individual Pension Plan and are still deductible.

THE OUTCOME

The client would now have a number of benefits as a result of implementing this structure. One benefit would be a deductible interest payment into a life insurance contract every year. These funds would grow tax-sheltered within the insurance contract and could be used to pass funds to heirs or can be leveraged in retirement to create tax-free retirement payments — an IPP with significant, defined benefit, and enhanced retirement benefits. What has been created as a result is a twofold retirement structure. By the use of an integrated plan, the client would have two streams of retirement funds: a defined benefit pension plan and a large cash value life insurance contract both built with deductions. In essence, this planning technique allows for the creation of several retirement structures with high tax efficiency.

THE POSSIBILITIES

Through planning, the client could potentially unwind his RRSP by making withdrawals on an annual basis equal to the interest payable on the policy loan. Therefore, although money withdrawn from an RRSP is taxable, the funds are used to pay deductible interest. The RRSP could potentially be exhausted by the time the client reaches age 69, which means the funds do not have to be transferred to an RRIF or annuity and withdrawn, since they would now reside as cash within a life insurance contract.

After many years of accumulating funds, the client has several choices as to how to utilize these funds for retirement:

1. The policy loan could be paid with outside funds and then leveraged with a bank for a bank loan or a series of bank loans.

2. After a period of time, the policy loan could be paid with internal cash that has accumulated within the insurance contract and then leveraged as in 1. above.

3. The client could use other retirement sources first, knowing that this cash is available in the future.

4. The client could make withdrawals directly from the insurance contract, albeit with certain tax consequences.

5. The client could potentially even sell HoldCo with the insurance policy asset within it.

As can be seen from the numerous choices, the client has the control, the opportunity and the flexibility to make choices that suit a desired lifestyle and with the capability of making the timing decisions on the client's own timetable.

If the funds are not needed, the client could pass the funds to the next generation or pay capital gains taxes with the insurance death benefit, having now accumulated excess funds that would not have been present otherwise. This could potentially make it very easy for the estate to be preserved into the hands of the next generation by providing funds to pay the taxes rather than using up a portion of the money the client built over a lifetime of hard work.

The flexibility of the concept lies in its simplicity. There is no financial underwriting for insurance policy loans. They are secured by the contract itself, and interest payments even have flexibility as to timing and amount. In fact, it is even possible to miss an interest payment once there are funds within the plan.

Moreover, the plan can be structured to fit the circumstances of most entrepreneurs and can even use cash-flow from the business to be built or can be placed within the all too familiar "bonus out and loan back" structure that is utilized by many principals of individually owned corporations or partnerships. The investments can be structured in numerous ways to fit the most conservative to highly aggressive investment goals. The plan is also available to high-income earning employees although without the Individual Pension Plan component. The OpCo/HoldCo planning is not always necessary but often works best depending on where the funds are located.

The universal life solution provides clients with a means to enhance their retirement, create funds for the future of their family and pass money to their heirs on a tax-free basis. All this is built with funds that are potentially deductible and which provide clients with the control, flexibility and capability of managing their own financial future.

Often, clients find pieces of the puzzle to enhance their future wealth creation goals, but it is rare to find a plan that can create a myriad of possibilities the way that this one can, especially in its flexibility. Isn't that what the nirvana of wealth creation should be all about?

Diagram 1. Universal Life Insurance with an Individual Pension Plan

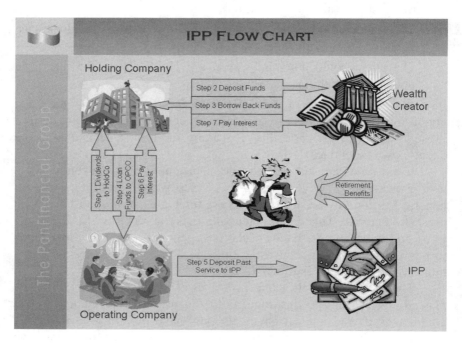

Diagram 2. Universal Life Insurance Without an Individual Pension Plan

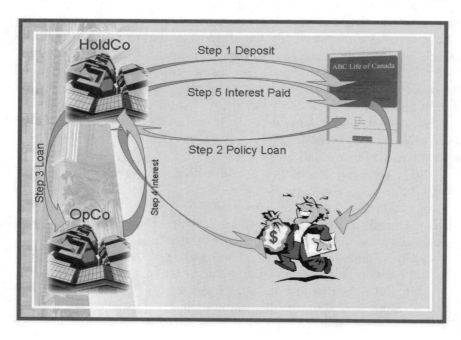

PART IV

THE 21ST CENTURY FINANCIAL CONSULTANT'S IPP CONCEPT PRESENTATION KIT

CHAPTER 20

THE 21ST CENTURY FINANCIAL CONSULTANT

Overview

This chapter offers an overview of how the financial planning industry has changed over the past two decades.

Learning Objectives

By the end of this chapter, you should be able to:

- understand what is required of financial planning in the 21st century;

- understand how to apply the Six-Step Financial Planning Process;

- understand how to select the right clients that will make for a stratifying career;

- understand your 150 and the power of a synergy group in your professional and personal life;

- understand the three compensation models for the 21st century financial planning professional for managing assets;

- identify what your next steps are.

WARNING: NEW LANDSCAPE AHEAD

Thomas S. Kuhn, a scientist, in his famed book originally published in 1962, *The Structure of Scientific Revolutions* (Chicago, Ill.: University of Chicago Press, 1996) first defined the term "Paradigm Shift". A "Paradigm Shift" is a revolutionary change from one way of thinking to a newer way of perceiving the world around us that allows us to accommodate changes in the world that the old model failed to address satisfactorily. This happens when one of the basic underlying assumptions we have been living with changes.

In 1987, the "four pillars" of the Canadian financial sector — banks, trust companies, insurance companies and investment dealers — fell down and all these independent sectors were allowed by the Canadian government to merge. Thus, the financial sector in Canada began its own paradigm shift over the last two decades and it continues on today. With this convergence of financial institutions, one-stop shopping for financial services is now possible for each Canadian consumer and new skills are required of the 21st century financial consultant.

The financial industry is constantly evolving. For many years, people turned to stockbrokers for money matters. Then, insurance agents entered the picture. Stockbrokers are now called financial advisors, and insurance agents are sometimes financial planners. There are independent financial planners, fee-only money managers and even accountants can invest client money at some accounting firms. It can be difficult to know what someone is really dealing with.

Investment advisors, insurance agents, financial planners and accountants should be aware that their practices are no longer competing with those of just other professionals in their respective industries. Traditional brokerage firms at Canada's largest banks own brokerage houses, and insurance companies are mobilizing their resources to become the semi-affluent client's primary financial advisor of choice in the 21st century by launching what they term as the family office.

These multi-billion dollar organizations are expanding their services to have teams of skilled professionals offering a wide variety of financial services. They have created huge teams of highly qualified Chartered Accountants (CAs), Certified Management Accountants (CMAs), Certified General Accountants (CGAs), Chartered Financial Analysts (CFAs), Certified Financial Planners (CFPs), Trust and Estate Planners (TEPs), Lawyers, Chartered Life Underwriters (CLUs) and Certified Employee Benefit Specialists (CEBS); placing these experts at the disposal of clients. These new players are taking aim at the traditional accountant's, insurance agent's, stock broker's and financial planner's clientele by evaluating a client's tax issues, preparing individual, corporate and trust tax returns and providing tax planning and other financial solutions.

In addition to offering the services mentioned above, the wealth management departments at Canada's largest financial institutions are offering expertise in areas that many accountants, insurance agents, brokers and financial planners are weak in, such as: debt consolidation, investment counselling, financial planning, succession planning, tax planning, estate and insurance services. In the process these new players, through their holistic approach to the financial planning processes, are uncovering and identifying clients' financial issues, and providing solutions to needs that these clients' financial advisors were unaware existed and/or had failed to address adequately and comparatively.

MAXIMIZING YOUR PROFESSIONAL VALUE AS A 21ST CENTURY FINANCIAL PLANNING PROFESSIONAL

Tom Nicolle, CA, CFA, is a very close colleague of mine and a financial professional whom I admire very much. Tom, who works from Halifax, Nova Scotia, has completed a very intensive study of the financial planning and succession marketplace in Canada. What his research shows is that for 21st century financial planning professionals to maximize their full intrinsic value, as in any other professional service, they will need to position themselves as a dominant player in a highly specialized niche market moving in the same expanding direction as market trends. By doing this, these advisors can be compensated based on the true value they create for their clients rather than on the time they spend working on a file, and these advisors can take advantage of a brand that recognizes them as the best in their field. When these forces come together, the true professional financial advisor has competitive advantages in the marketplace that bring both recognition and wealth.

Nicolle has determined that the 21st century financial advisor who takes advantage of the following three emerging trends in the financial services market will enjoy an abundance of opportunity:

1. The financial services industry predicts that in the next five to ten years, significant levels of wealth will change hands in Canada. It is estimated that much of this wealth is tied up in the equity of businesses whose owners need to plan their succession, and a large number of these businesses are valued between $2 million and $20 million, and are family-run enterprises.

2. There are more than 150,000 advisors competing for the management of the wealth of Canadians. Most of these people are generalists. Based on statistics from various professional organizations, it is estimated that less than one-half of 1% of these advisors are true professionals capable of providing the level of sophisticated advice required for succession planning. Successful advisors will need to focus on providing business as well as financial advice to business owners.

3.   Industry research suggests that there are two kinds of financial service companies that are highly valuable and profitable: those that are very large and benefit from scale and those that are niche boutique players with specialized expertise to enable them to boost profitability. There is a need for a specialized niche model that specializes in offering value-added succession planning services in the marketplace. However, this type of firm does not exist in Canada as of yet.

Nicolle believes that by taking advantage of these three trends, an advisor with credentials as both a business consultant and financial advisor will be positioned to maximize fully his or her true professional value in the 21st century marketplace.

21ST CENTURY CLIENT

Most people start by acknowledging they need some help with their money. That much we know for sure. What is less certain is what sort of help they need and from what type of financial planning professional they get that much needed help from.

To make things simple, financial help falls into two categories: financial planning and money management.

Financial planning is valuable and important. The key elements of good financial planning are retirement forecasting, tax analysis, insurance analysis, business succession planning and estate planning. Note that I did not say "investing". We haven't gotten to that yet.

Under the "Six-Step Financial Planning Process" advocated by the Financial Planners Standards Council of Canada (FPSCC), the 21st century financial professional continuously directs and monitors specific goals that a client has. For example, the traditional investment advisor is only going to monitor the performance of the product he or she has sold, but not make it part of the specific plan that is associated with the goal-setting process developed by the 21st century financial planning professional.

When a client initially meets with a 21st century financial planning professional, the client will find that some of the questions will not be financial. For example, when a client talks about financial independence and/or retirement, the 21st century financial planning professional might ask things like:

*   How do you spend your time?
*   What would you really like to do if you were financially independent?

- How will you stay motivated if you don't do the type of work you do now?
- How will you react to not having a job?
- How would your family be affected by your retirement and health issues that may have to be considered within the plan, such as your personal life expectancy due to previous disease or family history?
- Where would you like to live?

THE SIX-STEP FINANCIAL PLANNING PROCESS

Every human being has an innate desire, and skill, at perceiving the future. Albert Einstein said: "Imagination is everything. It is the preview of the life's coming attractions." By asking questions similar to those listed above, the 21st century financial planning professional helps his or her clients use future scenarios to make better choices today. Scenarios are not predictions; they represent, instead, possible alternative futures that will help an individual navigate the present and create his or her future.

The Six-Step Financial Planning Process is not science but an art, which is a disciplined way for the financial professional and the client to foresee alternative futures and make difficult decisions that will empower the client to adapt to the complex world we live in today.

This process properly applied empowers both the client and his or her advisor to question the client's underlying assumptions that the client has towards his or her family, health, future work-related circumstances, retirement and estate. What is an appropriate range of alternative scenarios? What decisions does the client have to make that are affected by these scenarios? Which decisions will leave the client much better off? Asking and answering these questions will provide the greatest possible benefit from the standpoint of developing and implementing the right financial plan that will fulfill a client's goals and needs at a particular point in time.

The 21st century financial planning professional is really the quarterback or facilitator of the architectural plans created for a client's present and future. In essence, what separates a traditional financial advisor from a 21st century financial planning professional is the training in the Six-Step Financial Planning Process that the 21st century financial planning professional will have received. Good financial planning is always more process than product.

Step one: The 21st century financial planning professional works with clients to clarify their present situation by collecting and assessing all relevant financial data such as lists of assets and liabilities, tax returns, records of securities transactions, insurance policies, wills, pension plans, business ownership and share structures, *etc.*

Step two: The 21st century financial planning professional will help clients identify both their clients' financial, personal goals and objectives as well as clarify their clients' financial, personal values and attitudes. These may include providing for children's education, supporting elderly parents, selling a business or relieving immediate financial pressures that will help maintain current lifestyle and provide for retirement. These considerations are important in determining the best financial planning strategy.

Step three: The 21st century financial planning professional will identify financial problems that create barriers to achieving financial independence. Problem areas can include too little or too much insurance coverage, or a high tax burden. The client's cash flow may be inadequate and may need to be reviewed. These possible problem areas must be identified before solutions can be found.

Step four: The 21st century financial planning professional will then provide written recommendations and alternative solutions. The length of the recommendations will vary with the complexity of a client's individual situation.

Step five: A financial plan is only helpful if the recommendations are put into action. Implementing the right strategy will help the client to reach his or her desired goals and objectives. The 21st century financial planning professional will assist clients in the actual execution of the recommendations, and in coordinating their implementation with other knowledgeable professionals, if necessary which might include lawyers, accountants, investment advisors, actuaries, trustees, mortgage brokers, bankers, venture capitalists and insurance agents. (By no means is this list of professionals mentioned above complete.)

Step six: The 21st century financial planning professional will provide clients with frequent reviews and revisions of their plans to assure that their goals are achieved. Clients' financial situations should be reassessed at least once a year to account for changes in their lives and current economic conditions.

Life's Main Questions

Several years ago I was introduced to the six questions that people ask themselves, as they enter different stages in their lives. The stage that someone begins asking each of these questions is usually tied to the individual's age and maturity. The 21st century financial planning professional, desiring to assist clients as they ask themselves these six questions, find that the Six-Step Financial Planning Process is their greatest ally in helping their clients reach answers to their specific life questions at a particular moment in time.

Life Question One: Who am I? This is an identity question. Individuals usually begin asking this question when they are small children. When we are born we have no identity, we are given our names from our parents, we are born into a certain place and culture to a family and we may assume the religion of our parents. Individuals answer this question by assuming different labels that describe who they believe they are, and this is how we identify ourselves.

Life Question Two: How do I fit in? Individuals begin asking this question usually when they reach their teens. It is a time when they try to figure out how they fit into their social and physical environments. When individuals begin asking this question in their development, they are highly influenced by their peers and are susceptible to peer pressure (*i.e.*, high school).

Life Question Three: What will I do? Individuals begin asking themselves this question usually in their early twenties. This stage occurs when individuals try to figure out what they will do with themselves for their career, and who they may or may not partner with. This question is different from Question One because it is concerned with the actions the individuals will take in their lives; this question is not an identity question.

Life Question Four: Who have I become? The question usually arises when individuals reach their forties. Individuals wake up and realize that they are no longer planning their lives, dreaming of what they will become when they grow up, because they are grown up. Some people transition to asking this question very gracefully; others do not. This question often leads individuals into the so-called "mid-life crisis". This is also a time when individuals become serious about planning their financial affairs.

Life Question Five: What have I accomplished? This question usually arises when individuals reach their mid-to-late fifties. Individuals realize that their working career is coming to an end, and a new stage of life is about to begin. At this stage individuals are getting ready to retire from work and enter their retirement. In the area of financial planning these people are putting their financial affairs in order to make sure they have enough income to support themselves when they no longer receive income from their own labour. For business owners this is the time when they start planning and implementing succession plans for their businesses.

Life Question Six: What will my legacy be? People start asking this question of themselves after they retire. They come to the realization that they are at the end of their lives. They begin to think beyond their mortal existence and start contemplating about what will they be remembered for and what legacy will they pass on after they are gone from this life.

Individuals asking this question are quite serious about gifting their time and money to people and causes they care about deeply. It has been said that those who begin asking this question of what will be their legacy, are the individuals who have the biggest impact on families, communities, society and the world long after they have departed. There is a Jewish saying that applies to many in this group asking Life Question Six:

"It is better to give with a warm hand than a cold hand."

SELECTING THE RIGHT CLIENTS THAT WILL MAKE FOR A STRATIFYING CAREER!

It is as true today as it was approximately 2500 years ago when Socrates, the ancient Greek philosopher, stated probably the most profound self-actualizing statement of all times:

"Know Thyself!"

Good financial planning cannot be reduced to technique; good financial planning comes from the identity and integrity of the financial professional. Technique is what you use until the authentic financial consultant arrives. In essence good financial planning comes from good people. As the author of this book I would also like to add as an addendum to Socrates' quote above for all those who choose to provide financial advice for their careers:

"Know Thyself!
&
Know Who You Can Best Serve!"

Our most valuable asset is our time, and it is wise that we spend our time where we will get the biggest bang for each second that we have been given on this blessed earth.

A financial planning professional that stays true to his or her core values and mission is a very attractive professional and the right clients will show up and appreciate them. How do you get people to share your core values? You can't. It is impossible. Just find people that are predisposed to share your values and purpose, attract and retain those people, and let those who do not share your values go somewhere else.

Our life span in the financial professions is relatively short and we need to be focused on those that we can help the most and who can help us as well achieve our independent personal and financial goals in our lifetime. Each professional relationship we have should be a win/win, where we share similar values, and goals and want the very best for each other.

Robin Dunbar, author of the ground-breaking book *Grooming, Gossip, and The Evolution of Language* (Cambridge, Mass.: Harvard University Press, 1996), convincingly argues that the purpose of human communication is to bond with others, and with those we communicate more often, the stronger our bonds are to those individuals.

Dunbar's research shows that the average person has an invisible social network of approximately 150 people, with whom the person would feel comfortable enough to have a cup of coffee if he or she bumped into a member of this group on the street. Dunbar found that the strength of social networks dilutes when these networks grow greater than 150 people. Yes, most of us know many more than 150 people, but we don't have the strong ties that we have to our 150.

Note: The research conducted by Robin Dunbar was used as the basis of Malcolm Gladwell's 2000 best-selling book The Tipping Point – How Little Things Can Make a Big Difference *(Boston: Little, Brown, 2000: reprinted with a new afterword by author, Boston: Back Bay Books, 2002).*

Robin Dunbar also found that within each person's 150, there is a core group of about 10-12 people who make up a smaller group of individuals whom we have an invested interest in and care dearly about. If something were to happen to anyone in our core group we would be deeply affected. We will discuss the Core Group and how we can use them to foster success in our professional careers in more detail when we explore "Synergy Groups" later on in this chapter.

So if there are a limited number of individuals with whom we can have quality relationships within our lives at any one time, especially during our careers, it is critical to know whom we can best serve as financial professionals and what clients to invite into our 150. There are spiritual vampires in our midst. By spiritual vampires I mean individuals who suck the living life force out of you when you are around them or when you think about them.

These are the clients and other individuals who when you see their names pop up on your caller ID, you don't want to talk to. To achieve longevity in any profession we should strive to be surrounded by spiritual angels, those individuals who give us energy, who we want to be around us and for them to succeed and they want us to have genuine success as well.

In a conversation I had several years ago with a colleague of mine, Derek Hill, CA, of Hill Kindly Group in Ontario, Canada, Derek shared with me that he has learned to group his professional and client relationships into three distinct categories:

Group One: Those individuals who only want to win and want you to be the loser in all your dealings with them. All that matters to these individuals is that they win and you lose.

Group Two: Those individuals who want to win and don't care if you win or lose from the relationship. If you win great, if you lose they don't care either way.

Group Three: Those individuals whose primary goal in all their personal and professional relationships is for win/win for everyone involved. The main goal of each of these individuals in their relationships is for everyone to come out a winner and for each party in a relationship, whether personal or professional, to always strive for that goal.

I believe that by taking the time to sit down with a pad of paper and categorizing each client, professional and personal relationship into Derek's three groups is a perfect place to begin to evaluate the people we have surrounded ourselves with. Very few people ever take the time to be honest with themselves, to consciously take stock of the nature of each of their relationships with others.

INVITING THE RIGHT CLIENT INTO OUR 150

Over the last two decades, I have continually redefined the criteria of the ideal clients to join my 150, clients that I can best help with the experience and skill set I have acquired, and who can help me achieve my specific goals in my life. I have come to my criteria by always asking myself the following four questions:

Question 1: What qualities do I want my perfect client to possess and demonstrate?

Question 2: What makes my perfect client tick?

Question 3: What do I want my perfect client to expect me to deliver and provide?

Question 4: What should I expect from my perfect client?

When you have found your own answers to these questions, you will know when a prospect will make a perfect client for your financial practice, and is a perfect candidate to join your 150. You will be able to recognize a perfect client the moment that you meet one. An immediate spark of attraction and connection between this person and you quickly leads to mutual respect and a profitable personal, and professional relationship follows.

Below I have provided the criteria I use to evaluate a potential and current client relationship. If my criteria works for you, use it: if it doesn't work for you, get rid of it. What is great about this financial profession is that you can build your own book of business however you wish, with whomever you wish, and be very happy and successful at doing it your way.

Clients who best benefit from working with our company are:

(1) those that trust us and appreciate our expertise in the fields of executive financial planning, wealth management, benefit plan design, investments, succession planning and estate planning;

(2) honest with us, and are willing to fully disclose their assets, values, goals and concerns;

(3) decisive and proactive with their financial decisions that affect their businesses, their families and their lives;

(4) extremely busy with their careers and businesses and don't have the time to manage their financial affairs and money themselves (they work in dynamic businesses and professional fields and enjoy what they do);

(5) oriented towards reaching goals such as wealth preservation, tax minimization and deferral, creditor protection, wealth accumulation, wealth distribution and being good private and corporate citizens (they have a responsibility to invest in the future, in themselves, in others and the community as a whole);

(6) referred to us by a partner or client who has benefited from our professionalism, skills and performance;

(7) those that have a basic understanding of tax planning, financial planning, succession planning and corporate benefit plans (these are businesses or individuals who are highly motivated to work with our team of financial professionals);

(8) those who fully understand the value of our services, advice and relationship (it is this mutual understanding that allows us all to be successful and profitable in both our professional and personal relationships).

Typically, our services are of most value to individuals who have at least:

- $200,000 or more of combined annual income;

    or

- $2,500,000 or more of net worth.

    Our services are of most value to companies with:

- $300,000 or more of combined annual income;

    or

- $2,500,000 or more of net worth.

SYNERGY GROUPS AND HOW THEY WORK TO MANIFEST YOUR SUCCESS

Richard Buckminster ("Bucky") Fuller (1895–1983), referred to as the 20th century's "Gentle Genius", a visionary and inventor, when asked to describe himself, said he was a "Verb" always in process. At the end of his life he had over 200 patents to his credit, he coined the phrase "Spaceship Earth" and was a pioneer in the worldwide environmental movement. His most famous invention was the Geodesic Dome (the golf ball shaped building located at the Epcot Centre in Walt Disney World, Florida), the most energy-efficient building ever designed in the world. Perhaps Bucky's greatest legacy was coining the word "Synergy" and being its biggest proponent during his lifetime, decades before it became fashionable in popular culture.

Synergy is "the phenomenon in which two or more discrete influences or agents acting together create an effect greater than that predicted by knowing only the separate effects of the individual agents": <http://en.wikipedia.org/wiki/Synergy>.

Combining the principle of synergy to our core group within our 150 we are acting on the premise that the combined energies of two or more like-minded persons is many times greater than the sum of the individual energies involved. In any great endeavour that you wish to succeed in, it is beneficial to ally yourself with others of like mind and purpose.

The pooling of your individual resources is very valuable. Through this process, invisible connections are also made between you. These give rise to this higher principle of the group mind that acts for the benefit of all involved. Yet, you should take great care of whom you allow into your synergy group because the opposite effect is also possible, where you unknowingly might have Spiritual Vampires in the midst of your core group who are sucking the life out of you. Individuals who knock you down not build you up.

It has been said that God created friends to make up for our families; thus, family will always be a part of our core group. However, our synergy group should consist of two or more persons (two to six is ideal) who meet regularly in an atmosphere of trust and harmony for the purpose of providing mutual support and encouragement and to believe for each other things which each, alone, may find difficult to conceive and believe in.

Melissa Giovagnoli's and Jocelyn Carter-Miller's insightful book, *Networlding: Building Relationships and Opportunities for Success* (San Francisco: Jossey-Bass, 2000) provides three useful questions that can help us populate our individual synergy groups with the right partners for our personal journeys.

Question One: Do we share the same values and goals? If an individual does not share our same values and goals we should seriously consider moving these individuals outside of our 150 and definitely out of our core group.

Question Two: Can we work together? Someone may share our values and goals but because of differences in personality and work styles we cannot work together. If these people are members of your core group you should move them to your 150 or even outside of that group.

Question Three: Is there opportunity for us to work together? We might answer yes to Question One and Question Two but at this moment in time there might not be an opportunity to work together on a project. If this is the case these individuals should be moved outside our core group and into our 150. However, if there is a genuine desire to create an opportunity amongst these individuals, they should be invited into our synergy group.

Synergy groups are not established so that individual members can solve each other's problems. Rather, such a group is established to surrender to the synergy that will be manifested in any problem areas. When such requests are fully and properly made of the synergy group, answers and solutions occur in the most amazing way. Opportunity is manifested and real success occurs for each member of the group.

Members of a properly put together synergy group feel a compulsion to make your problems their problems, your solutions their solutions, your opportunity their opportunity and your successes their successes.

Members of your synergy group have an invested interest in each member's success when the right group is put together and each member has an invested interest in the co-creation of business and personal opportunity for each other. A synergy group has the mindset that when one member succeeds in the group, all do. And real miracles happen.

THREE COMPENSATION MODELS FOR THE 21ST CENTURY FINANCIAL PLANNING PROFESSIONAL FOR MANAGING ASSETS

When a client hires a financial advisor, that client should know exactly how he or she will pay for that advisor's advice. This is the case whether a client is investing millions of dollars or just dabbling in the TSX.

It's also worth pointing out that until most financial advisors came along the financial advice that clients received probably cost them next to nothing. They got their information from reading *The Globe and Mail*, the *Toronto Star* or a mutual fund company's promotional material. Additional data may have come from watching television shows on ROBTV, attending a workshop hosted by one of the five large Canadian Chartered Banks or from talking to their dentist or friends and family.

This "free" information, incorrectly applied by a client, could turn out to be very costly. A client for life understands that valuable financial advice does not come cheap. He or she should be willing to pay for the right advice, from a qualified financial professional.

Several years ago, I read a short written piece by John Ruskin, the 19th century English social reformer, entitled "It's Unwise to Pay Too Much". This expresses my thoughts on the subject of the true value that the 21st century financial planning professional provides to his or her clients.

> It's unwise to pay too much, but it's unwise to pay too little. When you pay too much you lose a little money. That is all. When you pay too little you sometimes lose everything, because the thing you bought was incapable of doing the thing you bought it to do. The common law of business balance prohibits paying a little and getting a lot. It cannot be done. If you deal with the lowest bidder, it is well to add something for the risk you run. And if you do that, you will have enough to pay for something better.

Although some advisors may feel uncomfortable talking about how they earn their keep, it is vital that clients understand how the 21st century financial planning professional is compensated. Whether the 21st century financial planning professional is starting a new client relationship, or re-evaluating a current one, there are three basic models of compensation when providing the IPP solution or any other financial advice.

Model One: The 21st century financial planning professional can be paid on the commissions generated when a client makes transactions. One example of this approach is the stockbroker, who earns a commission every time a client buys or sells a stock, bond or some other product purchased through the broker.

Model Two: The 21st century financial planning professional may be paid according to the growth or shrinkage of a client's assets. For example, some advisors' fees are set as a percentage of a client's portfolio (*i.e.*, 1% a year). If a client's portfolio grows through appreciation so does the advisor's fee. If assets shrink, the fee follows suit.

Model Three: The 21st century financial planning professional may be paid by a client per project or by the hour (*i.e.*, a flat fee for an initial evaluation of a portfolio). The client is buying the 21st century financial planning professional's experience, expertise and time.

Each one of these compensation models rewards the 21st century financial planning professional in different ways. In the first model (the "transaction or commission" base) there is a financial incentive to generate transactions in a client's account. A commission-based financial advisor might determine that the most appropriate investment for a client is 100% allocation to T-Bills. But he or she may not be able to afford to tell the client this opinion because there is almost no commission involved to reward the advisor. Even though we put the needs of the client first and act ethically, the best interests of the advisor may not always match the best interests of the client.

When an advisor is using the commission compensation model, it's important to explain all of the commissions and fees they may earn from a deal. Full disclosure can help reduce any potential conflict of interest that may result from this model.

The 21st century financial planning professional whose pay is based on the size of the client's assets (model two) has an incentive to see those assets grow. Growth can come from appreciation of existing assets or from new assets that a client places under the advisor's management. If the client pays the 21st century financial planning professional a straight percentage of assets, then the client and the advisor both want to achieve exactly the same thing — making money.

A fee-only (model three) 21st century financial planning professional has an incentive to take as much time as necessary to do a client's work but has no incentive to steer the client to any particular product. Like other professionals who bill by the hour, there is an incentive to spend more time than necessary (the "over-billing problem") to complete any project.

To some investors, this "fee-only" approach appears to be the most expensive. For this reason, very few financial advisors have adopted the fee-only model. However, those who use this model have the potential benefit of obtaining increased referrals from other professionals in related financial fields. This occurs because accountants, lawyers and other professionals often feel more comfortable referring business to other professionals who are compensated in the same manner.

Investment advisors who earn their living by adopting model one (transaction or commissions) and model two (management fees on assets under management) can find it very profitable to work closely with a fee-only advisor (model three). A fee-only financial planning professional, for example, may discover new investment and insurance opportunities that the referring investment advisor can implement. Think of how an investment guru who writes a newsletter can work well with a model one or model two investment advisor. The guru is compensated on a fee-only basis (via a yearly subscription to their newsletter, for example), while the transaction or "fees on assets under management" 21st century financial planning professional helps to implement this advice.

Today's clients are becoming more knowledgeable about how financial professionals are paid. An advisor who dodges this topic or gives vague answers might find his or her clients looking elsewhere for advice.

As such, you must be willing to candidly discuss your methods of compensation.

The bottom line: Stand tall, and be proud of the value you bring to the table. Most importantly, be upfront with how you get paid for the valuable advice you provide. Great clients are willing to pay when they perceive that you bring value to their financial lives. Remember that as financial professionals all we truly have to sell is our time, whether we are compensated for it by earning a commission, fees on assets under-management, fee-for-service-only or a combination of these income models.

GOING FORWARD IN THE WORLD OF IPPs AND OTHER ADVANCED FINANCIAL SOLUTIONS IN THE FINANCIAL CONSULTING PROFESSIONS

In this new era financial professionals are being called upon to craft comprehensive solutions that will involve the services provided by brokerage firms, accounting firms, trust companies, banks, insurance agencies and financial planning firms. Financial and tax professionals that step up to the plate and fulfill the role of the new advisor will become the key gatekeepers to their clients while at the same time all the other professionals and organizations desiring to serve their clientele will become little more than subcontractors.

Those financial professionals that succeed in this new era will quickly identify their allies. They will build alliances with clients, other professionals that complement their services and organizations that will help them navigate towards the clear blue waters of success.

To succeed in this new era, financial professionals will have to place their focus on identifying and understanding a client's total financial life and create solutions that will solve a client's most important needs.

The best plan in the world is just a plan. Entrepreneurs and business people understand this intuitively. The key to success is not the plan; it is in the execution of the steps to reach the goals.

I once read an interview with Warren Buffett, founder of Berkshire Hathaway Inc., and someone I believe is the world's greatest investor. The interviewer asked Buffett if he was willing to share any of his personal investment strategies. Buffett laughed and said that everyone knows his strategy and his plan. It's been public knowledge since the beginning. He said that the reason he and his company are successful is that they execute the day-to-day details so that their plan becomes reality.

Today there is very little human knowledge that cannot be found in a book or on the Internet, awaiting those that have the time, interest and desire to learn. However, no one person can understand and successfully apply the total of this knowledge. The person who is sick might die before finding the information that can cure the illness, while a trained doctor, through specialized knowledge and experiences, can recognize the symptoms and effect a cure within a matter of hours or days.

The skilled 21st century financial planning professional can provide qualified wealthy clients with sound information and effective advice to ensure their financial health. Life is too short to find the right financial way through trial and error. Most people do not notice the symptoms of their financial illness until it is too late for them. In this busy and ever complex world people considering the IPP and other wealth solutions need to find knowledgeable experts that will deliver quality and value.

Remember, there are always people right now in this world accomplishing what we want to be doing, and these individuals can be our teachers to help us to achieve our desired outcomes. And there are others out in the world today that are looking towards us to be their mentors. The future is for the brave and bold, who set clear and specific career and life goals, who take action towards achieving their goals, who surround themselves with the right people and most importantly, who enjoy life!

"When the student is ready, the teacher will appear."

Lao Tzu's *Tao Te Ching*

CHAPTER 21

DEFINING THE PROFESSION: PROFESSIONAL FINANCIAL PLANNER COMPETENCY PROFILE

Cary List

Overview

This chapter discusses the new competency profile and lays out the entire scope of knowledge, skills, abilities and judgements that a Certified Financial Planner (CFP) professional must possess in order to be qualified to offer professional financial planning services to clients. It concludes by showing the complementary nature of the financial planning and accounting professions.

Learning Objectives

By the end of this chapter, you should be able to:

*   understand the Financial Planners Standards Council (FPSC) Professional Financial Planner Competency Profile for Certified Financial Planner (CFP™) professionals and how the profile will apply to financial planning professionals in Canada going forward;

*   understand how the Financial Planners Standards Council (FPSC) Professional Financial Planner Competency Profile for Certified Financial Planner (CFP™) professionals complements the profile and services offered by today's public accounting professionals.

THE NEW COMPETENCY PROFILE

When the Financial Planners Standards Council (FPSC) released its Professional Financial Planner Competency Profile for Certified Financial Planner (CFP™) professionals (the "Competency Profile", or

"Profile") in November 2006, it represented a quantum leap forward in defining the financial planning profession in Canada. The new Competency Profile lays out the entire scope of knowledge, skills, abilities and judgements that a CFP professional must possess in order to be qualified to offer professional financial planning services to clients.

While its most obvious application is to serve as the basis for the CFP certification examination, the Profile also serves as a guide to help distinguish the professional financial planner from other financial advisors and ultimately to establishing financial planning as a recognized profession in Canada and worldwide.

Since the Profile is performance-based, it clearly articulates the full set of capabilities required of a CFP professional in the performance of financial planning services, and will ultimately serve as a guide against which to measure how professional financial planners are living up to Canadians' expectations. The Profile will also help CFP professionals to validate their own skills and abilities. It spells out the extensive breadth and depth of capabilities that a CFP professional must possess, and should ultimately boost CFP professionals' own confidence in promoting the value proposition of professional financial planning and their role in the financial services community.

The Financial Planners Standards Council's Competency Profile is the culmination of a competency analysis project completed in 2005 as part of its regular review of the profession. It was developed by over 100 practising CFP professionals from across the country, under the leadership of FPSC, and with the guidance of independent certification experts. In the normal course of the competency analysis (often referred to as a job analysis or practice analysis by some professions) almost 1,000 CFP professionals were surveyed to validate the completed Profile.

Making a Difference Around the World

The draft Profile garnered significant interest from the international CFP community as well as other unrelated professional certification bodies. As a result, and in the interest of collaboration, the publication of the profile in Canada was delayed until input from these communities could be appropriately considered. During these consultations, FPSC donated the draft Profile to the international umbrella organization and owner of the CFP marks outside of the United States — Financial Planning Standards Board (FPSB) (of which FPSC is a member).

Through its leadership on FPSB's international standards committee, FPSC was able to ensure consistency between its competency standards and those of the international CFP community. The result is the first set of international competency standards for professional financial planners ever published. It reflects the extensive input of the international standards committee, numerous professional certification experts and many other external stakeholders.

FPSC's approach to the Profile is leading the international CFP community away from knowledge-based certification to competency-based certification. Such a move is necessary to ensure that this burgeoning new profession sufficiently addresses public expectations. While technical knowledge is critical for competent performance, the public must be able to expect a professional to have more than just textbook knowledge. This is because knowledge alone does not prove competence in any profession.

When expressed in terms of specific competencies needed for CFP professionals to provide appropriate solutions to their clients, the new Profile will help the public better understand the benefits of financial planning and the value of working with a CFP professional to help them meet their goals.

Defining the Difference Between Licensing and Professional Certification

The new Profile demonstrates the complexity and high levels of skills and knowledge intrinsic to the practice of professional financial planning. While Canadian financial services regulators play critical roles in protecting the public by imposing licensing requirements that are appropriately focused on the sale of product and related advice, the competencies detailed in the Profile for CFP professionals go well beyond those which may be required in offering product advice, and thereby lie outside the scope of current regulation. The Profile addresses the competencies necessary to meet the public's need for integrated professional financial planning services that range across a broad group of subject matter. The interrelationships among the many facets of financial planning are becoming increasingly critical to the financial well-being of Canadians, and the public increasingly needs to be served by professionals with the appropriate integration skills to meet those needs.

The New Profile Is One Critical Element in CFP Certification

CFP certification is based on *three sets of core requirements: Education, Examination and Experience.* Once certified, CFP professionals are then held to *three sets of professional standards: ethics*, as defined in the CFP Code of Ethics; standards of *competency*, as assessed by the CFP Examination and ongoing continuing education requirements; and standards of *professional practice*, as guided by FPSC's Practice Standards. Each of these requirements for CFP certification will be reviewed and reassessed by FPSC in the months and years ahead to ensure CFP professionals continue to meet the expectations set out in the Profile.

Since the spring of 2005, FPSC had been working with education providers to ensure that students are adequately prepared for the November 2007 Examination — the first exam that will fully reflect the Competency Profile. A new exam blueprint based on the Profile will be published concurrently with the Profile, and will present a clear guide for exam candidates. It will focus on what candidates should be expected to do competently, rather than solely on what they are expected to know, and will guide all future CFP examinations.

Developing the Profile

To ensure the establishment of a consistent and clear Profile of financial planning in Canada and around the world, the financial planning community needed to begin with a consistent definition for financial planning — one that would resonate with financial planners and their clients. This definition, as developed by FPSC and as agreed to by the international CFP community, is: "the process of creating strategies to help clients manage their financial affairs to meet life goals". It is the basis on which the Profile is built.

Armed with this definition, FPSC undertook an in-depth competency analysis to determine all that may be involved in the performance of financial planning services and the underlying skills, abilities and technical knowledge that a competent financial planner must possess to be able to perform the services as a true professional.

While the Practice Standards are critical to CFP professionals in guiding their process so that clients can expect a consistent financial planning experience, FPSC recognizes that financial planning is about much more than the application of a process. There must be a clear and explicit explanation of exactly what a CFP professional must be capable of doing throughout the process to ensure that the clients' objectives can be achieved.

The first step in the establishment of the Profile was to define in simplest terms, at the broadest level, the functions that planners perform. The professional CFP community identified three broad categories of functions: *collection* of information, *analysis* of information and *synthesis* of that information to achieve the desired result.

These functions were then examined with respect to each of the specific components of financial planning. "Components" refer to elements of financial planning with which people are generally familiar: *financial management, asset management, risk management, retirement planning, tax planning and estate planning*, as well as certain overarching *fundamental financial planning practices* that focus on the integration of information across multiple components — a key and distinct aspect of professional financial planning. Five core competencies were identified and then further defined in terms of every possible aspect of performance that may be required to demonstrate each competency. These aspects of performance are defined as "elements of competency", and are categorized within each financial planning component. There are over 100 elements of competency inherent in the Profile.

The Financial Planners Standards Council recognizes there are other skills intrinsic and fundamental to the demonstration of competent performance within all of these components that must also form part of the Profile. Specifically, a true professional cannot competently perform any of the specific functions of financial planning without applying certain generic professional skills. These skills are identified in the profile as core "Professional Skills" and are grouped within four categories: *ethical judgment, professional practice*, written and oral *communications* and *cognitive abilities*. These skills are fundamental to being a professional. In demonstrating any of the core competencies of professional financial planning, CFP professionals may be required to apply any one or more of these professional skills concurrently.

While FPSC does not anticipate testing professional skills explicitly as separate and distinct components on the CFP Examination, the assessments of these skills will be inherent in the examination questions that test any number of the core financial planning competencies.

The final and still critically important piece to the competency puzzle is *knowledge*. While knowledge itself does not define competency, one cannot be competent without possessing the requisite knowledge. Unlike traditional approaches to professional certification, requisite knowledge was determined *after* the component functions of financial planning were established. The task of defining requisite knowledge was relatively easy once the functions had been determined. We asked financial planning experts: "What might you need to know to perform each one of the particular activities?" The result was a number of domains of knowledge that are identified under one of 11 distinct categories.

The Complete Picture

Ultimately, the complete picture of financial planning can only be found by reviewing the entire set of competencies as they are set out in the new Profile. The Profile provides a comprehensive description of the full scope of expertise required of a professional financial planner and how a CFP professional can use it to provide sound, practical and unbiased advice across the broad range of subjects that in their entirety define the financial planning profession.

THE COMPLEMENTARY NATURE OF THE FINANCIAL PLANNING AND ACCOUNTING PROFESSIONS

The Profile articulates the complete set of knowledge, skills, abilities and ethical judgement required for competent performance as a professional financial planner. Together, these define competence as a financial planning professional, as demonstrated specifically by individuals who hold the CFP™ credential. There are currently in excess of 17,000 CFP professionals in Canada and over 100,000 worldwide. What makes these professionals different from other financial advisors is the competencies articulated in the new Profile. While there are a number of striking similarities between many of the competencies of a CFP professional and those of other financial advisors, a comparative review of each reveals the distinct nature of the financial planning profession, the value of financial planning and the value that financial planning professionals bring to client engagements.

All three Canadian professional accounting bodies representing Chartered Accountants, Certified Management Accountants and Certified General Accountants in recent years have released their own competency profiles. Like the Profile for CFP professionals, these documents clarify the expected knowledge, skills, abilities and ethical judgment expected of members of the respective professions they define. By examining these professional profiles together with that of the CFP, we can clearly see the similarities and differences between the financial planning and accounting professions. More importantly, the examination also reveals just how complementary financial planning is to these other professions.

A Professional Is a Professional Is a Professional ...

Intrinsic to specific competencies of the CFP professional are certain fundamental professional skills — judgment, professional practice, communication and cognitive abilities — that are, in many ways, common to all professions. For example, members of all three professional accounting bodies will be entirely familiar with, and already possess, virtually all of the skills identified under these categories. As these skills are what make a true professional, they do not serve to distinguish professional financial planning from accounting; instead, they help to demonstrate, at the highest level, the core skills and abilities common to both professions.

Overlapping Competencies

There exist several other more specific areas of competence that are shared by financial planners and accountants alike. The Financial Planning Competency Profile is divided into six core components: financial management, asset management, risk management, tax planning, retirement planning and estate planning. Of these six components, one — tax planning — stands out as a clearly overlapping set of competencies between the financial planning and accounting professions. Even here however, subtle differences do exist — accountants tend to have a greater focus on corporate taxation, while financial planners focus primarily on personal taxation. Accountants also share some competencies in the areas of retirement planning and financial management. This however is where the competency sets diverge.

What's Different?

While professional accountants are highly competent in tax and finance, they often have little training in many other personal financial matters. While highly competent in taxation, the non-tax issues related to asset management, risk management and estate planning fall well beyond the scope of the requisite competencies of professional accountants. Here is where the complementary nature between these professions begins to clearly emerge.

As the accounting professions grow and expand their core activities — assurance, financial accounting, finance and taxation — acquiring complementary competencies becomes increasingly valuable to the accounting professional. Responding to the needs of their existing clients, accountants are continually seeking new ways of better serving those clients, and adding more value to the engagement.

Consider the needs of the self-employed or small business owner. For these individuals, access to the breadth and depth of expertise available from a professional accountant who has earned CFP certification is invaluable. For this client segment in particular, financial planning and accounting clearly provide a tremendous complement to each other, to the benefit of the client. CFP certification helps accountants extend their expertise with these clients into the areas of asset management, risk management and estate planning. Additionally and more importantly, competence in the fundamental financial planning practices acquired through CFP certification helps accountants to understand and address the integrative nature of all of their clients' financial matters. With their already complementary skills, attainment of additional competencies that are unique to financial planning represents a logical and rewarding extension of the professional accountant's career path.

The complementary nature of the financial planning and accounting professions is one of the reasons all three professional accounting bodies support and endorse CFP certification and continue to be supporting members of the Financial Planners Standards Council (FPSC).

AND WHAT OF OTHER "FINANCIAL ADVISORS"?

The term "Financial Advisor" is often used to describe any and all individuals acting in some advisory or sales capacity within the financial services industry. Some terms — investment advisor, for example — are reserved for individuals licensed by specific regulatory authorities to advise on, or sell, specific types of products. The CFP Professional Competency Profile distinguishes the skills and abilities of a CFP professional from those of other financial advisors, and suggests an important relationship between professional financial planners and these other advisors.

As discussed earlier, competence as a CFP professional cannot be established without the key four professional skill sets — ethical judgement, professional practice skills, communication and cognitive skills. While these competencies are fundamental to financial planning and the accounting professions — in fact all professions — they serve to differentiate the CFP professional from all other financial advisors. Financial advisors may have these skills, but they are not required by their licensing bodies to possess them all. The aggregate of these professional skills are in fact beyond the scope required for proficiency within any financial services regulatory regime.

INTEGRATION MAKES ALL THE DIFFERENCE

While some of the fundamental components of financial planning share the nomenclature of services offered by other financial advisors — many investment advisors cover asset management advice; some insurance advisors deal with risk management and estate planning; some accountants deal with tax and retirement planning; and financial counsellors deal with financial management issues — these advisors are not necessarily competent in dealing with these components together, in an integrated manner, as is required of a professional financial planner. While each of these other advisors has demonstrated, through regulatory licence requirements, his or her qualifications to sell certain products or advise on specific matters generally related to those products, it is the breadth and depth of competencies articulated in the new Financial Planning Competency Profile that establish the unique nature of the financial planning profession and the CFP professional.

The Financial Planning Competency Profile reveals the important connection between regulated advisors and professional financial planners. The Canadian public clearly needs the services of both groups, and these groups clearly overlap.

The CFP professional's role is to develop strategies to help clients better manage their financial affairs, and since many of those strategies will by definition require advice regarding, and the purchase of, one or more financial products, the synergy between regulated product advice and professional financial planning is obvious. As a result, most CFP professionals are also licensed through a securities and/or insurance regulator, and most licensed securities and insurance advisors have either attained CFP certification or are working towards it.

IN SUMMARY

CFP professionals, accountants and other financial advisors with and without CFP certification must work together to assist Canadians in managing their financial affairs. The accounting profession neatly complements the financial planning profession for a distinct market segment. Likewise, financial services regulation must continue to work in concert, not in competition, with the financial planning profession and CFP certification. A clearer understanding of and respect for both the overlap and the differences in the competencies of each advisor group and of the distinctive nature of their skills and services will benefit all stakeholders of the financial services industry.

I invite you to see for yourself how the Financial Planning Competency Profile contributes to that clearer understanding. Visit <www.cfp-ca.org> to review the full Profile.

CHAPTER 22

THE "FEE-ONLY" APPROACH: THE CUTTING EDGE IN THE UNITED STATES — HOW U.S. ADVISORS PROSPER OUTSIDE OF WALL ST. BY PUTTING CLIENTS FIRST

Christopher P. Van Slyke

Overview

This chapter discusses fee-only financial planning. It outlines the main differences between the traditional commissioned financial advisor and the fee-only financial planner. It discusses the benefits of Canadian Public Accountants adopting the fee-only model to financial planning to meet their legal fiduciary duties to clients.

Learning Objectives

By the end of this chapter, you should be able to:

*   have insight into the unique value that fee-only planners create for their wealthy clients and their own practices;

*   learn from the experiences of one of the leading fee-only planners in the United States.

As the founder of Capital Financial Advisors, LLC, a successful and unique wealth management firm headquartered in sunny San Diego, California, I would like to share with you a practice methodology pioneered in the United States that may be highly suitable for use by Canadian Chartered Accountants (CAs).

First, I will give a bit of the history of the financial services industry here in the United States. Traditionally, large Wall Street financial firms have been vertically integrated. That is to say, that they owned the means of production (investment banks) right on through distribution and consumption (your local brokerage office). So, when investors wanted financial advice, they went to the local product company and asked them which product they should buy.

I would like to illustrate the problem with this arrangement by using car dealers as an example. If you go to the Ford dealership and ask the sales representative which car to buy, the sales representative won't tell you about the Toyotas, or even tell you which Ford is right for you. In fact, the sales representative will probably try to sell you the car with the largest profit margin for the dealer. Now, everyone knows this, and would not expect anything different from a car dealer. Well, that's exactly how things are at the large bank-owned brokerage firms here in the United States, where people mistakenly think they are getting a standard of care more akin to clients of a doctor, lawyer or CA.

Stockbrokers are not looking out for investors, though the public often thinks they are. Stockbrokers are trained primarily in sales, not tax, estate planning, debt usage, risk management, investments or retirement planning.

There has to be a better way, and there is. It's called the fee-only model. In 1983 an organization called the National Association of Personal Financial Advisors, or NAPFA, was formed. The following five core principles bound its members together.

- **Competency:** Requiring the highest standards of proficiency in the industry.

- **Comprehensive:** Practising a holistic approach to financial planning.

- **Compensation:** Using a fee-only model that facilitates objective advice.

- **Client-centered:** Committing to a fiduciary relationship that ensures the client's interest is always first.

- **Complete Disclosure:** Providing an explanation of fees and potential conflicts of interest.

The NAPFA business model is particularly well suited for Canadian CAs. For one thing, NAPFA Registered Financial Advisors must act as fiduciaries, and CAs are already acting in this capacity. Fee-only advisors are also prohibited from linking their advice to a product sale via a commission. From what I understand, CAs are prohibited from this practice as well.

Most of the wealth management advice in the United States is given by people who have not been accredited by recognized self-regulating bodies; thus, these people are ill-trained academically, ethically and professionally. The typical broker in a bank or brokerage firm is hired through an ad placed by an employer who requires the broker to have a high school education. The broker's primary skill set would be his or her ability to sell, which is where most of the "training" the broker gets from his or her employer is directed.

The modern fee-only firm requires the Certified Financial Planner (CFP®) designation of anyone giving advice. Contained within the CFP® requirement in the United States is now a minimum Bachelors Degree as well as specific financial planning coursework, 2,000 hours of personal financial planning-related work experience, a comprehensive two-day exam and, once the CFP® designation is earned, the successful completion of 30 hours of Continuing Education every two years. On top of that, NAPFA Registered Advisors double the 30 hours required by the CFP® Board to 60 every two years.

Though today's fee-only wealth managers may not have the golf game of a stockbroker, marketing is much easier because smart clients who are seeking true expertise will find you rather quickly by referral and reputation. You don't have to try too hard to sell people what's good for them. Plus, the firm is very easy to differentiate from the marketplace in its positioning and message.

The CFP® designation also lays the groundwork for true wealth management, which is the additional hallmark of a modern fee-only firm. Because the CFP® designation requires you to master knowledge in estate planning, tax, debt usage, risk management, investment and retirement, transition to a truly comprehensive and, therefore, superior service model is seamless. The vertically integrated product companies pay lip service to integrated comprehensive wealth management but because they don't hire qualified people to give the advice, they get what they hire — product salespeople.

Below is an illustration known as the Comprehensive Wealth Planning Wheel. It includes the services that 21st century financial planning professionals provide to each of their financial planning clients.

Another linchpin underneath the fee-only firm deals with compensation. Most of the industry links compensation to product sales in one way or another. "Do I need insurance?" the consumer asks. "Well, if I want to get paid, I better say yes", thinks the advisor. Even the so-called fee-based accounts offered by U.S. brokerages for asset management are rigged to produce excessive or expensive trading and proprietary product use. Without the fiduciary obligation and its disclosure requirements, this is, of course, not known by investors or their advisors.

We believe that advice must be separated from products for a truly client-centered experience. Therefore, we accept no compensation from anyone other than our clients directly. We receive no income from brokerages, insurance companies, lawyers, or mortgage brokers. We also accept no "soft dollars", which is an industry euphemism for secret non-cash payments such as free trips or brokerage research. Thus, many of the most problematic conflicts of interest involved in wealth management are eliminated. Where conflicts of interest do exist, they are clearly disclosed in writing as a stand-alone document rather than being buried deep in a contract, as is frequently done on Wall Street.

We generally link our fee either to the client's net worth or the client's investment account's value. Using this method, we have two incentives that clients don't seem to mind compensating us for. First, to keep them as clients, we don't use any tricks like propriety products or long-term contracts to make people stay. Thus, we must constantly strive to exceed the expectations of our clients. Second, since our fee is linked to their net worth or investments, we have an incentive to grow wealth so we can increase our pay as a reward.

All of this makes it much easier to act as a legal fiduciary. CAs are already acting in this capacity (as are doctors and lawyers), but most of the financial service industry avoids this status like the plague. Well, of course, if you are not going to hire qualified people and you plan to hide your compensation and agenda, you had better not be a legal fiduciary, right? Fee-only planners take a fiduciary oath and practise as registered investment advisors rather than stockbrokers. Registered investment advisors are fiduciaries by definition. This provides a level of protection and confidence for consumers, as well as creating a loyal trusting client base for advisors.

Though the fee-only model is ostensibly compatible with the business practices and skill sets of CAs, the experience Certified Public Accountants (CPAs) have had in adopting it in the United States has been mixed at best. Although what fee-only planners do looks easy, it must not be, because most CPA firms have had little success in comprehensive wealth management relative to the potential of their wealthy and loyal client bases.

My view is that there are two reasons for this. First, many CPA firms got stockbroker- and insurance-licensed (after pressuring and cajoling, their various professional regulatory bodies such as The American Institute of Certified Public Accountants (AICPA)) and ruined the trust they had built with their clients by giving what is essentially fee-only tax advice for years. As soon as clients saw that the CPAs were really just selling a product, they wanted nothing to do with that kind of relationship and wanted their old fee-only CPA back.

The other reason is that CPAs or Canadian CAs have a different skill set than those of us who come from the asset management and planning industry. Accountants tend be very much about today and yesterday in terms of preparing the tax return. In my experience, accountants are rather forensic as opposed to being forward-looking. Investing and planning take great courage and confidence, and advisors looking to lead clients in this way have a certain personality that is not usually found in accountants. Therefore, in most cases, either accountants in the United States have given up trying to offer comprehensive wealth management or else that financial planning business languishes in unfulfilled potential in its accounting practices.

While our firm has never partnered with an accounting firm, I have presented the idea of partnering to many accountants. It is my belief that rather than trying to do it themselves, the greatest potential for accountants lies in partnering with a fee-only wealth management firm that already has the infrastructure and talent to properly introduce and execute these services for existing CA clients.

In summary, CAs may want to look to the fee-only advice model promulgated by the National Association of Personal Financial Advisors in the United States as they contemplate offering wealth management services to their valued and trusting clients. The model is consistent in every way with the principles already established by CAs. Fee-only advice is fiduciary, involves no commissions and has high professional and educational standards. Furthermore, you need only to look a bit south to see a proven track record and lots of expertise.

CHAPTER 23

BUSINESS EXIT PLANNING & PREPARATIONS — CRITICAL LEGAL CONSIDERATIONS

Jordan Dolgin

Overview

This chapter addresses critical legal issues applicable to the process of "exit planning" for business owners.

    With a greater awareness in these areas, the professional is better equipped to assist his or her client and the client's legal advisors to (1) assess areas of vulnerability which a potential buyer might use to negotiate lower exit transaction values and (2) develop a plan for eliminating or mitigating the impact of such areas of vulnerability and thereby yield higher exit transaction values.

Learning Objectives

By the end of this chapter, you should be able to:

- understand the importance of legal aspects of exit planning preparations;

- identify some of the basic legal investigations necessary to getting organized in order to engage in proper exit planning;

- identify some of the more common business "skeletons" or "value threats" which can impact the exit planning process; and

- better assess the impact of "value threats" to a potential buyer and learn ways to eliminate, manage and/or mitigate their impact on the exit planning process.

INTRODUCTION

To the seasoned professional, any client who is undergoing the exercise of implementing an individual pension plan, retirement compensation arrangement and/or universal life insurance policy is already embarking upon the process of examining ways to extract value from his or her business on a "tax-preferential" basis and "better prepare" for his or her eventual retirement.

In my experience, clients who match this profile are often ready to consider a more holistic approach to a full exit from their business. Exit (or succession) planning will need to be tailored to the individual owner and to the nature of his or her expected or anticipated exit. The nature of the exit will ultimately depend upon the identity of the purchaser of the business.

Generally, there are three primary categories of purchasers to consider in any exit/succession planning exercise:

- family members (whether active or passive in the business);
- key managers/senior employees of the business; or
- a third party purchaser (which may be a strategic buyer such as a competitor or key customer/supplier of the business, or a purely financial buyer such as a private equity fund, merchant bank or angel investor).

GETTING ORGANIZED — WHAT'S IN YOUR CLOSET?

This part will quickly examine certain "places" where lawyers can and should look to assess whether a particular business may have problems or deficiencies which may give a potential buyer a reason to withdraw from negotiations, or ammunition to negotiate lower exit transaction values.

Public Searches

There are a number of publicly available searches which you can undertake against corporations and individuals when it comes to exit planning preparations. The more typical searches fall into the following categories:

- corporate existence/profile
- bankruptcy
- *Personal Property Security Act* (PPSA)

- *Bank Act*
- real property
- executions/court judgments
- litigation

Corporate searches will report on whether a given Canadian federal or provincial corporation has an "active status" and will also identify the subject corporation's current directors, officers, registered office address and a listing of publicly filed documents (such as articles of incorporation, articles of amendment, annual reports, *etc.*). It will be important to review these searches and to confirm that the applicable corporate information is accurate or to rectify any deficiencies. In some cases, this search will indicate that a given corporation's status is in "default" and permit the lawyers to rectify any governmental deficiencies prior to the applicable governmental authority taking any steps to prematurely terminate the corporation's existence or status.

Although hopefully not applicable, it is always desirable to obtain searches against key individuals and corporations to confirm that no filings have been made and that no proceedings either by a party seeking creditor protection or by creditors seeking enforcements of their rights against a given debtor are underway.

PPSA searches (and the equivalent searches in other relevant Canadian provinces or foreign jurisdictions where key business assets are located) will identify secured creditors of relevant corporations and individuals. Hopefully, the results of these searches will only show known current secured creditors, but surprises do sometimes appear. For example, sometimes a creditor who has been paid in full some time ago will continue to appear on this search if the parties forgot to process the necessary discharge before the expiry of the original registration period. Other times, a person may have filed a PPSA registration without the knowledge of your client (this person may be either a disgruntled unsecured creditor who did not get paid or a potential creditor whose deal was not concluded with your client). A potential buyer will obtain PPSA search results against the target business and its individual owners, so you might as well check these databases first and correct any inaccuracies well before your exit negotiations commence.

In Canada, security interests may sometimes be filed/registered by banks under federal banking legislation in addition to filings under the PPSA, and it is important to obtain these results as well to ensure they are accurate.

To the extent that real property (*i.e.*, land and buildings) is proposed to be sold to a potential exit buyer, it would be prudent to obtain full title searches and identify any issues which a buyer may object to or use as a basis to negotiate better exit pricing.

Any buyer will be concerned about existing litigation involving the target business (or its owners) and/or formal judgments obtained against the target business (or its owners). Litigation and execution searches will reveal any pending lawsuits or actual judgments which you and your clients will want to identify long before negotiations with a potential exit buyer commence.

Material Agreements

Every business enters into contracts (of varying degrees of importance) in order to govern its relationship with various key stakeholders, such as shareholders/founders, employees/contractors, customers, suppliers, landlords, equipment lessors and bankers, to name just a few. In the context of exit planning, these various agreements need to be identified, catalogued and reviewed to ascertain their impact, if any, on the exit planning process. For example, do these material contracts contain provisions which give a key stakeholder a right to terminate the contract if its approval is not first obtained prior to any "change of control" or "assignment" to a new party? In other cases, material contracts may not obtain consent or approval requirements, but may merely give a third party some favourable rights to increase prices, extend terms or obtain some benefit (*e.g.*, golden parachute) should a buyer terminate the agreement following the exit, *etc.* In any event, material contracts are clearly an area of critical examination for any client seeking to prepare for an exit transaction.

Note: Special consideration should be made in the case of company obligations under pension or other benefit arrangements. Corporate pension and benefit documentation should be carefully reviewed to ascertain how they may impact exit planning. For example, to what extent might unfunded obligations need to be "topped-up" prior to closing or what hidden charges or benefits might create a future cost to a buyer not otherwise known to it at the time of the exit closing?

Material agreements may also exist at the individual level in the form of personal guarantees which the owners have given to lenders and other key suppliers relating to the business. In such case, it will be important for these personal guarantees to be addressed as part of the exit transaction. Other types of material agreements which involve the individual owners include shareholder loans and corporate-owned insurance policies. A proper exit planning exercise will consider how these agreements need to be addressed with a potential buyer as well.

Apart from restrictions on ownership changes, material agreements should be reviewed from the perspective of "risk allocation". In cases where contractual terms involving customers of the business include limited warranties, liability exclusions and liability limitations, your client may be able to demonstrate fewer "customer skeletons" to a prospective buyer of the business.

Industry-Specific and Other Regulatory Considerations

Certain businesses will need to obtain and maintain key governmental licenses, permits and registrations under industry-specific municipal, provincial and/or federal government legislation. Proper exit planning will involve the identification and listing of these key licences, permits and registrations, and an understanding of any special conditions which a buyer may or may not be able to satisfy and/or whether or not these key licences, permits and registrations may be transferred to a potential buyer. Where a buyer is a competitor of the business, it will likely have its own industry-specific registrations, licences and permits.

Even in cases where there may be no unique industry-specific regulation which imposes any special licensing or permit requirements over the target business, it may be prudent for your client and your client's counsel to consider the impact of other Canadian federal and/or provincial legislation as part of your exit planning preparations. For example, notices and/or approvals from the federal Competition Bureau or Industry Canada under the *Competition Act* (Canada) or *Investment Canada Act* (Canada), respectively, may be required as part of the exit transaction depending upon the size of the deal and the size/residency of the buyer and seller. In the context of an exit structured as an "asset sale", the provisions of Ontario's *Bulk Sales Act* and *Retail Sales Tax Act* (among others) may also need to be considered.

Review of Corporate Records/Minute Books

Although every corporation is required by law to maintain its corporate records on an annual basis, many corporations do not have current and up-to-date minute books and corporate records. As part of any exit planning (and any tax audit planning), corporate minute books should be reviewed by counsel to ensure that the following matters are properly provided for:

- changes in registered office
- changes in board size
- changes in director and officer appointments and resignations
- issuances, redemptions and transfers of shares
- declaration of dividends and bonuses
- shareholder loans and loan security
- approval of material transactions/contracts
- authorization of articles of amendment and name changes
- approval of financial statements
- fixing/changing of fiscal year end
- appointment of accountants/auditors
- shareholder agreement approvals

While most minute book "deficiencies" can be rectified, it is important to identify these well in advance of any exit negotiation, particularly where the exit transaction is likely to take the form of a sale of shares, since the buyer will likely want certain legal opinions relating to share capital which your client's legal counsel may be unable to give unless the minute books are in proper condition and in good standing prior to the closing of the deal.

Review of Existing Corporate Structure

Proper exit planning preparations would not be complete without a thorough examination of the existing corporate structure of the target business and consideration of the various assets which are (or are not) intended to be sold to a potential buyer.

For example, if holding corporations constitute part of the corporate organizational structure, do the shares of the holding corporation need to be sold to the buyer in order to take advantage of any available capital gains exemption to individual sellers? If so, will a buyer likely be prepared to purchase the business at the "holding company" level? The answer is typically "yes", but the seller will need to be responsible for any "skeletons" at both the operating company *and* holding company levels.

Will non-core assets inside the holding company (or the operating company) need to be "cleared out" prior to the sale because they are to be excluded from the sale? If so, what are the tax implications of these purifying transactions?

If the sellers intend to retain key real property (held in a separate company) used by the business and lease that same property to the buyer as part of the deal, has a suitable lease been put in place before closing? If not, this will need to be addressed as part of the exit transaction.

IDENTIFYING SKELETONS — WHAT ARE YOUR "VALUE THREATS"?

This part will review the types of "skeletons" which, in my experience, are somewhat common and which the client's legal and other advisors should pay careful attention to as part of the exit planning process. In practical terms, you should really think of these "skeletons" not merely as unseemly warts or blemishes on the otherwise shiny complexion of the stellar business your client wants to present to a potential buyer, but as "value threats". By "value threats", these skeletons may either cause a buyer to completely abandon the sale process or (more likely) be used by a buyer opportunistically to extract better pricing or other deal terms from your client.

Minute Book Deficiencies

As mentioned above, a review of most corporate minute books will reveal minor (and often major) issues. Some of these problems are simply matters that have not been noted in the corporate records. In any event, they are most often able to be corrected if identified early enough. The area of greatest concern often relates to whether corporate shares have been validly issued, since many exit transactions are structured as share sales. Most buyers' counsel will (time permitting) insist on receive closing legal opinions from the seller's counsel pertaining to corporate existence and other typical minute book matters, so it is important to identify and address minute book deficiencies early in the process.

Asset Ownership and Encumbrances

Where the core value of a business rests with ownership of a key asset or group of assets, any problems with "title" to such asset will cause major issues with your client's buyer. The most obvious example of this is in the area of intellectual property and, in particular, ownership of the copyright subsisting in source code comprising software.

Under Canadian law and absent an express "assignment of title", ownership of the copyright subsisting in computer software remains with the author of the copyright. In the case of employees, the copyright created in the works they author belongs to the employer, but this is not the case with independent contractors. As a matter of practice, where a non-employee individual contractor and/or software development company built all or part of any key proprietary software used in and/or exploited by your client's business, you should ensure that some form of development agreement was signed and/or that intellectual property rights (*i.e.*, copyrights) were assigned from the developer to the owner of the selling company. Otherwise, title issues will likely arise and create significant problems for your client in executing an exit strategy.

Similar "chain of title" issues might exist with other key assets such as real property.

Additionally, as noted above, a review of the public search results might indicate certain "stale" PPSA encumbrances which will need to be discharged given that your client has long since paid off the debts owed to the applicable secured party. In other cases, registrations which were intended to only encumber specific assets (*e.g.*, motor vehicles or leased equipment) may have been filed to broadly cover all of your client's assets. In these cases, a buyer will want to see a letter from such secured parties confirming that their security does not extend to the assets being acquired by the buyer and that they release the buyer from any claims against such assets. Obviously, from a buyer's perspective, any unacceptable asset encumbrances will need to be addressed before closing, and your client will want to avoid any last minute surprises in his or her deal.

Share Capital Ownership Issues

Simply put, who owns your client's company? You are likely tempted to respond by saying "the client". However, consider the following questions:

- Were the legal formalities relating to any historical share redemptions or share purchases followed properly?
- Were any options or similar rights granted to any former employees, contractors or others early on in the evolution of the business?
- Were any creditors granted any rights to convert their debt into shares?

If the answer to any of these questions is "yes", your client may not be the 100% owner of his or her business, and there may be "phantom" owners who may surface during the exit process if you and your client are not careful in your exit planning.

Opportunistic Litigation

There are often a number of historical (or current) third parties who have unresolved disputes with your client and are just looking for some additional leverage to coerce a settlement. The exit process may be the leverage they are looking for. Once word gets out to the trade that your client is engaged in the sale process, all sorts of opportunistic plaintiffs may emerge from the shadows and commence real (or frivolous) litigation or complain to some governmental or regulatory agency.

Examples include:

- former employees or consultants who were granted stock options;
- former employees who were terminated under less than ideal circumstances;
- resentful competitors who have lost significant market share;
- former shareholders who sold out under less than ideal circumstances;
- large customers who may allege "product liability" issues; and
- large suppliers who may threaten to terminate favourable supply contracts.

Tax Audit/Reassessment Issues

One very typical and significant area of exit planning preparations involves assessing audit risk relating to historical income, commodity taxes and source deductions. This can be particularly problematic for businesses that have made extensive use of independent contractors or for businesses that have failed to collect and remit GST or PST. As part of any exit preparations, it would be prudent for the client's tax advisors to review the operations of the business for the past three to four years, as well as tax returns covering the same period, and comment on areas of possible audit risk which a buyer's tax advisors may identify and which may give rise to potential price negotiations.

Product Warranty/Liability Issues

Part of any exit preparations should include an assessment of any isolated and/or widespread issues of product liability and the warranty/insurance-related costs associated with those issues. As noted above, the extent to which customer agreements contain limited warranties, liability exclusions and liability limitations may assist in mitigating the costs of any product liability issues and thereby reduce the impact of these issues in any exit negotiations.

Environmental Issues

Whether your client is a landlord or tenant, environmental risks are becoming more prevalent; therefore, your client should review its operations and the history of the former tenants of the premises it occupies to ascertain whether any environmental contaminants may have been created, generated, used and/or disposed of within or in proximity to such premises during the past ten years. Depending on the facts, a buyer might be expected to ask for copies of any historical environmental audits and/or requisition its own environmental audit. Any negative results of such audit will be used by a buyer to seek price and other concessions from your client; thus, it would be best to discover any environmental issues long before a buyer is at the table.

Contractual Restrictions on Assignments/Changes of Control

As mentioned above, it is critical to identify any material contracts which may be adversely impacted by the completion of a sale of the business. If a buyer's interest is dependent upon, for example, the continuity of long-term customer contracts and/or a key supplier relationship, the cessation of such relationships may be fatal to your exit negotiations.

Regulatory Restrictions on Assignments/Changes of Control

As mentioned above, it is critical to identify any legislative restrictions and/or special conditions attaching to any existing permits, licenses and/or registrations held by the business which are not transferable to the buyer. Unless the buyer has its own licenses and/or can independently obtain them, the inability to transfer key permits to it may be fatal to any exit transaction.

Domestic/Foreign Law Risk

Depending upon the industry in which your client operates, and the nature of its products, services and/or customers, your client's business will be subject to a large number of domestic Canadian federal, provincial and municipal laws of either general or specific application. It will not come as a surprise to you that many businesses are non-compliant with some of these laws (although often it is to a degree which, on balance, will not have a material adverse impact on the business). However, a proper exit planning process should identify any areas or potential areas of non-compliance with general and industry-specific laws. More often than not, your client will be quite familiar with the laws affecting its own industry but less familiar with laws of general application (*e.g.*, provincial consumer protection legislation).

Moreover, many Canadian businesses have some level of foreign business activity. This may be limited to customers that are resident in other provinces or countries or may extend to the existence of employees or agents resident in such jurisdictions and/or some physical or permanent establishment in such jurisdictions. In these cases, the business may have extensive (and often valuable) business activities in such jurisdictions and be unknowingly offside various foreign business and tax laws. In such cases, the possibility of foreign legal risk may provide a buyer of the business with leverage to negotiate favourable price concessions and/or cause it to abort negotiations.

ASSESSING "VALUE THREATS" — SEE WHAT A BUYER SEES

Not every buyer will care about every "skeleton" to the same degree. While it is incumbent upon your client and your client's advisors to undergo the process of identifying potential "value threats" as I have identified above, it may not be practical (or possible) to incur the cost and time necessary to address all of these considerations, especially when the expected exit date is well into the future.

However, if for any given "value threat" your client is able to answer "yes" to any of the following six questions, then chances are that the particular threat should be addressed sooner rather than later:

- **Impact on Title:** Does it affect or impair the very ownership to the assets or shares which a buyer wants to acquire?
- **Nature of the Problem:** Is it a recurring circumstance (as opposed to an isolated or one-time event)?

- **Impact on Key Relationships:** Does it materially impair or threaten the existence of any valuable relationships which the business has with any key customers, suppliers or other stakeholders?

- **Cost to Fix:** Is the cost (in money's worth and time) to rectify the "skeleton" substantial?

- **Business Continuity:** Does it materially impair the ability of a buyer to continue to operate the business following the exit in the same manner in which your client operated the business prior to the exit?

- **Who Should Bear the Risk:** Is it a risk which no buyer is likely to want to assume, and which most buyers will expect a seller to fix or accept responsibility for?

STRATEGIC CONSIDERATIONS AND MANAGING "VALUE THREATS"

In light of the six questions posed above, the following are six basic strategic considerations aimed to assist you in discussing with your clients how to handle some of the "value threats" identified by the exit planning process:

- **Assess Your Negotiating Strength:** If you believe your client has (or will have) superior bargaining strength in the exit negotiations, you may (aggressively) take the position that your client need not address any "skeletons" at this stage, and address them only if necessary after the exit negotiations have commenced.

- **Don't Wait/Start Early:** In the case of any opportunistic litigation which this process identifies, it is often prudent (and less costly) to take steps to negotiate a settlement with the other party long before exit negotiations commence. As you can appreciate, the cost of settling will likely go up once the other party learns that your client is trying to sell the business.

- **Communications and Confidentiality:** Your client needs to take steps to carefully control the exit planning process and avoid leaks wherever possible.

- **Contractual Renewals, Etc.:** To the extent that the planning process has identified any negative contractual provisions which arise in connection with any exit or "change of control", your client should try to negotiate changes (or deletions) to these provisions as part of any contract renewal talks. Obviously, the new agreements which are being negotiated with new stakeholders from time to time should be reviewed carefully by your client's counsel to ensure that unfavourable exit provisions are not included in the final signed copies.

- **Be Proactive:** To the extent that your client is offside any important laws, consider the costs of compliance and implement corrective measures without delay and before these issues lead to litigation or regulatory action. Additionally, if there are any areas of inadvertent non-compliance with tax legislation, your client and your client's tax advisors should consider to what extent applicable tax fairness legislation or voluntary disclosure procedures might be used to reach a lower-cost resolution well before any exit negotiations commence.

- **Fix the Easy Ones First:** Your client may find that, for example, fixing minute book deficiencies and contacting old creditors to discharge stale PPSA registrations may be "low hanging fruit" in the process of implementing exit preparations.

PULLING IT ALL TOGETHER

You and your clients should consider exit planning as part of the other planning exercises undertaken in other parts of this book. Proper exit planning requires the client and the client's key advisors (including legal, tax, accounting, insurance, pension/benefits and financial) to identify key "value threats" to a successful exit, and to develop/execute a strategy to eliminate, manage and/or mitigate those threats for the sole purpose of helping the client to ultimately unlock upon exit the maximum after-tax liquid value from the client's business.

EXIT PLANNING PREPARATIONS — LEGAL CHECKLIST

The following is a non-comprehensive listing of pertinent legal matters to consider in the context of exit planning preparations:

A. Getting Organized — What's in the Closet?
- Obtain public search results
- Review material agreements
- Consider legislative/Regulatory licensing requirements
- Review corporate minute books

- Review corporate structure

B. Identifying Skeletons/Value Threats
- Minute book deficiencies
- Issues affecting asset ownership/Encumbrances
- Share capital ownership issues
- Opportunistic litigants
- Tax audit/Reassessment risk
- Product warranty/Liability issues
- Environmental issues
- Contractual restrictions on assignments/Changes of control
- Regulatory restrictions on assignments/Changes of control

C. Assessing Skeletons/Value Threats
- Consider impact on title to shares/Assets
- What is the nature of the problem — recurring vs. isolated?
- Is there any negative impact on key relationships?
- What is the cost to fix — material vs. *de minimus*?
- Can the business continue "as is"?
- Who should bear the risk?

D: Managing Skeletons/Value Threats — Strategic Considerations
- Assess your negotiating strength — will buyer let it slide?
- Neutralize potential litigants via early settlement
- Loose lips sink ships — preserve exit confidentiality
- Negotiate away third party approvals upon contract renewals
- Be proactive — address legal compliance issues early on
- Fix the easy ones first — begin at the beginning

CHAPTER 24

DEALING WITH POSSIBLE OBJECTIONS AND HOW TO PRESENT THE IPP SOLUTION!

Overview

This chapter serves as a primer for the financial professional to apply the concepts and principles behind value selling the IPP solution to prospective clients.

Learning Objectives

By the end of this chapter, you should be able to:

*   find your market;

*   deal with a prospective IPP client's objections to adopting this solution;

*   handle and neutralize a prospective IPP client's attempt to negotiate on fees;

*   present the IPP solution to a prospect in a way that he or she will see value and take action to receive the value of an IPP now.

FINDING YOUR NEW MARKET

"THE QUOTE", which I have read and heard, even borrowed, hundreds of times during the past two decades while being in the financial industry (and I am sure that if you have ever been to a financial advising training session or conference, or read a book on practice management or investing, you would have heard it, and even used it, yourself) with many variations, goes like this:

> When Willie Sutton the bank robber was asked why he robbed banks, he replied: "Because that's where the money is."

A financial professional who aims to provide financial services to the wealthy must know the fine distinction between someone who is affluent and someone who is wealthy. An affluent individual is a person who has a very good cash-flow statement. A wealthy individual is a person who has a solid net worth statement. Many people in our society confuse affluence and wealth. Great clients have both.

If you decide to be a serious IPP consultant, then there are plenty of hard decisions and tough calls to make, but it is definitely worth the time and effort to chart this course of action. For many financial advisors entering the IPP market, it is a pleasure for them to abandon low-end clients and to, instead, deal with serious clients with serious money to invest for the long haul.

In W. Chan Kim and Renée Mauborgne's book, *Blue Ocean Strategy: How to Create Uncontested Market Space and Make the Competition Irrelevant* (Boston: Harvard Business School Press, 2005), these two authors/consultants use the "blue ocean" metaphor to illustrate to their readers how companies can easily grow their businesses in practically competitor-free environments.

They define "red oceans" as market niches that have been well developed and are overcrowded by predators and competitors. When entering red oceans, you should be mindful that they are bloody and financially dangerous (*i.e.*, launching a new mutual fund company in 2007 in an already overcrowed industry with several thousand funds offered in the Canadian marketplace would be swimming in a red ocean). "Blue oceans" are untapped market spaces with the "opportunity for highly profitable ground-breaking growth for those who have the courage to step forward and take the plunge". Be mindful of the old adage:

> If you do what you have always done, you will always get what you have always gotten.

An advisor who chooses to offer the IPP solution to qualified prospects is one step closer to operating a financial planning practice in the blue ocean. Those advisors already providing IPP services know that they free up more time to develop deeper relationships with top-notch clients, which in turn earn a greater income for the advisor with far less effort.

To succeed in finding one's blue ocean within the IPP marketplace, a financial advisor will have to learn how to qualify the right clients, present the IPP solution and deal with a prospect's objections to implementing the IPP solution.

UNIQUE VALUE PROPOSITION (UVP)

Successful advisors the world over are aware of the unique value they bring to their clients. Each one of us has a unique value proposition to offer to those who have the ability to recognize and appreciate this value. Some people can immediately recognize a unique value proposition and act upon it, while others may not recognize it at first, but, through time and experience, will eventually come to recognize a unique value proposition and then act upon it. Yet others will never see the value in another, no matter how much time passes or how much may be done to prove that value. In our professional lives, many may be called, but a chosen few will be selected to work with the new 21st century financial professional.

This is why it is so imperative to keep in mind that when the new 21st century financial professional markets, what he or she is accomplishing is building a brand in the mind of his or her prospects and clients. In this competitive marketplace, only by building a brand can you differentiate your *unique value proposition* from your competitors. The simplest method to accomplish this is by contracting and narrowing the focus of services that your practice specializes in so that clients and prospects are not confused by what you do, and they know exactly what you do, how your services will benefit them and how to find you.

The difference between a flower and a weed is a judgement. Surround yourself with people who see you as a rose and not a dandelion.

PEOPLE PAY FOR VALUE, KNOW YOUR VALUE

Several years ago a CEO of a very successful multi-million dollar business wanted to redesign his company's logo in order to show the values his company stood behind. He visited over a dozen design studios and none of their design departments could come up with a logo that could express the message he was looking for.

After several months of looking for a design company that could help him, he was directed to a little boutique studio that had a reputation for coming up with design miracles. When the CEO arrived at this studio, he was met by the marketing team. They asked him what he was looking for, and the VP of Marketing said to the CEO that this sounds like a job for George.

At that moment, the VP of Marketing of the studio picked up the phone and called George into the room. George had been the head of the design department at the company for over 20 years. George proceeded to listen for two minutes as the CEO described what he desired the new logo to portray. George thanked the CEO and then proceeded to pull out his sketchpad and draw. At the end of two minutes, George picked up his sketchpad, showed the CEO his design and asked: "Is this what you have been looking for?"

The CEO immediately jumped up and said that it was exactly what he had been looking for all these months. The CEO then asked how much it would cost. George replied $100,000. The CEO gasped and then replied: "That is crazy! I saw with my own two eyes that you only spent two minutes drawing the logo." George turned to the CEO and calmly said: "It took me 20 years to be able to draw the logo in two minutes."

QUALIFY, QUALIFY, QUALIFY

When you provide a service, your main aim should always be to satisfy your client's need. This is why it is so important that the IPP is only presented to prospects and clients that have an inherent need for this solution. Why waste the time of both the prospect and advisor if the prospect has not been properly qualified?

My good friend Ian Baker, FCIA, FSA, Principal at Westcoast Actuaries Inc., has created an IPP Feasibility Study. This study will help the advisor determine whether the IPP prospect should be immediately eliminated or if the IPP prospect merits any further attention. The study asks the following 11 qualifying questions:

1. Does the Employee want a pension from a "Supersized RRSP"?

2. Does the Employer want larger deductions than an RRSP can provide?

3. Do the Employer and Employee want the IPP for the long term?

4. Is the Employee at least age 40?

5. Does a *bona fide* Employer-Employee relationship exist?

6. Does the Employee receive T4 income?

7. Is the Employee willing to follow investment guidelines?

8. Is the Employee willing to have IPP moneys locked in?

9. If the IPP is subject to provincial pension regulation, is the Employer willing to make regular contributions?

10. Is the Employer willing to make additional contributions if a triennial actuarial valuation reveals that investment earnings were less than 7.5% per year?

11. Is the Employer willing to forgo making contributions if a triennial actuarial valuation reveals that investment earnings were more than 7.5% per year?

If the prospect answers "no" to *any* question, then the advisor should simply state that the prospect is not a good candidate for an IPP at this time, and the advisor should move on to the next prospect. If the prospect answers "yes" to *every* question, then the next step is to show the prospect an IPP quotation. Thus, the advisor and prospect's time will be spent most efficiently.

Qualified IPP Prospective Clients and Where to Find Them

In the best selling book *The Millionaire Next Door*, written by Dr. Thomas J. Stanley and Dr. William D. Danko (New York: Pocket Books, 1998), the authors point out the difference between someone of affluence and someone who is wealthy. As mentioned earlier in this chapter, an affluent individual makes a great income and has a solid cash flow; however, individuals may spend more than they make and, therefore, their net worth is often very low. A wealthy individual has assets and saves more than he or she earns. Often advisors confuse affluent and wealthy individuals, but there is a difference, which must be understood by the 21st century financial consultant. Dr. Stanley and Dr. Danko describe the typical millionaire who lives next door as follows:

- Male, age 57, is married to his first spouse, with an average of three children.
- Two-thirds are self-employed business owners or professionals.
- Total average realized household income is $131,000 per year.
- Average household net worth including all personal and business assets is $3.7 million.
- On average, typical millionaires realize less than 7% of their wealth as their income. Hence they live well below their means.
- They live in neighbourhoods where they are outnumbered three to one by families that are not millionaires.
- They are extremely busy, spending between 45 and 55 hours per week working.
- They save and invest 20% or more of their household's income per year.
- They only hold about 20% of their family's wealth in publicly traded securities.

- Their most trusted advisors are their accountants, lawyers and financial planners. They overwhelmingly recommend that their children go into these professions to serve the wealthy like themselves.

SOME TIPS ON PRESENTING THE IPP SOLUTION TO QUALIFIED PROSPECTS

It is very important to understand that when communicating with a qualified prospect, our focus is not just on what we are saying; we should also be focused on how we are saying what we are saying. Our intended response from our prospects and clients is the sole purpose of our sales presentations. The quality of an IPP presentation is an inverse function of its length.

No one in the financial planning business ever became a great communicator of anything until he or she learned to transcend the facts of what is being sold and speak to the real needs of a prospect or client. Never state the attributes of the IPP in terms of what it is not.

The act of practising to perfect an IPP sales presentation is more important than all the sales training in the world, or, for that matter, the material contained within the pages of this book. An IPP sale is only made after the Q&A is done and you have gained conceptual agreement with the client that the IPP solution is best for him or her. Without this, the IPP for any client will not be maintainable and sustainable. Remember, there is no such thing as failure in the game of life; there is only feedback. Practice, practice and more practice equals success!

DEALING WITH POSSIBLE OBJECTIONS

Many prospects may believe that the cost of setting up an IPP is too expensive. Fees are often considered to be too high because the financial advisor presenting the IPP solution has not established an adequate matrix showing prospective IPP clients the cost they will incur if they do not set up an IPP. By that I mean a client has not been properly "educated" about the true savings being derived/generated. So the true worth of the IPP is not accurately understood. Consequently, the prospective client cannot possibly make a reasonable return-on-investment calculation, because the client does not truly understand the total return on his or her IPP investment.

I learned this first hand when I first began presenting the IPP solution many years ago. The cost of setting up an IPP was approximately $5,000, compared to having a self-directed RRSP with trust fees that ranged from $0 to $250 yearly. I quickly learned that I had to show the clients with their own numbers what the true short- and long-term costs would be if they did not implement the IPP solution, and use those same numbers to illustrate what the true benefit was going to be.

If prospective IPP clients say that implementing the IPP solution is too costly, it is best to immediately turn their resistance into a question about their perceptions of what constitutes value. Most financial advisors presenting the IPP solution today fall into the trap of focusing on the clients' reluctance to spend, rather than on their inability to see long-term value. Qualified clients may initially say no to the IPP solution for the following three reasons:

One: The perception of value by the prospect is too small, and the financial advisor has to re-educate the prospect about the true benefits. The prospect may be thinking in terms of one year, although the savings will be gained indefinitely.

Two: The urgency for the prospect is not sufficient enough to take action now. The prospect may believe that living with his or her current retirement vehicles is satisfactory. The financial advisor must be able to demonstrate that the prospect's retirement options are deteriorating and that every passing day causes more lost opportunity to save on taxes and compound more dollars in a tax-effective way for retirement.

Three: Say goodbye to discounts and special offers. The prospect appreciates the value of the IPP solution but wants to see if the financial advisor can be moved on fees because other people have been, or the prospect is simply a natural bargainer. If the financial advisor allows his or her fees to be moved, they will be.

Remember, successful business people know that the key component of cost-effectiveness is value. And if the prospective IPP client does not perceive value in your product or service, the lowest price for setting up and maintaining the IPP solution will mean nothing to them.

HOW TO PRESENT THE TRUE INTRINSIC VALUE OF THE IPP SOLUTION

When you present the IPP concept, the opening statement about this solution should define the client's core financial need. Articulating the IPP concept is the one critical and indispensable way to begin any IPP presentation. The IPP concept must be presented and seen as the solution to the client's problems. Always come to an agreement with the client that the need you are addressing is indeed his or her actual need. For example, the client is looking for a solution to reduce corporate taxable income and defer moneys for retirement in a tax-effective way.

Always stress to prospective clients what the IPP solution will do for them. By letting clients know what the IPP will do for them in achieving their financial goals you are presuming acceptance of the IPP solution by the client. If the prospect is properly qualified the IPP sales process is almost completed.

If the clients desire to know, share with them how the IPP works. In more cases than not the only people who want to know how the IPP works are the clients' public accountants. When you take your car to get fixed you want to know that you can trust your mechanic and that your car will start and go from point A to B without any trouble. Very few people actually want to know the inner workings of their automobiles and 99% of the time this is as true for their IPPs. What IPP prospects and clients want to know is that the IPP is sanctioned by Canada Revenue Agency (CRA) and that if they use you and your firm to implement and maintain the plan, that everything will run smoothly without a hitch.

Always go on the offensive in raising the issue of risk and limitations of the IPP solution. Don't be scared of telling your prospects and clients the risks and limitations of the IPP solution as you are closing your presentation. The limitations that are associated with the IPP solution were presented in detail in Chapter 2. By being honest with prospects and clients and sharing with them what the risks and limitations of the IPP are, prospects and clients will begin to see you as not just another sales person painting only the best-case scenarios. You will be seen as someone they can trust and want to do business with for a long, long time.

The key to becoming successful in the IPP marketplace is to always focus on the long-term value that the IPP solution will bring to the client. Focusing on output rather than input sounds simple, but you must have the confidence to approach selling the IPP solution in this way.

Lead clients to think in terms of the end by emphasizing, for example, how much more money the clients will have in their pockets at the end of 10, 15, 20 and even 40 years after they have implemented the IPP solution. By learning how to show clients how much greater their tax savings and tax deferral income will be if they opt for the IPP solution, you give the clients reason to act now rather than later.

The best way to get potential IPP prospects' attention is to speak in terms of the economic language they understand best, that of the bottom line and the impact of implementing or not implementing the IPP solution will have on their corporate bottom line and their retirement income.

In essence this converts buying reasons (emotion) into dollar-sized justifications, allowing the client to see in terms of Return on Investment (ROI). Successful advisors in the IPP market know how to move an IPP prospective client's attention to the outcomes of the IPP engagement and the impact the results will have on a company's long-term business plan and the IPP member's retirement plan. This avoids the task and commodity concerns and instead puts the focus on the results, which are near and dear to the IPP prospective plan sponsors' and plan members' hearts.

If a prospective IPP client is only certain of the cost of implementing the IPP solution but has a vague idea about the end results, the prospect may inevitably tip toward a lesser type of retirement plan such as the traditional RRSP, which would clearly be an outdated option for the properly qualified prospect to take. Consequently, it is incumbent upon the financial advisor to provide the client with the proper matrix with which to measure the IPP solution's results and convert those results into a calculable return on investment specific to the prospect's situation.

There are two types of metrics a financial advisor must prepare before attempting to achieve conceptual agreement with a prospect. These will empower the prospect to agree to implement the IPP solution:

1. *Short-term measures.* This includes the immediate savings that are generated when the IPP solution is created.

2. *Long-term measures.* This includes showing how much the prospective IPP client would be better off over the long term had he or she adopted the IPP solution.

Here is how to put these concepts to use.

Imagine you are presenting the IPP solution to a 55-year-old client named John Doe, who has owned an incorporated business since 1991 and has a T4 income of more than $100,000 and a marginal tax rate in Ontario of 46%. This client is serious about saving for his retirement during the next ten years. When he reaches 65 years of age, he plans to retire, and he is properly qualified for the IPP solution.

Step 1: When presenting the IPP solution to this client, you should show him the immediate short-term benefits created by implementing the IPP, which include a $161,851 deduction for his company and a non-taxable benefit for himself. Explain how this money will then compound tax-free within the IPP until it is withdrawn.

Step 2: Show how in the following year John Doe's company will be able to contribute on his behalf into his IPP $27,934, and these contributions will increase by 7.5% annually until he retires (the investment mix in his IPP earns 7.5%).

Step 3: Conclude this portion of your presentation by showing John Doe that when he reaches 65, he will have accumulated $815,583 in his IPP to provide him with pension benefits.

Step 4: Next, show John Doe how his situation would look different if he had chosen not to follow your recommendation to create an IPP for himself. This is called "lost opportunities!" Prepare an example of what his financials would look like if he had taken the same amount of money out of his company, after having paid his personal marginal tax rate of 46%. Then place what was left over into a non-registered investment earmarked for his retirement savings.

The first year after taxes, John Doe would be left with $87,400 to invest for his retirement. The following year, after taxes, he would make a $15,084 contribution to his non-registered retirement investment. His contributions into this plan would grow at 7.5% (the investment mix in his non-registered portfolio earns 7.5% and all growth of these investments are taxed at 46%).

Step 5: Show the client that had he opted for the non-IPP strategy at age 65, he would have only accumulated $351,113.

Step 6: Show the client that had he taken your recommendation to set up an IPP today, at retirement, based on the stated assumptions, he would have saved $464,470 more in retirement savings than he would have by investing in the non-registered investment.

Below is a table that shows the accumulated savings that the business owner in the example would have by opting to implement the IPP solution over not implementing the IPP solution.

Registered IPP Investments vs. Non-registered Investments Table

Years	IPP Annual Deposit (annually increase by 7.5%)	IPP Balance at the end of year (growth rate of 7.5%)	Non-Registered Investment Annual Deposit (annually increase by 7.5%)	Non-Registered Balance at end of year (growth rate of 7.5%)	Accumulated difference at the end of IPP year period
1	$161,851	$173,990	$87,400	$90,910	$74,451
2	$27,934	$217,068	$15,084	$110,250	$106,818
3	$30,029	$265,629	$16,216	$131,544	$134,085
4	$32,281	$320,254	$17,432	$154,958	$165,296
5	$34,702	$381,577	$18,739	$180,672	$200,905
6	$37,305	$450,298	$20,145	$208,881	$241,417
7	$40,103	$527,181	$21,656	$239,794	$287,387
8	$43,110	$613,063	$23,280	$273,637	$339,426
9	$46,344	$708,863	$25,026	$310,656	$398,207
10	$49,819	$815,583	$26,903	$351,113	$464,470

After you have presented these two scenarios to a qualified prospective client, and he or she still doesn't take action to implement the IPP solution, all I can recommend to you at this point is to quote Oscar Wilde when he said:

The definition of a cynic: "*A man who knows the price of everything and the value of nothing ...*"

And if that doesn't work, begin saying the "Serenity Prayer" by Reinhold Niebuhr (1892-1971):

God grant me the serenity to accept the things I cannot change; courage to change the things I can; and wisdom to know the difference.

CHAPTER 25

DELIVERING EFFECTIVE IPP SEMINARS

Overview

This chapter discusses the benefits of giving IPP seminars and the strategies to become an effective IPP seminar presenter. Learn how to gain IPP clients by giving excellent presentations. Understand the power you have been given with your gift of speech.

Learning Objectives

By the end of this chapter, you should be able to:

- understand the value of becoming an effective public speaker to help grow your practice;
- learn the lessons to deliver effective IPP Seminars;
- learn the strategies to turn public speaking engagements into consulting opportunities;
- understand the power of our speech.

THE VALUE OF EFFECTIVE PUBLIC SPEAKING

Becoming a good public speaker is easier said than done. It has been said that many people at a funeral would rather be in the casket than delivering the eulogy!

When I first entered my career in the financial service industry in the early 1990s, I lucked upon a book on successful marketing strategies for the financial service industry, which quickly became my Bible. One of its main tenets to achieving success as an advisor was to commit oneself to developing the art of delivering powerful and effective presentations.

These words have always resonated in my mind and have been my catalysis for wanting to learn how to speak comfortably in front of large groups and effectively communicate my message on whatever the topic might be at the time. During my journey over the last 15 years, I have been fortunate to have had the opportunity to deliverer over 400 work-shops and seminars and teach in the Certified Financial Planning (CFP™), Certified Employee Benefit Specialist (CEBS), Certified Human Re-sources Professional (CHRP) and Certified General Accountant (CGA) designation programs. What I would like to share in this chapter are some of the lessons I have learned about public speaking to help you on your own journey. If you choose to become an effective public speaker, you will learn how IPP presentations can help you tap into IPP business opportunities when delivering seminars to potential IPP clients and centres of influences.

HOW TO DELIVER AN EFFECTIVE IPP SEMINAR

Lesson One: You need to find your own style, and your own "voice", in a safe place, where you feel comfortable enough to practise. You can't copy someone else's style — it won't work for you. Lee Glickstein, a public-speaking guru in California, writes of "learning circles" in his book *Be Heard Now* (New York: Broadway Books, 1999). Learning circles are groups of people who meet in a supported environment to help each other find their own voice and become effective public speakers. Toastmaster's clubs also provide a good public forum and evaluation to help sharpen your skills. By just reading this chapter you will never become a great public speaker. There is no getting around practising the craft of public speaking. You have to get up and, as the Nike ad says, "Just do it!"

Lesson Two: You need to learn how to "read" your audience, and break through to the crowd. You do this by making connections with individu-als, not by looking at the group as a whole. In every audience, there are people who are really supportive, and you should make eye contact with them. Speak as if you are speaking to them directly and having a per-sonal conversation. These sympathetic listeners, these supportive people, will draw in the other members of your audience with their enthusiasm and interest. These chosen members of your audience will help you win over your entire audience. Try it the next time you get up and speak and I promise it will work miracles for you.

Lesson Three: When speaking, introduce yourself and tell a story about why you are there talking to them (how you came to be knowledgeable in your field, what you have learned and what you have to share with your audience today). That has to be communicated to your audience. At the very least, they want to be entertained, and they want you to succeed with your speech. It doesn't work when the speech is top-down, with you as the only person in the know. Remember, if people show up, it's because they want to hear your message. People want to feel connected, and as a speaker you need to learn to speak with your audiences and not at them.

Lesson Four: As a speaker, you need to be comfortable with the silences and pauses. It took me a long time to learn that when it is really quiet when I am speaking, this silence means that my audience is interested in what I have to say. I learned that when I heard noise from my audience while I was speaking, that meant I did not have the audience's full attention. It can get scary and unnerving when there is silence and you are the focal point of that silence. That can be the time that you begin to panic, get lost and forget what you want to say. I know it first hand. It has happened to me more than I want to recall. During those times I have trained myself to smile and look for a supportive face in the audience to encourage me to go onto my next thought.

Lesson Five: If you find yourself using "ums" and "aws", try to begin using "and" as a connector and an attention-getter instead. The word "and" allows you to transition effortlessly and smoothly from one thought to the next without missing a beat.

Lesson Six: I have learned that many of us, myself included, can't make people laugh at what we are saying, but we can allow them to find areas in our speeches to laugh at. This is done by making a statement and taking a pause. We may not have intended for something we said to be funny, but our audience might be laughing off their seats from what we have just said. Remember, the power of our pauses allows our audiences to participate and mentally catch up to us while we are making our IPP presentations.

Lesson Seven: Always keep your end in mind. You need to know what it is that you intend to communicate with your audience, and not be committed to a specific route to accomplishing your desired outcome. What if you are interrupted or the technology doesn't work for you? What then? You have to keep your presentation focused on the subject, in the room and on your message. By no means do I mean that you should not be committed to a proven process. When presenting many short IPP seminars I have always found it most effective to follow my own universal process to present seminars.

Lesson Eight: Last, and most important, is that when you are speaking to your audience about IPPs, or about any other subject for that matter, what you are selling is not your information, but the convictions that you have about your information and about your solutions, and, finally, you are selling yourself!

HOW TO GAIN IPP CLIENTS BY PUBLIC SPEAKING

Many times I have walked off the stage after delivering a speech for a little over an hour to a group of small business owners and their public accountants, and as soon as I have reached the bottom of the stage, a business owner has grabbed me and said, "I need to hire you now! Please let me call you later this week." The last time this happened I was asked to assist with the succession planning for a $25 million family-owned business.

From the very beginning of my career in the financial service industry I have always believed that professional teaching and speaking, apart from being lucrative in its own right, is the best method to gain access to extraordinary clients, and leads to very stimulating work. Below I have listed five strategies I have personally adopted to establish the environment of turning speaking engagements into lucrative financial consulting contracts. I would like to share them with you now.

Strategy One: Meet the Head Honcho

Always make it a point to meet the top person or people at the event to ensure that their objectives will be met, and to begin your formal relationship with them. Do not deal exclusively with the Public Accountant, CFO, HR professional or the workshop organizer, even if those are the people making the hiring decision.

Strategy Two: Make Sure and Do Your Homework

Find out about the organization and people you are making your presentation to. Learn as much about their history, business models, their people and all the pertinent information that you can gather before you make your speech. This research will empower you to make your speech relevant to your audience and future clientele. Great places to find this key information are corporate and association Web sites.

The best Web site to find information on key individuals on the Internet today is at <www.zoominfo.com>. This Web site has collected comprehensive information on over 32 million business professionals and 2 million companies across the globe in every industry imaginable. Best of all, this information is free. Another great Web site to gather quick information about financial topics that affect Canadians is <www.professionalreferrals.ca>.

Strategy Three: Know Your Audience

Ask the organizer of the event at which you will be speaking for permission to call several of the key individuals who will be attending. This strategy allows you to learn first hand the perspective of key people who will attend your talk, and the outcome they would like to achieve by listening to you. This allows you to prepare your presentation to create the greatest impact on your audience; that, in turn, will dramatically increase your ability to turn a speaking engagement into lucrative financial consulting work.

Strategy Four: Make the Call to Take Action, and Make Your Audience Know That You Are a Part of Their Solution

Describe the specific techniques, behaviour changes, new knowledge, new procedures or whatever is necessary for the group to make dramatic progress. Make it very clear that you have the specific experience in the area that you are talking about to assist them in accomplishing the needed transition.

Strategy Five: Always Follow Up

Bill Gates, founder of Microsoft, and author of *The New York Times'* bestseller *The Road Ahead* (New York: Penguin Books, 1996), states at the beginning of his book: "… we always overestimate the present and always underestimate the future." Not every time you make a presentation will it immediately turn into other business; have patience and opportunities will flow your way. Our lives might not change immediately as we hoped but when they do change, these changes are grander than we could ever have imagined.

Send either a letter or e-mail within a few days after your presentation to key people who were at the speaking venue. In these correspondences share your perspective on what was accomplished, and provide recommendations and suggestions on what can be done next to gain greater results. Let them know that you are available by offering your assistance both formally and informally.

Remember that public speaking is not for the weak at heart. Building public speaking muscles is only for those financial professionals who want to stand out above the crowd and be counted.

LAST THOUGHTS ON THE POWER OF OUR SPEECH

Each of us has been given a powerful gift. Every time we use this gift properly, we are showing an active display of our appreciation of this gift. Human beings were given three abilities that differentiate them from the rest of the animal kingdom — that of speech, a highly developed intelligence and the ability to tell a story.

Speech is not only unique to humans, but it is what makes us unique. While other animals on this planet possess some form of intelligence, only human beings have the ability to understand and analyze what is happening in the world around them and keep a distinct sense of self.

Our speech gives each of us tools to break down barriers and to connect us with others and to create and maintain relationships in a meaningful way. What differentiates us from other animals is our ability to express our thoughts, wants, emotions and insights with our language. Our language empowers us to bind time with others by sharing our experiences and insights, enabling others to learn from us without directly experiencing what we have shared with our words.

We should always be mindful that once we have said something out loud, our words bring about change in ourselves, others and the world as a whole. We should always remember these wise words attributed to Frank Outlaw, the founder of the supermarket chain BI-LO:

> Watch your thoughts; they become words.
> Watch yours words; they become actions.
> Watch your actions; they become habits.
> Watch your habits; they become character.
> Watch your character; it becomes your destiny.

Why is this so? In reality nothing has changed, yet the act of speaking has the power of changing how we feel, what we think and how we act in the world. Just saying something has the power of changing our world and changing the realities of those who hear our words. Speech then does create reality. It effects connections between ourselves, between one person and another, and our environment.

It is very important to understand that we, as thinking and speaking human beings, use little stories called metaphors to present suggestions and ideas to the unconscious minds of others. In hypnosis, this is a practitioner's most powerful and effective tool to cause change in his or her patients. A full acknowledgement of this power requires that the user of this tool accept all of the responsibilities that come from the understanding that our words and intent do bypass our listener's conscious mind. Thus, our words have the power to affect and change another's worldview forever. With this said, then, there is very little truth behind the old saying:

"Sticks and stones might break my bones but names will never hurt me!"

The word metaphor comes from the ancient Greek word "meta", which in the English translation refers to "a transfer of meaning from one thing to another". We use metaphors and symbolism to paint the picture of our communication for our listeners to derive meaning from our experiences so that they can interpret our meaning without us having to explain in literal terms, for example, an IPP is like an RRSP on steroids.

To make your audience understand and remember who you are, give them a visual, whether by invoking a strong image or by teasing out a scenario. The more abstract your service, the more technical or foreign your business, and the more imperative it is that you *anchor* your description in visual language.

The metaphor I prefer to use to describe my company's expertise is the following:

"At MerrickWealth.com we are financial planning and executive benefit architects for today's successful business owner."

What this metaphor implies to the listener is that those other people offering financial planning services are likened to carpenters and electricians: they are specialists in specific areas but are not skilled in putting it all together for what a successful business owner needs from a properly executed plan. That the building and selling of a business needs a specialist in design, implementation and management is something that everyone can envision, and that's the key to a positioning metaphor.

The use of our properly structured metaphors allows our families, our clients, our audiences, our professional colleges and our communities to come to their own interpretations and make similar connections from our metaphors to their own beliefs, values and circumstances. Our metaphors allow our listeners to come to their own understanding at their own level. This is accomplished by comparing unfamiliar facts with something simple the listener already knows. People learn more rapidly when the information relates to their own experiences.

Using metaphors and analogies in the financial planning industry allows us to distinguish ourselves in our listener's mind. A good analogy or metaphor can quickly anchor products and people into a prospect's or client's mind forever.

The power of our words should be very intimidating. One of my father's, Marvin S. Merrick's, lasting legacies to me that I would like to share with you now is the following wisdom:

"Once something is said, it cannot be taken back; it is nearly impossible to erase its effects."

Thus, we must invest the time to train ourselves to think before we speak. We ought to speak words that are properly motivated, that are directed, purposeful and well thought out.

Prior to speaking, we need to have the right intentions, have evaluated whether it is an appropriate time to speak and be sure that we are being sensitive to our audience. Our words need to be sincere. People sense the truth. They know whether a speaker speaks from self-interest or for the greater good. Words spoken from the heart will enter the heart.

"You must be the change you want to see in the world."

Mahatma Gandhi

CHAPTER 26

THE "WRITE" WAY TO DEFY GRAVITY AND MOVE YOUR FINANCIAL CONSULTING PRACTICE TO THE TOP

David Leonhardt

Overview

This chapter discusses how to create credibility through writing articles and books and how to successfully court media attention to grow your financial consulting practice.

Learning Objectives

By the end of this chapter, you should be able to:

- understand the pyramid to build credibility in prospects, clients, trusted advisors, colleagues and the public minds;

- understand how becoming a writer of articles and books will empower your financial consulting practice;

- learn how to successfully court the public media to grow your financial consulting practice.

THE PUBLIC CREDIBILITY PYRAMID

There is a hierarchy of public credibility that defies logic. If you are interested in logic, the next few paragraphs will provide you with endless fodder for philosophical debates. If, on the other hand, you are interested in expanding your IPP business, the next few paragraphs will provide you with endless fodder for moving up, defying not just logic but gravity.

The hierarchy begins at the bottom. The base of the pyramid is seeing your ad. If you place an ad, many people will see it, but few will call. Just above that base is receiving a cold call, which is not all that different from seeing an ad, except that there is a real human being and the opportunity to ask a question or two.

It's at the next level that gravity starts to act funny, where people hear you at a seminar. I'll go into what is funny about that in a moment. After that comes reading your article, and just above that, reading your book. We are still defying gravity, and increasingly defying logic, as we move up the pyramid.

The pinnacle of the pyramid is the media. Seeing your name quoted in a newspaper gives you superb credibility, and seeing your face on TV gives you the most. It's not for nothing that some marketers run infomercials just so they can put the "as seen on TV" moniker in their print ads.

Before giving you the information you need to make this hierarchy work for you, I suspect you want to know why this order defies logic. As with most of the sales process, and you are probably already aware of this, it is all about psychology.

Public speaking gives you more credibility than a cold call, even if the audience did not know you were going to be the speaker. Why? Because there is an assumption of credibility. Anyone can pick up the phone and call you, or place an ad, but not anyone can convince someone to let you speak. Even if it is your own seminar, the credibility of speaking over a cold call or an ad defies all logic.

One step up the pyramid, reading your article, a prospective client assumes that you had to go through a certain triage to get that article printed. So even if you typeset the article yourself and have it reprinted so that it resembles a magazine article, your credibility rises with the article. Why this defies logic is that you cannot be untruthful in an ad or in a cold call, any more than you can in an article, but logic has nothing to do with it.

A book carries more weight than an article, no pun intended. Somehow being a published author is more credible than being merely a published writer. It doesn't matter if you self-publish, an author is more of an expert than a cold-caller. Period.

But the ultimate expert status is conveyed upon those who appear in the media, particularly television, which acts as the great filter of truth. Never mind that everybody says, and knows, that you can't trust everything you see on TV or read in the news; we all believe it anyway. Yes, after hundreds of media interviews on several dozen topics, from weekly local reporters to national news anchors, I can tell you that what really happens, and how much of the true story gets into the media, varies immensely from broadcast to broadcast or from article to article.

Yet, in the absence of other information, I assume that what I read or see is true. My knowledge does not interfere with my psychology, and it won't interfere with your target market's psychology, either.

Your mission to build credibility with wealthy clients is to get into the media when you can. And when you can't, hand them in person the ultimate calling card: your book. Business cards are a dime a dozen, almost literally. Hand your book to a prospective wealthy client and/or their trusted advisors, and offer to autograph it. Watch your sales conversion rate rise.

HOW TO WRITE A BOOK

Even if you can't write, you can be an author and a highly credible one. The first step is to come up with an idea. What special aspects of financial planning and taxation will your book be about? It needs to be more than just a run-of-the-mill how-to manual. It needs to be a little different. Put your personality into it. If you can make it visionary, you strike gold. Why? Because your wealthy clients count on you to do more than just understand the current regulations and landscape. They want you to ensure they are positioned well as the regulations and landscape change.

The next step is to organize your thoughts. Are you having problems doing this? Get a freelance editor to coach you. As the head of a freelance writer/editor agency, I can tell you that there are many brilliant people who cannot organize their thoughts for a book or an article — even if they can deliver superb reports to clients and dazzling sales pitches to prospects.

The next step, which is very important in any sector, such as in the financial service industry, where regulations prohibit hiring a ghost-writer, is to write. Never mind whether you can spell. Never mind whether English is your first language or your twenty-first. Never mind if you feel insecure about writing. Just write.

If you happen to be a brilliant writer, you might be able to write your whole book. If not, that's where a freelance editor comes in. If your book is reasonably well written to start with, any competent editor will do. If your writing is really poor, you will need an editor with writing experience.

What the editor will need is at least 25,000 words of the main ideas you want to get across. An editor can bulk it up and make it read well, but the editor cannot add any information that by regulation must be written in your own words. Make sure the editor understands the boundaries of the regulations within the financial industries.

When your manuscript is complete, go to any printer who specializes in books. These printers can arrange for cover art and typesetting. Ask first to see three samples of books they have recently printed. It is absolutely important that the artwork look professional and that the print quality is impeccable. More prospective clients will judge your credibility on the quality of the printing firm you hire. Defies logic, right? Well, if you can't even choose a good printer, how can these potential clients expect you to assist them with their finances?

If a whole book is not in the cards, a quicker and less expensive route is to have a feature-length article prepared. Again, the same principles apply to the writing, although only about 800 words need to be written for a 1,600-word article. "Copies" of the article should be printed on full-colour, two-sided glossy paper, just as if they were printed for insertion in a magazine. Staple the sheets together and slip them into your information folder for each prospective client.

HOW TO GET IN THE MEDIA

Much harder than becoming a published author is to become a media spokesperson. Where do you get the credibility with the media? Where do you start? Hint: it does not involve writing a news release. The first step is to identify the media venues you want to or think you can get quoted in. Think long term. If you are thinking about getting quoted next week, you have already lost the battle.

Next, find out who controls the news. It is usually not the on-air personality, but rather a producer. At a newspaper it might be the assignment editor or the specific reporter whose byline you see.

Follow their work religiously. Whenever they report on a topic you feel falls within your scope of expertise, write a short note. The note should not be critical. It should always be helpful. For instance, if the reporter missed some basic information, rather than criticize the piece's lack of depth, offer to share some additional information that could help with future stories.

Suggest a meeting, especially if that gives you the chance to pass along a copy of your book.

It might take several meetings, but after a while you will be seen as a good source to quote or interview on financial planning or related topics. Of course, it might lead to nothing. Getting into the news is about building relationships — friendly relationships, true, but most of all, professional relationships, based on the journalist deciding that you are a credible source of information. If a journalist doesn't like the colour of your hair, and that stands in the way of a relationship, there is very little you can do. Similarly, if journalists already have a good source they like to call on, there is very little you can do. But if the opportunity is there, it is up to you to forge that relationship.

So you can defy gravity, along with people's logic, by moving up in the hierarchy of credibility. For obvious reasons, the higher you climb, the harder you have to work to get there. Maybe getting your face on national TV will not bring the ROI you wish. At least consider how far up the ladder you want to climb — speaking at seminars, writing articles or books, being interviewed for newspaper or TV — defying logic and gravity and increasing your business.

CHAPTER 27

THE THREE RETIREMENTS

Gilles R. Marceau

Overview

In this chapter, you will learn about the three stages of retirement.

Learning Objectives

By the end of this chapter, you should be able to:

* understand the three stages of retirement and learn how to integrate the Individual Pension Plan, retirement compensation arrangement and Health and Welfare Trust to optimize an individual's gold years.

Most self-employed professionals and business owners in their mid- to late 50s concern themselves with providing retirement income during their lifetime. And with a third of their lives still left to live, many are beginning to realize their needs are different as they think about the various stages of life they will transition to, be it semi-retirement, full retirement, or retirement at the end of their lives.

We call these stages "the three retirements".

FIRST RETIREMENT — SEMI-RETIREMENT

The *First Retirement* encompasses trading "at work time" to "do the other things I want to accomplish in my life". At this point, the driving force is not money but internalized feelings of accomplishing other goals in one's life.

For the most part, our culture defines its members by what they do, not by who they are. Our identities are often dependent upon our occupations and/or what we own. "Being" rather than "doing" must become the primary focus of our lives in order to enjoy this stage of retirement. The

First Retirement is all about the transition to "being". This means that true wealth is time!

This may mean you need to find tax-effective ways in which to bridge the income gap without using those assets required to support a longer-term income stream when full retirement arrives. More on this later!

The Retirement Compensation Arrangement — The Unknown Tax Strategy

The retirement compensation arrangement (RCA) gives the business the opportunity to achieve maximum tax relief while maximizing the owner's retirement income. As importantly, the income stream can be matched on a year-by-year basis to the owner's personal requirements.

RCAs were introduced by the Department of Finance as an unregistered supplemental retirement plan established by a company to provide additional retirement benefits beyond that provided through a Registered Retirement Savings Plan/Deferred Profit Sharing Plan and/or through a Registered Pension Plan.

Statistics Canada in its January 1, 2003 research paper entitled "Pension Plans in Canada" identified that from a modest start in 1991 (249 trusts and $200 million in assets) the value of RCAs as of the end of 2001 grew to 2,051 trusts with $5.3 billion in assets.

Contributions were nearly $1.1 billion in 2001, with the total number of potential beneficiaries at about 12,000 persons in 2001.

RCAs are very flexible in that:

- The funding of the RCA can be tied into the company's accomplishment of corporate profitability, thereby enabling the company to make RCA contributions when the funds have been earned. Such funding is tax-deductible for the company in the year the contribution is made.

- A business owner or self-employed professional who started the company/practice 30 years ago and incorporated only in 2006 can obtain service for every year he or she has been in the business/practice.

- There are no requirements for when the pension must start. While registered plans (*e.g.*, RRSPs) must start income by end of the year in which the self-employed individual turns 69, RCAs have no requirement. Thus, they are excellent in meeting the variable income needs of the business owner if "stop and go income" is required to support the First Retirement Stage.

- Participation in the RCA does not generate a pension adjustment nor does it affect or reduce RRSP room. It is a supplemental retirement program.

- There are no restrictions on investments.

This *First Retirement Stage* involves a transition to a new way of living and requires a period of adjustment. If an individual wishes to maximize his or her options, it is necessary to take control of the future, to the extent that this is possible. What can be controlled should be controlled. Life choices can then become a real possibility with the individual determining the direction of his or her life, rather than wandering aimlessly into the future.

This trade-off between "*at work time*" and "*doing the other things I want to accomplish in my life*" can be referred to as "the semi-retirement period".

It is a period that most self-employed individuals will enjoy until they arrive at that period in time in which their energy levels do not permit them to "keep such a pace". The natural aging process begins to affect a person's ability to continuously do.

SECOND RETIREMENT — FULL RETIREMENT

The *Second Retirement* relates to "slowing down" due to the aging process. The topic of aging is one that many prefer to avoid. Yet, it is a process all of us must go through. We can prepare for aging only if we talk about it. While it may be difficult for some people to picture a situation 20 years in the future, it is an essential discussion to ensure that personal plans also address potential needs.

For example, during the *First Retirement Period*, decisions about where to live may be based on work-related factors. At the *Second Retirement Stage*, the housing decision becomes part of the individuals' personal planning choices. Whether individuals remain in their current homes or communities ultimately depends on what they want out of life.

To be old and dependent is an ugly existence in a culture that values youth, productivity and functionality. Western culture does not appear to like its elderly, and this may be another reason why many people do not actively plan for this part of the life cycle. Planning for it means we must face its inevitability.

The Second Retirement should allow a smooth transition that takes into consideration the aging process. The Second Retirement should include the ability to cope with life, to maintain emotional well-being, to continue to make valued contributions to all facets of life and to *feel worry-free financially*.

The objective in the *Second Retirement Phase* — full retirement — remains unchanged. It is to create wealth for retirement sufficient to maintain a person's lifestyle *for the last 25-30 years of life without having to worry about outliving one's money and to accept life as it is and make the best of it*. This stage is defined through the following question:

"What else, other than work, defines you?"

The Individual Pension Plan — Another Relatively Unknown Tax Strategy — Creating a Guaranteed Income Stream You Cannot Outlive!

Historically, many business owners have maximized their RRSP contributions, hoping that investment growth and the sale of their business would provide the retirement income required to maintain their current lifestyle.

Unfortunately, RRSPs have not performed well, and business owners are realizing (as they approach full retirement) that their businesses are not easy to sell.

The solution could be an Individual Pension Plan (IPP).

Legislation governing IPPs provides twice the savings room (contributions) for suitable business owners/professionals by providing 50% to 75% more retirement income than RRSPs.

The IPP legislation may be an appropriate way to maximize retirement income for the owner while giving the business the opportunity to achieve maximum tax relief.

The structure of the IPP is that of a defined benefit pension plan for one or more people. There is a promise of a specific income stream based upon years of service and earnings. Thus, there is downside protection. In the event that the plan suffers lower than expected returns, the company has the ability to make additional tax-deductible contributions to adequately fund the plan. By their structure, defined benefit pension plans usually provide 40% more income than a normal RRSP.

THIRD RETIREMENT — RETIREMENT AT THE END OF LIFE

The *Third Retirement* represents that stage in which our health may affect our finances.

For example, the effects of possible long-term health care needs on an investment portfolio that is designed to provide income to the surviving spouse or the provision of alternative living accommodations to the spouse who can no longer care for himself or herself on a day-to-day basis are significant lifestyle-related issues that will have significant effects on the capital/income requirements. While this stage may be an uncomfortable subject, you need to get through the reluctance barrier to ensure that you have plans that anticipate real potential situations.

A recent RBC Insurance/Ipsos-Reid survey found that 34% of respondents were worried about the cost of care in their old age.

How a Health and Welfare Trust and/or Retirement Compensation Arrangement Can Be Used to Fund Future Health Care Expenses

RCAs are essentially not regulated by Canada Revenue Agency as long as they are "reasonable" and not camouflaged salary deferral arrangements. Any pension promise of under 100% of pre-retirement earnings is reasonable. Thus, a $200,000 per annum business owner can create a $200,000 per year pension.

This limit may allow you to take into consideration any future health care costs that may be a significant part of the retirement plan. On the other hand, you may prefer to establish a Health and Welfare Trust (HWT), which is specifically set up to pay current and future medical expenses.

Both the RCA and HWT contributions are tax-deductible to your company in the year they are made. The difference is that benefits payable from the HWT are tax-free, whereas income from the RCA is taxable. The health spending account converts health care expenses into 100% business deductions.

The HWT Is a Benefit That Can Also Be Enjoyed Today

All traditional health care costs, like dental, prescription drugs and vision care, are eligible, but the HWT extends to cover the rest of your costs: family orthodontic, cosmetic and restorative dental, laser eye surgery, cosmetic surgery and even long-term care costs for elderly dependants. This may allow you to put more aside for the future.

ONLY YOU CAN BE YOUR LIFE'S ARCHITECT

When you know what you want to accomplish, then you can make the appropriate decisions relating to the financial support of your retirement needs.

LIFE IS NOT A DRESS REHEARSAL

Life is about taking charge and control to accomplish those things that are important to you. It is only when individuals take responsibility by making a major effort to solve their problems, adapt to changing circumstances and look forward to the future that they can say they have done a total job of retirement planning.

This can best be achieved if your planning incorporates the same process for personal retirement planning as that which we use for business planning: you want to become a successfully retired person.

CHAPTER 28

THE FINANCIAL PLANNING PROFESSIONAL'S WORK MANIFESTO FOR THE 21ST CENTURY

Overview

This chapter asks provoking questions that will help the 21st century financial professional chart his or her own course for his or her life and career.

Learning Objectives

By the end of this chapter, you should be able to:

- be on your journey to asking yourself the thought-provoking questions discussed in this chapter;

- have some insight into what type of life and career you aim to have going forward.

THE FINANCIAL PLANNING PROFESSIONAL'S WORK MANIFESTO FOR THE 21ST CENTURY

In the Information Age, the only thing we can count on is change itself. After more than two decades in which millions of people's working lives have been disrupted by corporate outsourcing, downsizing and re-engineering, individuals have come to realize that Canadian companies can no longer offer them job security for life.

In the New Economy "we have a better chance of getting a gold watch from a street vendor than we do from a corporation", said one former Vice-President of Human Resources with 20 years experience, who had been let go due to corporate restructuring.

Before globalization and the information age, the old trappings of success were a secretary, a company car and a corner office. These are now things of the past. Today, we are all responsible for managing our own careers. All jobs, whether contract or permanent, eventually end and should be viewed as temporary.

Signs of career trouble have also changed. In the old economy the rules of success were simple — one would receive incremental promotions every few years. If you did not get a promotion, or were offered partnership in your firm, you would have taken that as a warning that your job might be in jeopardy. Over the last few years the warning signs have become much more subtle. So in this new era we must become aware of these signs and be prepared for change.

QUESTIONING UNDERLINING ASSUMPTIONS

It is important for each and every one of us from time to time to question why we do what we do. When I think about questioning our underlining assumptions, I am often reminded of a story about a newlywed couple that drives home this point to me, and I hope it helps you as well.

One evening a husband came home as his new wife prepared dinner. That night they were having roast beef. He noticed that his wife had cut off the ends of the roast beef and thrown them in the garbage. He found this very puzzling so he asked his wife why she had cut off the ends of the roast beef and put them in the garbage. She politely replied that this was the way her mother had "always" prepared roast beef. After receiving her answer, he wisely decided to follow the advice his father had given him on the day of his wedding, which was to pick your battles wisely, so he let it go.

About six months, later the husband was having dinner at his mother-in-law's, and the main dish she was preparing that evening was roast beef. He noticed that she had also cut off the ends of the roast beef and put them into the trash can. He shook his head as he remembered the conversation he had had with his wife several months before and decided that he would ask his mother-in-law why she made roast beef this way. So he asked, and his mother-in-law replied that this was the way her mother, his wife's grandmother, had made roast beef when she was a little girl. He was more confused then ever, so he let it go.

Several months passed, and his wife's grandmother flew in from Florida to visit the family. At dinner one night when the entire family was gathered together, the husband, still puzzled over the roast beef mystery for almost a year, turned to his wife's grandmother and asked her:

"I was wondering why, when your daughter, my wife's mother, was young that when you made roast beef you cut off the ends and threw them out?"

The grandmother laughed out loud at the top of her lungs. After she settled down a bit, she turned to him and began to tell him the story that when she first got married, she and her husband were so poor that the pot that she cooked in was too small to fit an entire roast beef in, so she had to cut off the ends so it would fit in the pot.

Asking the right questions is sometimes more valuable than the answers to your questions. Ask yourself the key questions below to provoke insight into what drives and motivates you — embark on the journey of taking ownership of your career and destiny.

Are you learning? If you can't say to yourself that you have learned anything of value in the past year, nor do you think that you will learn anything of value next year at your job, you should be concerned about your position. In the New Economy our greatest assets are the new marketable skills we acquire. When your learning stops at your present job, you have to be prepared to leave and move on. This rule applies even when a promotion might be involved. If your job has become easy for you to do, remember either your position can be automated or someone else can be hired to replace you for a lot less pay.

Educators have identified four stages of learning that everyone acquiring a new skill set must pass through to achieve mastery of those new skills. The financial industry is constantly evolving, requiring you to be a life-long learner. As you grow as a person and transition from one way of doing to moving to the next level, it is helpful to identify what stage you are at on your learning curve, so that you can consciously direct your course of study towards mastery. These distinct stages of learning are as follows:

(1) *Unconscious Incompetence* — We are not aware that we can't do something.

(2) *Conscious Incompetence* — We know that we can't do something.

(3) *Conscious Competence* — We can now perform the new task but we have to really think about it. This is a state of concentration.

(4) *Unconscious Competence* — We no longer have to think about the skill. This is the stage when we can pay attention to other things and new learning while still performing the skill.

If your job were advertised in the career section of the newspaper and you applied for it, would you get it? If you were applying for your current position would your firm be looking for the skill set that you currently have?

Has your current firm taken advantage of you? Were you asked to sacrifice long-term career growth for very short-term gains that only benefit your firm and not you? For example, a Chartered Accountant wants to learn forensic accounting but is encouraged by senior partners at the firm to stay put and continue doing audit, while others in the firm are paid to learn these skills. If you have answered yes, your firm has stopped investing in you and you are expendable!

Do you know what you contribute to the bottom line of your firm? How about your contribution to your firm's success? If you are not able to describe what you do and how it benefits your firm from the time it takes for a traffic light to turn from red to green, most likely your partners and your clients can't either.

What would you do if your job vanished tomorrow? Can you honestly say that you have invested enough into yourself and your career by developing marketable skills, built contingency into your plans and developed support networks to help you through a transition to new career opportunities?

Do you enjoy what you do for a living? Life is too short to live the delayed life plan — doing the things you don't like, in hopes that one day you will be living your true life plan. There are two major flaws with this type of thinking. One, will you know when it is time to switch to living your true life-plan? If you have not taken any steps towards making your dreams happen today, what makes you think you will embark on your true life path tomorrow? And two, do you really have all the time in the world to make this change? Do you believe that you will be the only one in human history to live forever? Ask yourself: "Have I accomplished anything in my life that has real meaning to me, my family and the greater community as a whole?"

Sure, many of us suffer from the collective illusion that by continuing our delayed life plan we are earning a living and this is the best we can hope for in this lifetime. But if our hearts are not into our work, are we not just making a "dying" for ourselves? If each day we lose a little more of our dreams, our self-respect and ourselves, what type of legacy do we create?

Do you know what you stand for, and what your core values are? Have you ever sat down and asked yourself what you stand for, and what you believe? Values are the principles and standards we set for ourselves either consciously or unconsciously. These are the qualities that we consider worthwhile to fight for, to uphold and to even die for.

A perfect example of someone who has a very concise value system is a gentleman named Major G. Scott Bowman, founder and headmaster of Robert Land Academy (RLA). Major Bowman had a vision in his mind's eye in the early 1970s to turn a 168-acre pig farm in the heartland of the historic Niagara Peninsula in Ontario, Canada into a school for boys, based on a military theme that would reinforce the importance of organization, teamwork, discipline and personal responsibility. These boys would become true citizens in the very sense of the word to their communities, nations and the world. They would value their responsibilities and obligations to their society and know that each right and freedom they enjoy needs to be earned, respected and appreciated every day of their lives. Major Bowman believed that these values were strongly missing in our modern day society.

Major G. Scott Bowman is a direct descendant of Robert Land, who was a United Empire Loyalist during the American Revolution, an early settler of the Niagara region and a man of significant character and achievement. The Academy was named after Robert Land in honour of his spirit of independent resourcefulness, courage and responsibility.

Students admitted to the Academy are chosen for their potential for success. Students admitted to the Academy have, while trying to succeed in the public school system, experienced difficulties related to attitude, concentration, focus and respect. Today as a testament to Major Bowman's vision, spirit and values, stands "Robert Land Academy, an Island Oasis in a Sea of Mediocrity". Today, from nothing more than one man's vision, determination and hard work stands a school, physically resembling a British colonial fort, that has helped thousands of boys become contributing members to our society. Major Bowman's vision has become a model for hundreds of other schools and institutions around the world.

The driving force behind Major Bowman's creation and success of RLA has been the value system that he first wrote down on a napkin over 35 years ago, when the idea of the school was only a vision in his mind. The Academy emphasizes five core values in everything it strives to teach to its students, within and beyond the bounds of the class: *Loyalty*, *Labour*, *Courage*, *Commitment* and *Honour*. As the excerpt from the Academy's parents' handbook explains below (reprinted with the explicit permission of Robert Land Academy):

The Five Values of Robert Land Academy

Loyalty as a concept is self-explanatory. How one makes it tangible as a value determines the nature of one's conduct. Modeling plays an important role. It is paramount that loyalty is displayed to each other and the Academy. We expect loyalty as a matter of course and it is rewarded when displayed. The necessity and benefits of loyalty to something outside and other than oneself must be demonstrated in a concrete fashion, through verbal explanations and providing opportunities to demonstrate its value in life situations. By graduation, each Cadet should understand and be capable of displaying loyalty to something greater and other than himself.

Labour for Robert Land Academy Cadets entails far more than the routine performance of menial jobs. We are committed to labour as a way of life and to the importance of fulfilling one's life work with an attitude of self-respect as well as respect for the labour of others. We view life itself as labour, in the sense that one must work for what one earns, whether rights or remuneration. This is not to say that we believe life to be drudgery; rather, as Robert Land himself believed, life is a toiling after the best, in the realms of work, rest and play. We instill this value in our Cadets by demanding from them their best in all activities. All Cadets share in the work done at the Academy, and their work must meet our standard of excellence. Our Cadets also labour in academics, life skills and extra curricular activities, and again, they must labour to be the best they can be.

Courage: Our Cadets are taught to have the Courage to speak their minds, act on their convictions and be able to finish what they start, despite hardships. With courage our Cadets will learn to master their limitations and exploit their strengths in order to achieve maximum success. It should be noted that courage is not the absence of fear, but its conquest. The person who has never been afraid has never had to display courage.

Commitment is perhaps the most fundamental of our values. Robert Land's life was based on a commitment to principles and institutions, which were not accepted universally. For this he suffered considerably. Commitment breeds endurance in adversity, a necessary attribute for anyone seeking success. Cadets must learn that commitment means binding one's self to someone or something else, and that such binding is both necessary for one's development and beneficial to one's personality. Cadets will be taught to show commitment to each other, to the Academy and its values, and to excellence in all their endeavors.

Honour: Cadets at Robert Land grow to Honour themselves, their families, their friends and the Academy. The service theme facilitates the development of all of the values in our Cadets, especially honour. Through the continual insistence of honour for the values of our Academy, our Cadets will learn respect for a code of conduct that will stand them in good stead for the rest of their lives. The honour associated with the life of Robert Land should be a fine example to the entire Robert Land community.

By no means do I imply that you should adopt or accept the five values of Robert Land Academy. However, what is important is to understand the importance of becoming conscious of what your core values are and that you never stray from what you know is right for your community, your family and friends, your clients and you.

After you become conscious of your core values, it is very important that you begin to rank and prioritize them in importance to you. This theory was put to the test at a recent workshop I ran in Toronto for financial planners. The attendees were given an exercise to write down what they valued most and then to list them in order of importance to them. One of the participant's came up with the following "value system", which I would like to share with you now as an example:

Sample "Value System"

(1) I believe in the importance of health, as long as I am healthy my universe is open to me.

(2) I believe that an individual should strive for personal control over his or her own destiny. I know that this personal power for me only comes after I have taken ownership of my own life, attitudes, dreams and hopes. Life is not a dress rehearsal!!! If it is to be, it is up to me!!!

(3) I believe my happiness and success in my life will be based on the quality of my relationships with others. Less is more! Quality is better than Quantity! Depth not breadth!

(4) I believe in life, that if money can solve a problem, it truly is not a problem!

(5) I believe life is too short and one should find balance with family, friends and work in a synergic way so one can get the most out of his or her human experience. As the old saying goes "don't sweat the small stuff because in the end it's all small stuff".

(6) I believe through ongoing financial planning and continually putting my plans into action, I will only then be moving in the direction of turning my dreams into my living reality.

(7) Money to me is something I choose to trade my life energy for. I place no limit to my energy. Nor will I let outside influence and forces place a limit on me either.

(8) I choose that the role money is to play in my relationships with others is to foster creative, stimulating and productive mediums of exchange. If we do not all win in a relationship it

is not a relationship I choose to be in. I believe true power is having the ability to choose my relationships and associations.

(9) I believe that we should all strive to play great financial offence in how we earn our living and to play equally, as well, defence in how we store our wealth.

Do you have a written plan of how you are going to specifically achieve your most important financial and life goals?

"Where there is no vision, the people perish."

Proverbs 29:18

Most people spend more time planning a vacation or a car purchase than planning their life and financial future. The average person will work 90,000 hours in his or her life, yet spends less than 24 hours asking himself or herself what he or she wants to accomplish in his or her lifetime, or what his or her legacy will be.

The Ancient Greeks often compared men to ships. However, most do not have rudders, so they go this way and that way and eventually end up crashing on rocks. Any route will do because they don't have a plan. But those who do have a plan make life look so easy for the rest of us. They go from one port to the next, from one success to the next success. If you don't have a plan for your life there are plenty of other people who will step up to the plate and make decisions for your life. Is this what you want?

All highly successful people I have ever worked with have had very clearly defined, written life, career and financial plans. They believed implicitly and unshakably in their plans and were impervious to external circumstances. So they didn't alter their plans every time the wind changed direction, and continued to work their plans steadfastly, no matter how long it took, until their plans inevitably succeeded. People succeed because they believe and they are believed!

There is no substitute for a good step-by-step, goal-oriented plan. A Harvard study in 1952 showed that 3% of the graduates had written out their career goals in a plan. Twenty years later, in 1972, those same 3% were worth more than the other 97% of that 1952 class. Remember, these were Harvard graduates; the wealth of that 3% must have been staggering! That's the power of setting a goal, having a plan and working the plan.

What is your purpose in life? Viktor Frankl, an Austrian psychiatrist, heir to Sigmund Freud (1865-1939), who was the father of psychoanalysis, and a survivor of Auschwitz and the Holocaust, wrote about his experiences in the Nazi death camps in his 1946 book *Man's Search for Meaning: An Introduction to Logotherapy* (Boston: Beacon Press, 1963). In this book he describes what he observed in Auschwitz of humans' free will and character. He tells the story that no one survived in the camps for a prolonged period of time unless he or she had a reason to live, be it for revenge, to find loved ones or to tell his or her story.

Frankl observed that each person needs to be fulfilled as a human being, to have a purpose and to have a meaning for his or her existence. Frankl developed an entire modern movement in therapy based on his experience called Logo therapy. Logo in Greek means "meaning". The aim of Logo Therapy was to help people find their purpose in life and to help them live out their purpose. To be truly successful in your life it is absolutely imperative that you find your meaning for your life and live your purpose to the fullest. Frankl believed if a person discovered his or her "why" to life, once this was done the "how" of his or her life would fall into place.

> "The last of the human freedoms — to choose one's attitude in any given set of circumstances, to choose one's own way."
>
> Victor Frankl — *Man's Search for Meaning*

TAKE THE QUANTUM LEAP

In the introduction to James Carse's book *Finite and Infinite Games* (New York: Ballantine Books, 1987), he introduces and then defines that "there are at least two kinds of games. One could be called finite, the other infinite. A finite game is played for the purpose of winning, an infinite game for the purpose of continuing the play".

It absolutely makes a world of difference whether we consider ourselves as pawns in a game whose rules we call reality or as players of the game who know that rules are "real" only to the extent that we have created or accepted them, and that we can change them.

The first step is understanding that any relationship or process can be characterized in "finite" or "infinite" terms. The second step is recognizing that characterization is almost always a matter of choice and that, by choosing to see a relationship as "infinite", you can redefine it in a meaningful and healthy way.

I have observed that when people see life as an infinite game and are living out their life purpose, they come up with more ideas, see more associations between ideas and see more similarities and differences among things than people who see life as a finite game. What emerges is more of a partnership ordination towards family, friends, work, communities, environment and ourselves.

It has been said that when a person has one way of doing something, he or she is stuck; if that person has two ways, he or she is in a bind; and only when that person has three or more ways of doing something, he or she has true choice. The Chinese symbol for "crisis" has a duel meaning, which also translates into the word "opportunity". Each player in the game of life who is perceptive enough to see himself or herself playing in an infinite game has the uncanny ability to see through all crises as opportunities to continue play. So all that happens to this kind of person in life is a part of the play, and there are no failures in the mind of this kind of player; there is only feedback so play can continue.

Fred Alan Wolf, in his award-winning book titled *Taking The Quantum Leap: The New Physics for Nonscientists* (New York: Harper Perennial, 1989), describes a quantum leap as:

> The explosive jump that a particle of matter undergoes in moving from one place to another … in a figurative sense, taking the quantum leap means taking a risk, going off into uncharted territory with no guide to follow.

In 2001, a few days after 9/11 and after I had had my own epiphany that my business model would need to change if I were going to continue to prosper in the financial industry going forward, I just happened to be watching a television interview with Sir Paul McCartney. Call it synchronicity or not, but when the interviewer turned to McCartney and asked him how he, John Lennon, George Harrison and Ringo Starr started writing their now classic songs for the Beatles that defined a generation, contained within McCartney's answer to the interviewer's question was the insight I had been searching and longing for, of how an individual could live an authentic life.

Paul McCartney answered with a short story. He told the interviewer that when the Beatles were getting started, in 1961, they performed 92 days straight in Hamburg, Germany, where they perfected their talents. At the beginning of their tour, the Beatles were little more than a cover band, playing other bands' top 40 hits.

McCartney recounted how frustrated both he and John Lennon were feeling because many of the bands that the Beatles were performing with were going on stage just before them and playing the same cover songs. So out of this great frustration and some creative flare both McCartney and Lennon found their own voice and made their own quantum leap. One night just before they were to go out on stage to perform, they decided to work on a song that McCartney had written sometime earlier. Together they jotted down some lyrics and improvised a melody.

That cold night in April 1961, the Beatles sang "Love Me Do". It is that little momentous event when the Beatles started writing their own music and performing it themselves that made all the difference. Perhaps if the Beatles had not performed that single authentic act, we might not be experiencing their genius today.

Little seemingly unconnected events can create huge changes half way around the globe. The best way to understand this concept is by adopting the metaphor that is used to explain Chaos Theory known as the Butterfly Effect: a butterfly fluttering its wings in China could set off a tornado in Texas.

Now, ask yourself, are you making a change today that will make all the difference in your life today and tomorrow, and will cause you to have your very own butterfly effect?

BE A LIFETIME LEARNER!

If you have read this far, congratulations, you have completed a long unique journey, considering that 80% of U.S. families did not buy or read a book last year (source: Jerold Jenkins, online: <www.jenkinsgroupinc.com>). In January 2007, *The CSI Exchange*, the Canadian Securities Institute's online magazine, reported that "according to a number of studies, business people who read at least 7 business books a year earn over 2.3 times more than people who read only 1 book per year". The report stated that the reason why readers earn more money than non-readers is because they receive "a constant stream of new ideas and strategies they can use to help their careers, their clients and their companies".

Joseph Campbell (1904-1987), who was considered the world's greatest scholar in mythology, was the author of *The Hero with a Thousand Faces*, commemorative ed. (Princeton, N.J.: Princeton University Press, 2004), which inspired George Lucas to write his *Star Wars* script in 1975. Campbell, through his years of studying the world's mythology, came to the understanding that there is very little human knowledge that has not been spoken or written before. Human wisdom that seems new is actually "old wine in new bottles". The things not known is the history not studied.

There is nothing that has not been thought of before. Our minds do not create thought; we amplify it. Our minds can be compared to radio receivers; if we have the right equipment we can tune it into the wisdom of the world. All the wisdom of the world has been written down somewhere in the annals of great literature, and this is mankind's greatest accomplishment and legacy.

Ideas are like viruses of the mind. A profound thought once spoken or written down has the ability to replicate itself and be passed on from one mind onto the next, and from one generation onto future generations. Every idea that enters our mind has the ability to influence our behaviour. History has shown that good ideas always prevail and endure over bad ones in the long run. Aim to tune your mind to great ideas and vaccinate yourself from evil ones.

> "People with extraordinary minds, talk about ideas.
> People with average minds, talk about events.
> People with simple minds, talk about other people."
>
> Anonymous

I have personally found that the books I treasure the most and recommend to others are the ones that say the things that I have been thinking and did not have the right words to properly express myself at the time. These are the books that have provided me with a language empowering me to crystallize my own thoughts and beliefs. These are the books that have a prominent place in my library.

Returning to the discussion of Joseph Campbell, there is a famous story about him when he was a college professor. At the beginning of each course, Campbell would give out a large reading list to his students. Several weeks into one of his classes, a student raised her hand and asked, "Professor Campbell, this is not the only class we are taking. How do you expect us to read all the books on your reading list in one semester?" Campbell turned to his class and replied, "I am not expecting you to read all these books this semester; you have the rest of your life to discover them."

This book will have achieved its primary purposes if you finish it with a brand new kind of lexicon and have many more meaningful and insightful questions than you started out with. Your thirst for more knowledge has expanded exponentially. As mentioned throughout this book, a question is ten times more valuable than its answer because when you formulate the right question, what you have accomplished is the focusing of your attention and the presupposing that an answer to your question is out there for your own discovery. Depending on how much importance and how exact your question is will determine how much energy you expend to find out your own unique answers.

An act, a deed and a word have the power to change our world and the worldview of others. When I begin teaching either a financial planning course or a workshop, I always preface my talks by sharing with my students and participants that I am not any smarter than they are. I have, however, been on the path a little longer, and if they have the desire, and the determination to invest their most precious asset, their time, they will be further along the path and know a whole lot more than I. And I look forward to becoming their student.

Each Remembrance Day in Canada, on the 11th hour of the 11th day of the 11th month, we are asked to stop for a minute to reflect on and remember those courageous men and women who served in our armed forces and laid down their lives in war so that today we could all live in peace and enjoy all the rights and freedoms they fought for, and so that we could enjoy a free and democratic society. Every fall across Canada, primary school children are taught and recite "In Flanders Fields", the poem written by Lieutenant-Colonel John McCrae (1872-1918), who had fallen while serving our country during World War I. This legacy belongs to all of us and is a call for both you and me, together, to take up the torch from those who have come before us.

> In Flanders Fields the poppies blow
> Between the crosses, row on row,
> That mark our place; and in the sky
> The larks, still bravely singing, fly
> Scarce heard amid the guns below.
>
> We are the Dead. Short days ago
> We lived, felt dawn, saw sunset glow,
> Loved, and were loved, and now we lie
> In Flanders fields.
>
> Take up our quarrel with the foe:
> To you from failing hands we throw
> The torch, be yours to hold it high.
> If ye break faith with us who die
> We shall not sleep, though poppies grow
> In Flanders fields

My father, Marvin S. Merrick (1939-1999), just before he died in March 1999, bequeathed to me his Ethical Will, his spiritual legacy, which he had accumulated throughout his lifetime, and which he believed was important enough to be passed on after he was gone so his values would live on. In one of the last conversations that I had with my father, he imparted the following wisdom:

> "One's only concern and focus should be on what one has in his pockets and not in the pockets of others. The grass might look greener in someone else's yard, but those lawns need to be manicured as well. Have the wisdom to truly know and appreciate that the grass is always greener on your side of

the pond, to always be proud and satisfied with what one has and not to be-grudge others for having or not having. Most importantly, it is our responsi-bility and obligation to take care of that which one loves and to enjoy the best life possible while helping and not harming others. What you do does not define who you are. The world is a looking glass on the self; what one puts before it, is what is reflected back from it. If life serves you up lemons, make lemonade."

THE POWER OF NOW

A successful career in the New Economy results from having a résumé that describes a person with fewer titles, but many more employers and experiences. Whether you are employed permanently or are a sole practitioner, it helps to see yourself as a self-employed person who is always of the mindset of turning work into his or her vocation and purpose — being inwardly directed and outwardly focused. Having a self-employed mindset prepares you mentally for the likelihood of becoming unemployed, looking for new opportunities and turning your dreams into your living reality!

We can all learn from the moral contained within the children's story of the "Tortoise and the Hare". The slow and the steady always win the race. A major influence on Warren Buffett's investment philosophy was the investing legend Philip Fisher (1907-2004), author of the 1958 investment classic *Common Stocks and Uncommon Profits* (New York: Wiley, 2003). Fisher believed adamantly in never investing money with a man who had never fallen flat on his face, broken some bones, knocked out a few teeth and failed miserably at least once in his lifetime, and then pulled himself up by his own bootstraps through shear inspiration, determination and perspiration. This individual was a creative force to be reckoned with and could be counted on as a leader in the land of the living.

This type of person, Fisher believed, had an indelible spirit, a moral compass and a strong defining character (an infinite gamer at his or her very best). This was the kind of person whom Fisher wanted on his team and would invest his and his clients' money in for the long haul because this type of person had shown through adversity that he or she would not allow himself or herself to be counted out, and was a serious player in the game of life.

One of the main tenets behind Kabbalah, the mystical side of Juda-ism, is the understanding of the "Bread of Shame", which means that you cannot keep what you have not rightfully earned. The only way to be deserving of what you have is to be a proactive force for the purpose of not receiving for the self alone. This belief is in sync with Dr. Laurence J. Peter's (1919-1990) Peter Principle, which became popularized in the late 1960s.

The Peter Principle states that we rise to the highest level of our incompetence and no higher. So by combining both ideas behind the "Bread of Shame" and the "Peter Principle", you and I have as much success, money and fame that we can handle at this moment in time because there is a lesson to be learnt first before we will consciously or unconsciously give ourselves permission to move onto the next level in our maturing process.

If we aim to achieve more in our life, we will first need to prepare ourselves so we feel deserving of all our successes. So when opportunities present themselves, we will have all the resources needed emotionally, intellectually and physically to identify, act on, incorporate, appreciate and enjoy that which we have learnt. Having acquired new wisdom as a part of who we are at our core will allow us to act appropriately in applying this new wisdom. Only then will we be able to put those experiences and knowledge behind us, allowing us to move on to the next level in our life's quest. The ancient sages teach us that the way out of a rut is to be creative and to give to others. The "ideal" in life is a virtue of good.

At the end of your days, the person whom you will have to answer to for all the things you did or did not do will be you. It is better to regret the things you did than the things you did not do, and live life to its fullest. You are a very powerful person, but first you need to believe this yourself.

"You'll See It When You Believe It"

Dr Wayne W. Dyer

The time is now! It is time to take your own "Quantum Leap" in your life and your career! People are frightened of change because they don't feel they have any control. Remember, you are the producer of your own life; you pick the projects, finance them and choose the directors, writers and actors. You are the one and only unifying and defining principle during your journey. When you take aim at the stars and if you only find yourself walking on the moon, remember you will be in the company of only a few people within human history to have accomplished such a feat. The best place to begin your journey is where you are right now. From the sturdiest foundations the tallest structures are built.

A picture might be worth a thousand words, but we all know that an experience is worth a trillion of those. By taking one step forward *today* towards your authentic self and your true purpose in life, the universe will open up to you and make the other 99 steps towards you. It has been said that those who fail to plan, and fail to act, plan to fail. When your life and financial goals are important enough for you, there can be very little that stands between you and your success.

This book is titled *The Essential Individual Pension Plan Handbook*, which is a very fitting name because the word "pension" receives its origins from the Latin word "pensare", meaning to "weigh carefully". Each of us is given one life to live, and as *individuals*, it is absolutely *essential* that we *plan* and *weigh carefully* everything that we choose to do with our gift called life.

As I finish writing this book, which has been a true labour of love, I am reminded of my children and their favourite bedtime story: Dr. Seuss's (Theodor Seuss Geisel, 1904-1991) last book published just before he died, *"Oh, the Places You'll Go!"* (London: Picture Lions, 2003). This was Geisel's lasting personal message to future generations.

With any journey as important as your life, this ancient Chinese proverb can be very fitting to be mindful of as you go forward:

"The thousand mile journey begins with the first step!"

EPILOGUE

At the beginning of 2005, Peter Merrick began a very engaging dialogue with Mort Shapiro, President of Morden S. Shapiro & Associates Inc. Management Consultants, and a fellow columnist at *The Bottom Line*. Their talks focused on how the roles of the public accountant and financial planning professional were in the process of being redefined as they converged upon one another. What follows is a revised reprint of their two articles that appeared in the October 2006 issue of *The Bottom Line* newspaper, a LexisNexis publication. Shared within these articles are some of the insights that were gained from their lengthy discussions that continue on today.

"Thin Ice" (Article One)

Mort Shapiro

In recent years clients' needs have become increasingly varied and sophisticated, particularly so in the areas of wealth accumulation, management and preservation. Satisfying these needs has become increasingly complex in today's taxation and regulatory infrastructure. At the same time, clients have become more knowledgeable and aware and increasingly tend to focus on maximizing their economic well-being by managing their financial affairs as effectively as possible.

It's important for public accountants to understand that if clients have needs, they'll find ways to satisfy those needs. The areas of wealth accumulation, management and preservation are no exception to this rule. Although it may seem logical to many clients that their accountants would address these needs, such is not always the case. And unfortunately, when accountants do address these needs, they often do so with a deficiency of knowledge and expertise, which feeds the following "thin ice" factor.

THE "THIN ICE" FACTOR

It's well recognized that today's public accountants practise in a litigious environment. Risk management is a mantra in the business world. To render advice without sufficient expertise or knowledge is akin to skating on "thin ice". Not only does it create a real vulnerability from a litigation viewpoint, but it also exposes the practitioners to a possible breach of their professional rules by not sustaining their competence in those areas on which a client relies on them due to their professional status. The reality is that whether or not they realize it, most public accountants are constantly practising in the areas of wealth accumulation, management and preservation and are often on "thin ice" when they do so.

It's because of these concerns, that in this issue I join with my fellow columnist Peter Merrick to address a common "thin ice" scenario which I encounter in the course of my work in the world of public practice.

THE PROFIT DISTRIBUTION TRAP

In the all too common annual "how shall we distribute/allocate this year's corporate net income?" meeting, practitioners tend to focus on traditional salary/bonus/dividend mixes which are based on the integration of personal and corporate tax rates and are designed to minimize current tax burdens and maximize (to some extent) the availability of disposable after-tax income in the present. However this traditional practice now often requires new levels of knowledge and expertise in order to keep the practitioner from giving inappropriate advice.

For many clients, traditional strategies are often recommended without an appropriate workup of a client's goals, needs and wishes (for the short-, medium- and long-term periods). Even if this has been done at some previous date, circumstances may have altered a client's strategic goals.

Every profit distribution strategy has within it an implicit strategic plan. The "thin ice" develops when the implicit plan is not known to or appreciated by the client, who, with choices available to him/her may have chosen to achieve some alternative goal, need or wish which might not necessarily have minimized current tax burdens and maximized (to some extent) the availability of disposable after-tax income in the present.

The accountant's dilemma may be rooted in any or all of the following factors:

- The client's current goals, needs and wishes (for the short, medium and long-term periods) may not be known to the accountant, who then uses conventional planning strategies (*i.e.*, maximizing tax-paid disposable income when much of it ends up being redundant cash, but outside the client's corporation) which may not be well aligned with the client's goals.

- The accountant may not be aware of strategies and techniques that are available to achieve alternative goals (*i.e.*, the broad range of insurance products, deferred compensation plans and other such vehicles).

- The accountant may not have the skills needed to guide the client through an intensive inward-looking process to develop a personal strategic financial plan (*i.e.*, to identify and evaluate quality of life and life cycle events which must be addressed and reduced to very practical financial terms and then explored at an emotional and psychological level).

- The client may not be prepared to pay the accountant to explore his or her personal financial goals, needs and wishes (*i.e.*, "just tell me how to do it").

The accountant's vulnerability is rooted in the eventuality that clients may discover, after the fact, that they had choices as to how they could have managed their wealth differently, which choices you as their accountant did not present to them. It's possible that even had alternatives been presented to the clients, they would have chosen the path recommended by you as their accountant. But they or their heirs or legal representatives will be tempted to attack you for, at the very least, not having informed them of their alternatives (*i.e.*, you took away their opportunity to make a choice).

I've asked Peter Merrick to address this example of the annual profit distribution strategy, and comment on the traps into which accountants all too easily fall. After familiarizing yourself with Peter's cautionary words, I invite you to consider using the following self assessing checklist (this can be applied to an individual accountant or to a firm as a whole):

- Do I realize what goals and objectives are implicit in the financial recommendations that I make to my clients? (*i.e.*, what is being primarily achieved by my recommended strategy?)

- Do I lead my clients through the process of developing goals and objectives for a financial strategic plan?

- If yes:
  - Do I have the appropriate skills to do so (*i.e.*, interview skills/counseling/mediation if dealing with a family unit, *etc.*)?
  - Do I have appropriate expertise and knowledge to appreciate what alternative strategies are available to achieve a broad range of goals and objectives (*i.e.* the latest developments in legal and tax regulations/new and emerging financial products)?
- If no:
  - Do I communicate in writing to my client the range of goals that my recommendations do and do not achieve?
  - Do I have the client confirm in writing that I have recommended that they undertake the process of developing goals and objectives for a financial strategic plan OR that I have made such a recommendation and they have rejected it?
- Whatever my responses were to the foregoing self-assessing questions, do I do these things on a regular, periodic basis so as to be satisfied that the information with which I am working is current (*i.e.*, the birth of a child/the illness of an aging parent/the development of a medical crisis/disability, *etc.*)?

The opportunities for delivering real value to clients are there for the taking as are the traps for delivering poor, incomplete or (as your client might argue) incompetent service. These opportunities flow from real needs which real clients have. To ignore them is to ignore the reality of the world in which you practise.

Be mindful of the fact that any attacks on your performance in this arena will generally come from persons of wealth. And they usually have the financial wherewithal to be serious attackers.

Readers should consider whether any of the strategies outlined by Peter Merrick would have been appropriate for one or more clients, either to adopt or at the very least to consider. If there are such scenarios and if they were not adequately considered, then you may have (unknowingly) been practising on "thin ice".

Mort Shapiro, B. Com., FCA, CMC, and Peter Merrick, B.A., FMA, CFP, FCSI, address these areas together through their newly formed group, Rockhaven Financial. Mort can be reached at (905) 513-3736 or <mshapiro@shapiro-inc.ca>.

How to Skate Around Thin Ice
(Article Two)

Peter Merrick

In this month's column Mort Shapiro has posed several thought-provoking questions. He's asked me to address his scenario from the perspective of a Certified Financial Planner (CFP), in order to provide public accountants with some fresh insight.

I personally find it useful to keep in mind that in this developing era of convergence, most client financial problems are multi-dimensional. Efficient solutions tend to reach beyond the scope of the traditional public accountant's skill set.

Most clients' issues, be they strategic business planning, estate planning, succession planning, charitable giving, investments or insurance issues are as significant to the client as their tax issues. In order to successfully service their clients' needs, public accountants must ensure that they are capable of considering this broad range of concerns.

Mort has asked me to examine the common profit distribution trap from the perspective of this broader landscape. This trap usually arises during the annual review meeting between the public accountant and his or her client. The traditional question inevitably arises: "How shall we distribute/allocate this year's net corporate income?" Many public accountants fall into the trap of recommending a stand alone salary/bonus/dividend mix without considering the alternatives. This single dimension strategy is built on two underlying assumptions:

(1) No obvious tax-planning opportunities exist for corporate-held investments funded from undrawn net income and so there tends to be a reluctance to leave funds in the corporation.

(2) The client is often presumed to wish to maximize the quantum of after-tax dollars in his or her hands today.

The problem with the latter assumption is that the accountant will likely have assumed this to be the client's goal without having explored its validity. In fact, the clients' goals may not be tax-driven at all. The accountant's exposure, which flows from the traditional assumption, is rooted in today's common client expectation that their accountant is capable of providing overall advice on the client's long-term financial welfare and is a knowledgeable and capable strategic thinker.

Mort Shapiro has identified the annual net profit distribution meeting as a "thin ice" scenario. He speculates that a problem could/will arise if clients subsequently learn that they had other options (other than the salary/bonus/dividend mix recommendation made by the accountant) that would have better suited their needs by yielding greater overall benefits for them and better supporting the clients' goals in both the short and long term.

Opportunities often exist whereby corporate funds created from undrawn net income can compound tax-free within the company or/and tailed executive benefit plans. These opportunities are often viable and complementary to the traditional salary/bonus/dividend mix strategy. These alternatives are available through financial solutions which may take the form of: corporate class money-managed products, corporate interest rate swaps, retirement compensation arrangements, individual pension plans, corporately owned universal life insurance, and health and welfare trusts. (This is not an exhaustive list of the alternatives.)

CORPORATE CLASS MONEY-MANAGEMENT PRODUCTS

This is a strategy whereby a third party money-management company invests the client's corporate funds. This investment structure allows a business to invest its funds in tax effective investment type accounts that allow for the switching between fund classes of shares within the same fund corporation without triggering capital gains for the client corporation. As with many vehicles, there are limitations: assets will attract tax if they are withdrawn from the third party money-management company.

CORPORATE INTEREST SWAP

An *interest* rate *swap* contract consists of exchanging two types of investment instruments without actually exchanging these investments. This is a strategy whereby the client purchases units in a fund held by a third party money-management firm. The money market returns will be taxed as capital gains only on sale. Funds invested in such corporate interest rate SWAPs allow the business to have access to this money in a secure way while at the same time delaying the taxation of the returns on such moneys and leveraging the deferred tax dollars.

INDIVIDUAL PENSION PLANS (IPP) AND RETIREMENT COMPENSATION ARRANGEMENTS (RCA)

Owners who are employed by an incorporated business should consider creating a "Supersized RRSP" in the form of an Individual Pension Plan (IPP) or a Retirement Compensation Arrangement (RCA). Contributions to these two vehicles for older clients will exceed the maximum allowable RRSP limits, are fully deductible by the sponsoring company and are a non-taxable benefit for the individual. Increases in the total value of the assets held in the vehicle are tax-deferred until withdrawn. IPPs and RCAs offer the potential for significant amounts of additional tax-deferred income to be set aside for retirement.

CORPORATELY OWNED UNIVERSAL LIFE INSURANCE (UL)

UL provides tax-sheltered growth within a policy. A corporate-owned life insurance contract can tax shelter large portions of a company's retained earnings in the cash value potion of the UL policy provided that the premiums are not deducted. The business owner can then access these funds personally or for use in the business during his or her lifetime by collateralizing the policy through loans from a bank.

For example, the individual might borrow funds annually in order to increase his or her retirement cash flow. Appropriate documentation and guarantee fees must be in place in order to avoid a personal (deemed) benefit. Any related bank loan would be repaid automatically at the death of the insured business owner from a portion of the policy proceeds. At the same time, a credit to the corporate Capital Dividend Account (CDA) would be created equal to the full policy proceeds.

HEALTH SPENDING ACCOUNTS (HSA)

An HSA is a bank account created by the corporation to be used and whose deposits are available exclusively for health care expenses. By having an HSA, business owners are able to convert health care expenses into 100% business deductions equal to the deposits into the HSA in the year. Payments of these health care expenses are treated as a non-taxable benefit to the business owner. The business owner determines the contribution amount each year and also determines how to spend the benefit dollars. Unlike traditional medical and dental plans, if the deposits are not spent in the current year, then the funds remain in the account, available for future use. In essence, "if you don't use it, you don't lose it".

THE BOTTOM LINE

As Mort Shapiro has suggested, if clients' needs are not being satisfied by their accountant, then there is a very real possibility that the clients will have those needs satisfied by someone else and may attack their accountant if a strategic opportunity has been lost. Today's public accountant should at least be aware of options such as those noted above and should be prepared to bring these alternatives to their clients' attention in the event that they would address client needs beyond the traditional salary/bonus/dividend mix recommendation. Such service is the best strategy for avoiding "thin ice".

In order to ensure that you are satisfying your clients' needs, consider asking them the following question:

"What do you want to achieve this year with your money?"

Make sure that your clients understand your question. This question should elicit whether the clients' goals for their money in the current year are for consumption, retirement or estate purposes. Each type of goal requires a different set of tailored solutions, which may or not include the traditional salary/bonus/dividend mix recommendation.

This question also implies that the practitioner should ask the same question each year because as every public accountant knows, life changes and so do clients' needs and goals from year to year. If a public accountant fails to identify and address these new changes in the goals and direction of a client's life, then that practitioner risks skating on "thin ice".

Peter Merrick, B.A., FMA, CFP, FCSI, and Mort Shapiro, B. Com., FCA, CMC, address these areas together through their newly formed Rockhaven Financial. Peter can be reached at (416) 854-1776 or <peter@merrickwealth.com>.

APPENDIX A

CONSULTING, SEMINARS AND WORKSHOPS

Peter Merrick, B.A., FMA, CFP, FCSI, is one of Canada's most sought-after financial and employee benefit professional consultants and speakers. His pioneering insight and work in the areas of tax minimization and deference solutions and employee benefit plan construction have made him the first choice for CAs, CGAs, CMAs, lawyers, financial advisors and organizations seeking a high-profile expert, consultant, keynote speaker, or seminar leader whose message and skill set will transform corporations and individual lives, creating tangible results and restoring commitment and productivity in these uncertain times. Peter's extraordinary seminars and consulting services are fully customized through a unique research process, rich in practical content that your people can use immediately.

Learn more about Peter's consulting, seminars and workshops. Visit his Web site at <www.MerrickWealth.com> or contact him at <peter@merrickwealth.com> or (416) 854-1776.

APPENDIX B

NEHEMIAH

When I sometimes become discouraged and I believe that the world is falling apart around me, and perhaps I will not meet my goals, I remind myself of the story of Nehemiah. Just the name Nehemiah is enough to give me the strength to stay the course to achieve my life goals whatever the obstacles that are placed in front of me. Nehemiah helps me to remember that the important things in life are not easy but are worth achieving.

Nehemiah is a character found in the Old Testament of the Bible. His story to me is the most inspirational in the entire Bible. Nehemiah's story begins in Persia around 446 BC. Here, Nehemiah is a young man who is the King's royal cupbearer at the palace, a very important position.

One day at the palace, Nehemiah met up with some travellers from Jerusalem and heard about the disrepair that had fallen upon Jerusalem, the city of his forefathers. His heart filled with sadness. For many days after this, he couldn't eat or sleep, as he couldn't stop thinking about Jerusalem. The King watched Nehemiah as this was occurring, and one day the King approached Nehemiah and asked:

"Nehemiah, why are you so sad these last few days?"

Nehemiah explained to the King that he had learned that Jerusalem had fallen on tough times, and he desired to do something to help it rise from its ashes. The King replied:

"Nehemiah, you have been a loyal servant for these many years, I give you my permission to go to Jerusalem and become the governor of Judea."

On Nehemiah's arrival, he began to survey the city secretly at night, and formed a plan for its restoration. He looked at what could be accomplished, something that would unite the people of Jerusalem. Nehemiah saw that there were great holes in the walls of Jerusalem. He decided that fixing the walls was the project that would unite his people and begin the restoration of the city of his forefathers. The next day, Nehemiah stood up in front of all Jerusalem and proclaimed that he and all who would join him would work to fix the walls, and this would begin the rebirth of Jerusalem and unite its people. Immediately, some of the people saw the value of what Nehemiah planned to do, and joined with him right away. Others who were complacent or threatened by Nehemiah's goal started saying:

"Nehemiah you are crazy, it can't be done, why try?"

Nehemiah replied by restating his goal of fixing the walls of Jerusalem. He focused on his goal and those who supported the goal, and on the restoration and resurrection of an entire people. After the project began, those who had an invested interest that Jerusalem stay the way it was began to try to sabotage the work that was being done. Nehemiah did not become discouraged; no, he focused even more on his goal, and those who supported this goal. He innately knew that this goal was greater than any one person.

Those who tried to stop the work of restoration realized that it was going to happen. Those people made continuous calls to Nehemiah to cease his work and to come meet them to discuss the situation. Nehemiah did not allow those who had tried to co-opt the project of fixing the walls; he stayed focused on the goal and those who supported the goal. Nehemiah and those who had supported him, at great personal risk, and with skill and energy, completed fixing the walls within six months after he had first stood up and stated his goal.

Nehemiah's action is accredited with the return of the Jewish people to Israel after their long exile in the Persian Empire and is seen as the catalyst for the building of the Second Temple.

What I learned personally from the story of Nehemiah, and what we can all learn from Nehemiah, is that it is important to set goals that are greater than ourselves, that are accomplishable either in our lifetime or in future generations.

There will always be people who support us in achieving our goals, and there will always be others who are threatened and fearful of us achieving our goals. Those threatened by us achieving our goals at first may try to discourage us and then may attack us. After they come to terms with the fact that we cannot be put off our chosen path, they may try to pretend that they are beginning to accept our goals in an effort to distract us.

What is very important for us to always remember is never to get distracted from what we know in our hearts to be right for us and to stay committed to our goals, values and ideas, to remain focused and to appreciate those who give us our support while we are journeying towards our goals and destinations. Remember:

"Nehemiah"

Appendix C

It Couldn't Be Done

Edgar Albert Guest (1881-1959)

Somebody said that it couldn't be done,
But he with a chuckle replied
That "maybe it couldn't," but he would be one
Who wouldn't say so till he'd tried.
So he buckled right in with the trace of a grin
On his face. If he worried he hid it.
He started to sing as he tackled the thing
That couldn't be done, and he did it.

Somebody scoffed: "Oh, you'll never do that;
At least no one ever has done it";
But he took off his coat and he took off his hat,
And the first thing we knew he'd begun it.
With a lift of his chin and a bit of a grin,
Without any doubting or quiddit,
He started to sing as he tackled the thing
That couldn't be done, and he did it.

There are thousands to tell you it cannot be done,
There are thousands to prophesy failure;
There are thousands to point out to you, one by one,
The dangers that wait to assail you.
But just buckle in with a bit of a grin,
Just take off your coat and go to it;
Just start to sing as you tackle the thing
That "cannot be done," and you'll do it.

CHIEF SEATTLE'S LEGACY IS A WARNING TO US ALL!

In December 1854, Chief Seattle of the Suquamish Nation in Washington State's Puget Sound, after whom the city of Seattle is named, delivered what is considered by the Social Responsibility Movement as one of the most insightful environmental declarations of all time. Chief Seattle's speech was given on behalf of his people in response to a proposed treaty offered by the United States that called for the Suquamish Nation to sell two million acres of its ancestral land for $150,000 (U.S.), and to then be relocated to a reserve.

Chief Seattle's Thoughts (1786-1866)

How can you buy or sell the sky, the warmth of the land? The idea is strange to us.

If we do not own the freshness of the air and the sparkle of the water, how can you buy them?

Every part of this earth is sacred to my people. Every shining pine needle, every sandy shore, every mist in the dark woods, every clearing and humming insect is holy in the memory and experience of my people. The sap which courses through the trees carries the memories of the red man.

The white man's dead forget the country of their birth when they go to walk among the stars. Our dead never forget this beautiful earth, for it is the mother of the red man. We are part of the earth and it is part of us. The perfumed flowers are our sisters; the deer, the horse, the great eagle, these are our brothers. The rocky crests, the juices in the meadows, the body heat of the pony, and man — all belong to the same family.

So, when the Great Chief in Washington sends word that he wishes to buy our land, he asks much of us. The Great Chief sends word he will reserve us a place so that we can live comfortably to ourselves. He will be our father and we will be his children.

So, we will consider your offer to buy our land. But it will not be easy. For this land is sacred to us. This shining water that moves in the streams and rivers is not just water but the blood of our ancestors. If we sell you the land, you must remember that it is sacred, and you must teach your children that it is sacred and that each ghostly reflection in the clear water of the lakes tells of events and memories in the life of my people. The water's murmur is the voice of my father's father.

The rivers are our brothers, they quench our thirst. The rivers carry our canoes, and feed our children. If we sell you our land, you must remember, and teach your children, that the rivers are our brothers and yours, and you must henceforth give the rivers the kindness you would give any brother.

We know that the white man does not understand our ways. One portion of land is the same to him as the next, for he is a stranger who comes in the night and takes from the land whatever he needs. The earth is not his brother, but his enemy, and when he has conquered it, he moves on. He leaves his father's grave behind, and he does not care. He kidnaps the earth from his children, and he does not care. His father's grave, and his children's birthright are forgotten. He treats his mother, the earth, and his brother, the sky, as things to be bought, plundered, sold like sheep or bright beads. His appetite will devour the earth and leave behind only a desert.

I do not know. Our ways are different than your ways. The sight of your cities pains the eyes of the red man. There is no quiet place in the white man's cities. No place to hear the unfurling of leaves in spring or the rustle of the insect's wings. The clatter only seems to insult the ears. And what is there to life if a man cannot hear the lonely cry of the whippoorwill or the arguments of the frogs around the pond at night? I am a red man and do not understand. The Indian prefers the soft sound of the wind darting over the face of a pond and the smell of the wind itself, cleaned by a midday rain, or scented with pinon pine.

The air is precious to the red man for all things share the same breath, the beast, the tree, the man, they all share the same breath. The white man does not seem to notice the air he breathes. Like a man dying for many days he is numb to the stench. But if we sell you our land, you must remember that the air is precious to us, that the air shares its spirit with all the life it supports.

The wind that gave our grandfather his first breath also receives his last sigh. And if we sell you our land, you must keep it apart and sacred as a place where even the white man can go to taste the wind that is sweetened by the meadow's flowers.

So we will consider your offer to buy our land. If we decide to accept, I will make one condition — the white man must treat the beasts of this land as his brothers.

I am a savage and do not understand any other way. I have seen a thousand rotting buffaloes on the prairie, left by the white man who shot them from a passing train. I am a savage and do not understand how the smoking iron horse can be made more important than the buffalo that we kill only to stay alive.

What is man without the beasts? If all the beasts were gone, man would die from a great loneliness of the spirit. For whatever happens to the beasts, soon happens to man. *All things are connected.*

You must teach your children that the ground beneath their feet is the ashes of our grandfathers. So that they will respect the land, tell your children that the earth is rich with the lives of our kin. Teach your children that we have taught our children that the earth is our mother. Whatever befalls the earth befalls the sons of earth. If men spit upon the ground, they spit upon themselves.

This we know; the earth does not belong to man; man belongs to the earth. This we know. All things are connected like the blood which unites one family. *All things are connected.*

Even the white man, whose God walks and talks with him as friend to friend, cannot be exempt from the common destiny. We may be brothers after all. We shall see. One thing we know which the white man may one day discover; our God is the same God.

You may think now that you own Him as you wish to own our land; but you cannot. He is the God of man, and His compassion is equal for the red man and the white. The earth is precious to Him, and to harm the earth is to heap contempt on its creator. The whites too shall pass; perhaps sooner than all other tribes. Contaminate your bed and you will one night suffocate in your own waste.

But in your perishing you will shine brightly fired by the strength of the God who brought you to this land and for some special purpose gave you dominion over this land and over the red man.

That destiny is a mystery to us, for we do not understand when the buffalo are all slaughtered, the wild horses are tamed, the secret corners of the forest heavy with the scent of many men and the view of the ripe hills blotted by talking wires.

Where is the thicket? Gone. Where is the eagle? Gone.

The end of living and the beginning of survival.

APPENDIX E

PENSION SPEAK

Learning a language is akin to acquiring a new code cipher. "Pension Speak" refers to a language that is spoken by individuals who have developed a mastery in Canadian pension, tax, accounting and actuarial terminology. You will encounter many terms as you delve into the world of Individual Pension Plans and other advanced planning solutions, and the aim of this appendix is to provide you with a working lexicon of the most commonly used terms and concepts.

Glossary

2/3 Pensionable refers to pre-1990 pensionable service recognized after June 7, 1990. The maximum pensionable benefit limit for pre-1990 pensionable service funding is $1,150 (two-thirds of $1,722.22) for years up to and including 2003, and two-thirds of the maximum pension limit for years after 2003.

Accountant is a tax professional, who keeps, audits, and inspects the financial records of individuals or businesses and prepares financial and tax reports. In Canada there are three recognized accounting professional designations, which are Chartered Accountant (CA), Certified General Accountant (CGA) and Certified Management Accountant (CGA).

Accrual Accounting is a form of accounting that matches revenues to expenses at the time in which the transaction occurs rather than when payment is received.

Accrual Rate is the rate usually specified in the benefit formula of a defined benefit pension plan as a percentage of earnings, at which pension benefits are earned. Example: 2% of pensionable earnings for each year of service restricted by the defined benefit maximum pension limit.

Accrued Benefit Obligation is the actuarial present value of benefits attributed to an IPP member's service performed as of a specific date.

Active Member is a member of an IPP to whom a pension benefit has accrued under the provisions of the plan during the year that contributions to the plan have been made.

Actuarial Assumptions are the estimates of future events that will impact upon the cost and obligations of the employer to provide a retirement benefit. These events may include administration costs, rate of return on IPP assets, mortality tables, Income Tax Regulations, Average Indexed Wage and retirement age.

Actuarial Gains and Losses are the changes that occur in the accrued benefit obligation of the IPP assets as a result of experiences that differ from the actuarial assumptions.

Actuarial Valuation is the report by an actuary of the financial strength of an Individual Pension Plan.

Actuarial Valuation Report (AVR) is a report that determines the funding level of a pension plan as of a specific date and the appropriate contributions to be deposited into the pension fund for the periods between the next actuarial valuation.

Actuary is a person who is a Fellow of the Canadian Institute of Actuaries. Actuaries are business professionals who apply their knowledge of mathematics, probability, statistics, and risk theory, to real-life financial problems involving future uncertainty.

Additional Voluntary Contributions (AVC) are typically described as additional funds set up inside a Registered Pension Plan (RPP) that are in addition to the prescribed amounts set out in the RPP plan text. AVCs are not subject to the locking-in provisions found in Registered Pension Plans.

Administrator is either a person or a body of persons with the ultimate responsibility for administrating an IPP. In most cases the administrator for an IPP will be the trustee or the employer.

Annual Information Return (AIR) also referred to as a Form T244. An annual Information Return is a form that must be filed with CRA every year for each Registered Pension Plan in Canada within 180 days of the plan year-end. The AIR reports activity that occurred within an IPP during the past year and the health of the plan. If an AIR is filed late, penalties may be charged to the IPP by CRA.

Annuity is a contract between an individual and an insurance company for a guaranteed interest bearing policy with guaranteed income options.

Applicable Pension Laws refer to the requirements based on the *Income Tax Act*, *Income Tax Regulations* and all statutes of Canada and provinces of Canada that apply to IPP.

Asset is approved property held with the Individual Pension Plan.

Asset Allocation refers diversifying investments in different categories such as cash, fixed income, and equities.

Assets Under Management (AUM) refer to the total investment funds that are managed by another.

Average Indexed Wage (AIW) is the measure of the average weekly wage published by Statistics Canada.

Beneficiary means the person or persons legally designated by the plan to receive any benefits payable under the Plan as a result of the IPP member's death.

Beta refers to a stock's exposure to the overall market and its sensitivity/volatility in relations to the overall market.

Blue Ocean is a term referring to a metaphor that illustrates how companies can easily grow their businesses in practically competitor-free environments.

Bread of Shame is a main tenet in Kabbalah, the mystical side of Judaism, which means that you cannot keep what you have not rightfully earned; the only way to be deserving of what you have is to be a proactive force for the purpose of not receiving for the self alone.

Bridge Benefit is also referred to as a CPP Offset. A temporary supplement to a pension, usually paid from the early retirement date until the normal retirement date of age 65 or death, whichever comes first.

Business Case is a document and/or presentation that advocates a solution based on its ability to improve the client's business and retirement objectives, and framed according to the executive decision-making criteria. Typically it includes tangible benefits, intangible benefits, risk assessment and financial analysis, while achieving a strong sense of strategic alignment.

Butterfly Effect is a metaphor used to describe the main principles behind Chaos Theory, where little seemingly unconnected events can create huge changes half way around the globe. The Butterfly Effect Metaphor: a butterfly fluttering its wings in Brazil could set off a tornado in Texas.

Canada Revenue Agency (CRA) administers tax laws for the Government of Canada and for most provinces and territories and various social and economic benefits and incentive programs delivered through the tax system.

Canadian-Controlled Private Corporation (CCPC) is defined under the *Income Tax Act* (subsection 125(7)) as a corporation that has been incorporated in Canada and where the majority of outstanding shares are held by Canadian residents.

Career Average Earning Defined Benefit Pension Plan is a pension benefit that the IPP will pay out to a plan member based on his or her entire career average earnings during which he or she was eligible to acquire pension credits from the plan. Each year is treated equally in the weighting of the career average and capped at the CRA prescribed pensionable amount. Career Average Earnings are used to calculate the total annual pension benefit that a connected person will get from his or her IPP.

Cash is money invested in T-bills, and in chequing and savings accounts.

Catalyst is the change agent that provokes and speeds up significant change or action.

CICA Handbook, Section 3461, Employee Future Benefits, are the accounting standards set by the Canadian Institute of Chartered Accountants that oblige companies to make changes in several key areas in their financial reporting in relation to IPPs and other defined benefit pension plans. Accrual accounting is required for retirement and post-employment benefits. Organizations operating in the private sector are required to accrue the cost of all employee future benefits including Individual Pension Plans.

Common Law Partner is a person of the opposite sex or the same sex who is the natural or adopted parent of the IPP member's child. The common law partner has been in an intimate relationship with the member of the IPP and has been cohabiting with the member for 12 consecutive months or lived with the member previously for 12 consecutive months.

Commuted Value refers to the amount of money that needs to be set aside today, at current market interest rates, to provide sufficient funds to pay for a pension when a plan member retires. It shows how much a benefit is worth today. Commuted values express the lump sum value of a promised benefit, usually from a defined benefit pension plan. The commuted value takes into account the benefits, interest and mortality rates.

Company refers to an employer who sponsors an IPP for an owner, executive or employee.

Connected Person is a person who owns directly or indirectly 10% or more of capital stock in a company or a related corporation. It also includes a person who does not deal at arm's length with a company. This includes a spouse or a common law partner.

Consumer Price Index (CPI) measures monthly and yearly changes in the cost of 300 goods and services commonly bought by Canadians.

Contract for Insurance refers to IPP funds that are held under a contract with an insurance company. If the Administrator of an IPP elects to have IPP money held with an insurance company the administrator of the IPP will not have to appoint trustees to administer plan assets.

Correlation refers to the relationship that two or more securities have to one another.

Cost-of-Living Adjustments refer to the adjusted salaries and pensions based on changes in the CPI. Typically salaries and pensions are adjusted annually.

Credited Service is the continuous service that a member of a plan has accumulated from the effective date and during which the company made contributions or has deemed to make contributions on behalf of the member of the IPP.

Creditor is either a person or legal entity to whom money is due.

Cultural Creatives are a new subculture in society who care deeply about ecology and saving the planet, about relationships, peace, social justice, self-actualization, spirituality and self-expression. Such individuals have a burning desire to have their values reflected in their careers, investments and community.

Current Service Cost refers to the expenses connected with the funding and the administration of a defined benefit plan on an annual basis.

Custodian is the entity that actually holds the assets inside the IPP. The custodian can either be an insurance company or a formal trustee or a three-party trustee.

Decision-Making Paradigm is the overall business condition or paradigm that affects how companies make investment decisions. The paradigms are: cost, strategy, operations and restructuring.

Deemed Registration of an IPP is deemed registered with CRA January 1st of the calendar year that an application to register an IPP has been made.

Deferred Income Plans are retirement savings plans recognized and registered with CRA that allow immediate deductions for employed individuals or their companies where taxes paid on the money in these plans are not taxed until withdrawal. These plans include RPPs, RRSPs, RRIFs, LIFs, LIRAs, LRIFs and Locked-in RRSPs.

Deferred Pension refers to when a member's employment or pension plan terminates and the pension benefit is not payable until pensionable age.

Deficit may occur in an IPP because the fund returns in the plan were lower than anticipated due to AIW rising faster than expected, or for any other reason. As a result, the actuary will require additional contributions to be injected into the plan in order to finance the deficit. Note that this deficit may be amortized over a maximum period of 15 years.

Defined Benefit Maximum Pension Limits (per Year of Service) are the following: 2006 ($2,111), 2007 ($2,222), 2008 ($2,333), 2009 ($2,444), 2010 (indexed to the average wage).

Defined Benefit Pension Plan (DBPP) is a traditional pension plan registered with CRA that pays workers a specific monthly benefit at retirement. These plans either state the promised benefit as an exact dollar amount or specify a formula for calculating the benefit. Within these plans, the contributions are not defined, but the benefits are defined.

Defined Contribution Pension Plan (DCPP) is a registered pension plan with CRA and is governed under the federal and provincial Pension Acts depending on the province a DCPP is registered in. A DCPP is also referred to as a money purchase plan. In these plans the contributions are defined but the amounts that will be withdrawn are not defined.

Designated Plan is a pension plan where more than 50% of the pension creditors are for a specific person. These individuals are active members of a pension plan who are connected persons to the employer of the plan or who earn two and one-half times the year's maximum pensionable earnings (YMPE).

Disability is the inability to work due to illness or injury.

Disability Insurance is a form of health insurance that provides periodic payments when the insured is unable to work as a result of sickness or injury.

Due Diligence is the formal process of investigating the background before taking action in a business deal.

Early Retirement is the date prior to a member's Normal Retirement Date, when the member actually retires. This date can be the first day of any month within 15 years of the member's Normal Retirement Date and no earlier.

Earnings mean the amount of pensionable earnings as defined in the IPP text that is used to calculate pensionable benefits earned.

Effective Date is the date that an RPP is considered to be registered with CRA. This date is outlined in IPP documents. This date cannot be before January 1st of the year that the application for registration of the IPP is made to CRA. The Effective Date also refers to the date that the membership into an IPP is terminated.

Efficient Frontier refers to every risk level having a corresponding optimal combination of asset classes that maximizes returns.

Employee Profit Sharing Plan (EPSP) is a form of employee compensation that is established to enable employees to share in the profitability of an employer.

Employer Health Tax (EHT), previously known as OHIP in Ontario, is paid by employers who exceed a certain payroll amount to the Ministry of Health. The amounts paid by each employer goes towards covering health care for Ontario residents who hold a valid Ontario Health Card. Once a business's payroll reaches $400,000 (whether it takes five months or five years to reach) it must pay EHT.

Equities are ownerships in companies.

Ethical Will is the spiritual legacy, values, insights and principles closest to a person's heart that he or she wants to bequeath to his or her heirs.

Excess Surplus represents the lesser of 20% of the actuarial liabilities or the greater of 10% of the actuarial liabilities and two times the contributions for current service. The actuary will require a contribution holiday or a decrease in contributions if the IPP is in an excess surplus position.

Factor of 9 is a pension credit formula used to determine the pension credit in a defined benefit pension plan. The Federal Government created the Factor of 9 to equalize the tax assisted savings between all Defined Contribution Pension Plans and RRSPs to Defined Benefit Pension Plans. The Factor of 9 states that for every $1 of defined benefit pension benefit promised to a member, the government considers that $9 of funding will be required. However, this relationship is an average over a plan member's entire working career. To calculate the Factor of 9 the benefit earned by the member of a DB plan to determine an IPP member's PA is to multiply the defined benefit promised to the member of the IPP in a year by 9 then subtract the PA offset (9 × benefit − $600).

Fair Market Value (FMV) is the price that the open market would pay in a normal time period in a transaction between arm's length (non-related) seller and buyer.

Fiduciary is any person or entity that has any power or authority over the control, management or disposition of the funds of any employee benefit plan including anyone who provides investment advice for a fee or has discretion with respect to the administration of a plan.

Fiduciary Duty represents a very high level of standard of care in dealing with assets on behalf of a beneficiary. If the duty and standards are not met, the offending fiduciary could be legally liable for the consequences.

Final Average Earning Defined Benefit Pension Plan is the pension benefit that is paid out to the IPP member based on length of service that is pensionable and the average earnings of the IPP member for a stated period of time. This formula can only be used for a non-connected person. Usually the best IPPs for non-connected members are based on an average of the top three earning years that are capped at the CRA prescribed pensionable amount.

Finite Games are games played for the purpose of winning.

Fixed Income is money invested in GICs, bonds and mortgages.

Four Pillars refer to the four sectors of the Canadian financial sector: banks, trust companies, insurance companies and investment dealers.

Group Insurance refers to insurance coverage for several people under an insurance contract.

Health and Welfare Trust (HWT) is an arrangement where an employer remits an amount to a trustee for the benefit of an employee. HWTs allow employers to make tax-deductible contributions into the trust for medical and dental-related coverage on behalf of an employee and his or her dependants. All approved medical and dental expenses allowed to go through the HWT are non-taxable benefit for the employee.

Health Spending Accounts (HSA) are health and dental spending accounts set up by an employer for an employee to pay for medical and dental expenses. Contributions into an HSA by an employer are a deductible expense and a non-taxable benefit for the employee. HSAs come in two forms in Canada, Health and Welfare Trusts (HWT) and Private Health Service Plans (PHSP).

Henson Trust is a trust that is created by the parents' Will. Only available since 1989, when the case after which it is named was upheld by the Ontario Court of Appeal, it places estate assets in the care and control of a trustee to be administered for the benefit of a beneficiary. Inheritances placed in a properly prepared Absolute Discretionary Trust are not the asset of the child and will not affect provincial benefits.

Hybrid Plan refers to a Registered Pension Plan that has features of both defined benefit pension plans and defined compensation pension plans.

IIS Form is a Risked-Based Pension Investment Monitoring Program and Investment Information Summary Form that has been mandated in Ontario to be submitted every year by sponsors of IPPs to the Financial Services Commission of Ontario (FSCO).

Income Tax Act (ITA) is the primary source of all income tax legislation in Canada. The ITA lays down the rules of taxation in Canada.

Income Tax Regulations (REG) are complements to the ITA. The REGs specify the terms and conditions of applying the ITA.

Indexing refers to the pension increases for a pension plan member or the member's survivors. It is calculated each year using Consumer Price Index (CPI) data published by Statistics Canada. The increases are based on a comparison of the 12-month average of the monthly CPI for the year just ended, to the 12-month average of the monthly CPI for the previous year.

Individual Pension Plan (IPP) is a defined benefit pension plan for just one employee as defined in section 147.1 of the Canadian *Income Tax Act*. IPPs provide senior executives and business owners with the opportunity to achieve maximum tax relief combined with a maximum Registered Pension Plan (RPP).

Infinite Games are games played for the purpose of continuing the play of the game.

Initial Value Message is a statement of value an advisor could bring to a prospective IPP client based on prior experience and success in a particular market segment with similar companies and individuals. It is used early in your sales process to generate interest in a discussion.

Investment Management Fees (IMF) are the fees that clients pay a financial institution to manage their investment assets.

Investment Manager is an individual or organization appointed by the trustee or administrator of an Individual Pension Plan to manage the assets of the plan pursuant to federal and provincial laws and regulations pertaining to the investment of pension assets.

Investment Policy Statement (IPS) refers to the written guidelines that are used for the IPP's long-term financial and investment decisions. It generally includes investment objectives (return requirements and risk tolerance), constraints (cash requirements and timing issues) and guidelines for achieving an IPP's objectives.

Kabbalah is the mystical side of Judaism.

Lifetime Retirement Benefits are benefits promised to be paid to members of defined benefit plans from the time the benefit starts paying to the time of the member's death and the death of the member's spouse.

Locked-in Plan is a registered plan where money has been transferred from a pension plan to a personal registered retirement account where there are restrictions to accessing the money to ensure that there will be an income stream during retirement for life. Lock-in Plans include Life Income Funds (LIF), Lock-in Retirement Accounts (LIRA), Locked-in Retirement Income Funds (LRIF) and Locked-in RRSPs (LRRSP).

Logo is derived from the Greek word for meaning.

Logotherapy is a therapy that focuses on helping individuals find their meaning/purpose in life.

Luck is when preparation meets opportunity.

Matching Service is the contributions to fund an IPP for non-connected persons for years of service prior to 1991.

Member/Participant is a designated employee of a company who is deemed or has been deemed to have contributions made to a RPP.

Metaphor means to transfer the meaning from one thing to another.

Modern Portfolio Theory shows how to create a frontier of investment portfolio that aims at maximizing investment returns and minimizing investment risk.

Money Purchase Plan is also referred to as a defined contribution pension plan. This is a registered pension plan with CRA in which the contribution amounts are defined but the benefits of the pension received at retirement are not defined. Contributions limits are set for 2006 ($19,000), 2007 ($20,000), 2008 ($21,000), 2009 ($22,000), 2010 (indexed to the average wage).

Morbidity refers to the incidences of disability in a given population.

Mortality refers to the incidences of death in a given population.

Mythology is the study of cultural stories.

Normal Retirement is the first day of the month following a member's 65th birthday.

Office of the Superintendent of Financial Institutions (OSFI) is the Ontario entity making sure pension plans governed by the Ontario *Pension Benefits Act*, R.S.O. 1990, c. P.8, comply with this Act.

Paradigm Shift refers to a revolutionary change from one way of thinking to a newer way of perceiving the world around us that allows us to accommodate changes in the world that the old model failed to address satisfactorily.

Participating Employer is an employer that has made or is required to make contributions to an IPP for an employee or former employee.

Past Service Pension Adjustment (PSPA) reduces an individual's RRSP deduction limit for any pension benefits earned in a year after 1989 for the following year through the reporting of a Pension Adjustment (PA).

Payback is the time it takes to recover the amount invested, commonly expressed in months or years.

Pension Adjustment (PA) is a plan member's total pension credits earned for the prior year. A PA reduces the amount that a member can contribute into his or her RRSP. For IPPs, the PA is nine times the approximate amount of the annual pension accrued in the year for defined benefit pension plans, minus the Pension Adjustment Offset. It should be noted that the PA reported for Defined Contribution Pension Plans and Deferred Profit Sharing Plans is equal to the actual dollar amounts invested in those plans.

Pension Adjustment Offset is the minimum level of RRSP room that someone is given. Up until 1996, it was $1,000, and then from 1997 to the present, it has been $600 per year for a member of a Defined Benefit Pension Plan. The Pension Adjustment Offset gives a member of a Defined Benefit Pension Plan a minimum RRSP contribution room for any given year.

Pension Adjustment Reversal (PAR) restores RRSP contribution room for an employee that was terminated from a registered pension plan (RPP) or a deferred profit sharing plan (DPSP). PAR increases a former RPP and DPSP member's RRSP room by the difference between the total employee's PAs that were reported while a member of these plans and the actual pension transfer value to an RRSP. A PAR is calculated based on when membership in the plan is terminated The RRSP room generated by PAR can be used by the individual to make RRSP contributions in the year of termination or it can be carried forward for use in future years.

Pension Benefits Guarantee Fund (PBGF), which is available only in Ontario, was created to offer limited protection for the over one million DBPP members within Ontario's borders. If a DBPP in Ontario has insufficient funds, the PBGF will guarantee only the first $1,000 per month of pension benefits. This fund does not protect designated plans such as the IPP.

Pension Credit is the value of a pension benefit that a member of a plan earns under an IPP in a calendar year. Pension credits are totalled to determine an IPP member's PA with his or her employer.

Pensionable Age refers to when a member of a pension is entitled to an unreduced pension.

Pensionable Service refers to the number of years that a member of a defined benefit pension plan has accredited to his or her retirement since becoming a member of a plan.

Peter Principle was developed by Dr. Laurence J. Peter (1919-1990) and became popularized in the 1960s. It states that we rise to the highest level of our incompetence and no higher.

Portability refers to the right to transfer locked-in or vested benefits to another registered plan when a member leaves the service of an employer.

Postponed Retirement is the earliest of the first day of the month on which the member actually retires after his or her Normal Retirement Date and December 31st of the calendar year in which the member reaches the age of sixty-nine (69).

Private Health Services Plan (PHSP) is an account that is similar to that of an HWT with specific limits in terms of contributions and a two-year forfeiture from date of deposit for making claims.

Projected Unit Credit Funding is a funding method that takes into account all the benefits that may be paid under a fund for a member of an IPP. A level of contributions is set so it covers both the benefits that have already accrued and benefits associated with membership in the future. Projected benefit funding methods include individual funding, aggregate funding, attained normal age funding, and entry age normal funding.

Pro-Rata Method is a formula used for the division of IPP assets during the divorce of a married couple. Formula divides the value of the IPP assets on the date of legal separation based on how long the couple were married and pension credits for the IPP were earned. Once this amount is determined, assets are split between the divorcing spouses according to the prescribed provincial and federal matrimonial asset division rates.

Provincial Pension Regulators (PPRs) administer their respective provincial Pension Benefits Acts.

Prudent Person Rule as it applies in this book refers to the restrictions and the discretion that a prudent person would have seeking to achieve a good investment return while achieving the preservation of capital.

Qualifying Transfer is a direct transfer of a lump-sum amount from an unmatured RRSP, a money purchase plan, locked-in plan or a DPSP. A qualifying transfer is made to pay for all or part of the cost of the past service benefits related to the PSPA.

Qualifying Withdrawal is an amount a member of a Registered Pension Plan is allowed to withdraw.

Quantum Leap is the explosive jump that a particle of matter makes in moving from one place to another. In a figurative sense, taking the quantum leap means taking a risk, going off into uncharted territory with no guide to follow.

Real Property is land and buildings.

Reciprocal Transfer Agreement is an agreement between two or more plans to transfer an appropriate sum of money from the pension fund of one employer directly to the pension fund of another, to fund benefits of an employee who leaves the first employer to enter employment with the second employer.

Red Oceans is a term that refers to market niches that have been well developed and are overcrowded by predators and competitors.

Registered Pension Plan (RPP) is a pension plan that has been set up by an employer and registered by CRA to provide specified employees with a pension when they retire. An RPP exists when there is a formal arrangement between an employer to contribute on behalf of an employee to a trust.

Registered Plans Directorate is a special division in CRA, responsible for all program activities related to the provisions of the *Income Tax Act* for the registering and monitoring of employee pension plans, retirement savings plans, retirement income funds, deferred profit sharing plans, supplementary unemployment benefit plans, education savings plans and registered investments.

Registered Retirement Savings Plans (RRSPs) are savings plans for individuals, including the self-employed, that have been registered for the purposes of the federal *Income Tax Act*. RRSP contribution limits are based on earned *income*. RRSPs provide retirement income at retirement based on accumulated contributions and return on investment in the plan. Contributions to an RRSP are tax-deductible, the *investment income* in it is tax-deferred and payments from it are taxable. Annual contributions are limited to 18% of earnings up to a maximum of $18,000 in 2006.

Remuneration refers to all salaries, wages, bonuses, vacation pay, honoraria, commission, taxable allowances, the value of taxable benefits and any other payment that a member of an IPP receives as an employee of a sponsoring company.

Retirement Benefit is the benefit paid out to a member of a pension plan on a periodic basis.

Retirement Compensation Arrangement (RCA) is a plan defined in subsection 248(1) of the *Income Tax Act*, providing supplemental pension benefits to owners/managers and key employees of incorporated businesses. Contributions to an RCA are 100% tax deductible by the employer and are not taxable for the employee until the money is withdrawn from the RCA.

Retiring Allowance is amount of money that an employer pays to an employee in recognition of long service with the company or an amount paid for loss of employment or position. CRA may allow the taxpayer who receives a retiring allowance to defer part or all taxes on the amount by making payment into an RPP or RRSP if certain criteria are met.

Return on Investment (ROI) is defined as net income divided by investment. ROI is often used in a general sense referring to the overall return on investment of the IPP initiative for both the sponsor and the member of the plan.

Risked-Based Pension Investment Monitoring Program and Investment Information Summary Form (IIS Form) is a form that must be submitted every year by sponsors of IPPs to FSCO. This form allows FSCO to reduce the risk of members of individual pension plans not receiving the benefits promised.

Salary is the active income an employee receives for providing service to an employer.

Salary Continuation Plan (SCP) is a form of disability coverage that may yield favourable after-tax results as compared to traditional private disability insurance policies. The premiums for an employer are a deductible expense and the benefits when paid out to the disabled employee are taxable.

Shareholders' Agreement refers to an agreement between all of the shareholders about how the company should be run and the application of the rights of the shareholders. This acts as a contract between the shareholders. The company itself is not bound by it, as it is not a party to the agreement.

Socially Responsible Investing (SRI) refers to investing strategies that apply three main components: screening, shareholder advocacy, and community investing.

Solvency Requirements is a calculation to determine the funding requirement to properly fund a defined benefit pension plan if it is to be terminated and wound up.

Specimen Plan is an IPP text that has been pre-approved by CRA. Specimen Plans are used heavily by administrators or consultants who market IPPs. An approved Specimen Plan document uses the same terminology and identical wording for all sponsors of IPPs registering IPPs, who have used the same consultant or administrator. When an IPP uses an approved Specimen Plan, CRA will quickly register the IPP as soon as it has been determined that the IPP plan matches the Specimen Plan. Specimen Plans for IPPs have within them approved IPP text, funding formulas and other documents.

Sponsor is a company that sponsors an IPP for an employee. IPPs can only be sponsored by incorporated businesses or incorporated professional corporations.

Spouse is a person who is married to an active IPP member, inactive IPP member or retired IPP member.

Statement of Investment Policies and Procedures (SIPP) must be provided each year by sponsors of pension plans registered with the Province of Ontario to the Financial Services Commission of Ontario (FSCO). A written Statement of Investment Policies and Procedures must be submitted that meet the guidelines of the Office of the Superintendent of Financial Institutions (OSFI). This documentation is used to help ensure that individual pension plans are operating in the best interests of plan members.

Surplus in an IPP will not require a contribution holiday or a decrease in contributions if the IPP surplus does not result in an *excess* surplus.

Synchronicity refers to any apparent coincidence that inspires a sense of wonder and personal meaning or particular significance to the individual or individuals experiencing an event. Synchronicity means a coincidence that an individual finds meaning in.

Synergy is the phenomenon in which two or more discrete influences or agents acting together create an effect greater than that predicted by knowing only the separate effects of the individual agents.

T10 is the form that reports the Pension Adjustment Reversal to CRA on the behalf of the former RPP member. The T10 restores the RRSP room that was reduced as a result of membership in a pension plan or DPSP terminated, and the member is no longer entitled to a portion their pension benefits.

T1004 is a Past Service Pension Adjustment Certification Form.

T1007 is a CRA Connected Person Information Return Form.

T244 is a CRA form in which the IPP Annual Information Return is reported to CRA.

T3P is an IPP Trust income tax return. The T3P must be filed within 90 days after the year-end of the Trust. T3Ps must be filed by the IPP trustee(s). If this form is late, CRA can impose penalties for filing late. T3Ps only have to be filed by IPPs that have formal trust agreements. If investments of an IPP have been invested in a contract of insurance such as in a segregated fund, there is no T3P filed.

T4 is a slip that reports an individual's earned income from his or her labour.

T4PS (profit-sharing) is a slip issued to employees of a company that participate in a company's employee profit-sharing plan.

T510 is a form that the sponsor/administrator submits to CRA when applying to register an IPP. This form is an application for registration of a pension plan. This form indicates that an IPP is a designated plan. Once an IPP has been given plan status, it continues to hold this status unless CRA changes its status.

Tailored Individual Pension Plan (TIPP) is a defined benefit plan created for an individual where the PA is inappropriately low in relation to the benefit promised by the pension. CRA frowns upon TIPPs and for plan sponsors and members of plans that have been deemed TIPPs. An IPP designated as a TIPP runs the risk of being deregistered.

Tangible Benefit is a benefit that can be monetarily quantified.

Terminal Funding may occur if the member of the IPP retires prior to age 65. Then the plan could be amended to provide an unreduced pension plus a bridge payment from early retirement to normal retirement. Terminal Funding creates an underfunded liability and an opportunity for a company to make further contributions to an IPP.

Third Party Administrator is an organization that processes health plan claims but does not carry any insurance risk.

Transfer refers to the act of conveying the title of property.

Transfer Factor is a formula that is used to determine how much money CRA will permit to be transferred on a tax-deferral basis from an IPP to an LIRA, RRSP, LIF or LRRSP without triggering taxes. This formula is based on the age of the IPP member.

Triennial Valuation is an actuarial valuation that must be filed with CRA every three years that reports the strength of a registered IPP. The valuation is used to set current service contributions for the next three years. It also determines if the plan has a surplus or deficit. Based on the Triennial Valuation, it is determined whether the IPP will meet its benefit obligations or not.

Trust is a legal arrangement in which one person or entity (settler) transfers legal title to a trustee (fiduciary) to manage the property for the benefit of a person or institution (beneficiary).

Trustee(s) can be a trust company or at least three individuals, who live in Canada, who are charged to promote the financial security of a pension fund through sound investment policy and practices. If an IPP has been set up with a Trust Agreement instead of using a contract of insurance, a T3P tax return must be filed with CRA within 90 days of the year-end of the Trust.

Unfunded Liability occurs when there are fewer assets in the IPP fund to meet the IPP's pension benefit obligations.

Unique Value Proposition (UVP) refers to the unique value an advisor offers to his or her clients. However not everyone has the ability to appreciate this value. Advisors are called up to work with those clients who perceive this unique value.

Valuation is an actuarial examination of a pension plan to determine whether contributions are being accumulated at a rate sufficient to provide the funds out of which the promised pension can be paid when due. The valuation shows the actuarial liabilities of the plan and the applicable assets.

Value-Added Method is a formula for the division of IPP assets during marriage breakdown. The formula subtracts the value of the pension earned before the legal union of the couple from the value of the pension at the time of the official separation. Once that amount is determined, the split of the IPP assets occurs at the prescribed provincial and federal matrimonial asset division rates.

Value Assessment is the consultative process of identifying the business impact of an investment, according to the client's decision-making criteria, and assembling the business case that explains it.

Value Assessment Methodology is a methodology for selling that focuses on how you produce value for clients.

Value-Based Pricing is based on the value of the product or service to the client, not the cost of production.

Values are the principles and standards we set for ourselves either consciously or unconsciously.

Vesting means that a member of a pension is entitled to get the pension benefits that he or she has built up according to the pension plan formula.

Wind-up is the process whereby an employer discontinues a defined benefit pension plan.

Year's Maximum Pensionable Earnings (YMPE) is the average Canadian national wage determined and adjusted yearly by Statistics Canada and reported by CRA. The YMPE is the maximum amount of annual earnings, not including reductions for the year's basic exemption, upon which benefits and contributions for purposes of the *Canada Pension Plan* and *Quebec Pension Plan* are based. The 2007 YMPE has been set at $43,700.

INDEX

ACCOUNTANT
certified financial planner, as, 226-28
CICA Handbook Section 3461, 72-73
fee-only financial planning and, *see* FEE-ONLY FINANCIAL PLANNING
support of, 72

ACTUARIAL CALCULATIONS
actuarial valuation, *see* ACTUARIAL VALUATIONS
connected vs. non-connected person, 85, 88
employer contributions, 97-98
ITA requirements, 86
past service benefits, eligibility, 89-90
pension limits, 86
pension plan governance, determinations by CRA, 87
professional standards of CIA, 88
provincial regulators and, 87
RRSP deduction limit lost condition, 89-90
valuation reports, 53, 88

ACTUARIAL VALUATIONS
assumptions of, 53
going concern calculations, 94

maximum funding calculations, 91-93
reports, 53, 88
solvency valuation, 94-96

ACTUARY, 43

ADDITIONAL FUNDING
see FUNDING

ADDITIONAL VOLUNTARY CONTRIBUTIONS, 129-33

ADMINISTRATION REQUIREMENTS AND PROCESS, 48-49

ADMINISTRATIVE SERVICES ONLY INSURANCE *see* EMPLOYEE INSURANCE

ADMINISTRATOR OF IPP, 38-40
duties of, 39-40
preliminary determinations by, 38-39

AGE
contributions factor, 25
retirement date age, 67
retiring allowance, 71
transfer factor, 70-72
under 40, 29